Aaron H. Stern

BREAKING THE JUMP

BREAKING
THE JUMP

THE SECRET STORY OF PARKOUR'S
HIGH-FLYING REBELLION

JULIE ANGEL

Aurum
Press

Quarto is the authority on a wide range of topics.

Quarto educates, entertains and enriches the lives of
our readers—enthusiasts and lovers of hands-on living.

www.QuartoKnows.com

First published in Great Britain
2016 by Aurum Press Ltd
74—77 White Lion Street
Islington
London N1 9PF

A catalogue record for this book is
available from the British Library.

ISBN 978 1 78131 554 5
Ebook ISBN 978 1 78131 633 7

1 3 5 7 9 10 8 6 4 2
2016 2018 2020 2019 2017

Typeset in Chaparral Pro by SX Composing DTP, Rayleigh, Essex
Printed and bound by CPI Group (UK) Ltd, Croydon, CR0 4YY

Contents

Foreword

'You start practising Parkour,' my new buddy Neal told me, 'and whole nights disappear.'

I already grasped what he meant, even though I'd only gotten my first glimpse of Parkour about ten minutes earlier. I'd been shopping in a drugstore near my home in rural Pennsylvania when I looked out the window and spotted two guys leaping around on the handicapped railings. They were still there when I came out, and as we talked, they explained how this weird French guerrilla sport had taken hold in the middle of Amish farm country.

'I got into it because I was so fat,' Neal began. He'd begun partying after high school and by age twenty had bloated from one hundred and seventy-five pounds to two hundred and forty. One afternoon, he was in a nearby park watching some strangers 'kong vault' picnic tables. They'd charge a table, plant their hands and shoot both feet through their arms like gorillas. They talked Neal into giving it a try. He was shocked to discover that once he got over his fear, he could master skills that at first looked impossible.

Well, maybe not *master*. 'You're on this endless trajectory where you're always getting better, but it's never good enough,' Neal said. 'That's what's so exciting. As soon as you land one jump, you can't wait to try it again. You're

1

always looking for ways to make it cleaner, stronger, flow into your next move.' Neal became a regular member of this local Parkour tribe and joined them in their late-night rambles across the city. The best time to train is after midnight, he explained, because by dark the city is all theirs. Whenever a police car prowls by, they drop to the ground and bang out push-ups. 'No matter what time it is, no one bothers you if you're exercising.' Within a year, Neal was able to scramble to the roof of a three-storey building and crouch high on a flagpole.

'Just like Spider-Man,' he told me. To himself, he'd said, 'You're back!'

Two weeks later, I was the one facing the impossible. I wiped my palms and weighed my chances against a six-foot brick wall outside a Wells Fargo bank. It was lunchtime rush in downtown Lancaster, and people swarmed past us on the sidewalk. 'You've got to learn to shut out distractions,' Andy Keller told me. 'Forget who's watching you. Forget where you are. Just focus and *go*.'

Andy is one of America's few trained-in-Europe Parkour coaches, and by a bizarre twist of luck, he lives twenty miles from my house. I'd kept thinking about that comment Neal had made, the one about feeling just like Spider-Man, and I'd finally decided to give Parkour a try for myself. Who wouldn't want to be able to skitter up the sides of buildings? And frankly, if a double-stuffed slacker like Neal could forge himself that quickly into an American ninja warrior, how hard could it be? Age isn't on my side – I'm twice as old as Neal – but that's another theory I wanted to test: maybe Parkour is what human strength is really all about. Because logically, the one thing we rely on for survival – the way birds rely on flight and fish depend on fins – would be the one thing we're all good at, men and women, old and young alike. Most of the recreational sports we get excited about now are kind of phoney. They were created by men, for men, to show off what men do best, and they have just about zero connection to any natural human function. They're a guy pride parade. So is it possible that Parkour, with its emphasis on agility and creativity instead of bulk and brute force, is really the tightest link we have in sport to our evolutionary past?

I knew one way to find out. If Parkour really is Our One True Natural Sport, it has to be immune to the two Ts: time and testosterone. A skill is only natural if it's accessible to *everyone*, regardless of age or gender. It would make no sense if, for instance, only teenage male geese were fast on the wing; pretty soon, the sky would be full of lonely ganders wondering why they couldn't find dates or due south. So is Parkour really gender-neutral? I got my first clue when I came across an extraordinary YouTube clip created by Julie Angel, the author of this book and an artist with a genius for capturing the soul and sinew of Parkour. The video is called *Movement of Three*, and it opens with three young women strolling through a north London housing project. They're just giggling around in baggy sweats, looking like they're in the mood for something pumpkin-spiced after Bikram. Suddenly, they burst into action: in little more than two minutes, they cat-leap up and over a seven-foot wall, land precision jumps on two-inch guard rails, execute a hand-to-hand traverse along a rooftop railing, and then two of them catapult themselves through a swing-set while the third squats on the bar above their heads, blowing soap bubbles. *Movement of Three* is a fast-moving masterpiece, a sort of time-lapse display of how average women can use Parkour to turn themselves into an aerial urban-assault team.

'It's not magic,' Andy Keller told me when we got together for our first session. He and his buddy, Adam, showed me what they meant by getting me started on a basic Parkour move called a turn-vault. We headed into an alley behind a tyre repair garage and ran toward a chest-high cement wall with a metal guardrail on top. Andy and Adam planted their hands on the rail, swung their legs over, then twisted their hips so they turned one hundred and eighty degrees and landed facing back the way they came. 'Very handy for jail breaks,' Adam pointed out.

I tried the same thing, but my knees clanged into the bar and I dropped backward. *Ugh.* Humiliating. But Andy quickly pinpointed my problem: poor butt boost. Like most people, I've lost my taste for being weightless in space. We all used to love it, which is why every kid destroys his parents' box spring at some point and would trade a sibling for rope swings, trampolines, diving boards or sliding boards. But grown-ups keep warning you that you'll get hurt, recess monitors yell at you to cut it out, and over time you grow so nervous about falling down that you forget how to jump up. Watch anyone over age twenty attempt a cartwheel: a nine-year-old girl goes straight vertical and takes all the time in the world, while the twenty-something rushes through and barely gets his feet off the ground. The higher our hips, the more anxious we get.

So Andy started me over again, this time by breaking the move into individual pieces. We planted our hands on top of the waist-high guardrail and turned ourselves into desktop drinking birds: head dropped down, ass tilted up, boosting our butts higher and higher and spending longer each time supporting our weight on our hands. For a two-second manoeuvre, it's got a lot of moving parts: one palm faced out, the other in, your knees pressed together and your elbows locked out straight. After three reps, my knees were higher than the rail; after five, I suddenly twisted, swung over the rail, and executed a turn-vault without even thinking. It just seemed so natural.

'Man, I could do nothing but this all day,' I said. Even that little taste of Parkour was the perfect combo of *kaizen* and kid-on-a-swing: you want to keep smoothing the move, like a sushi chef obsessing over his tuna slicing, but you don't mind because, you know, you're flying over walls like a fugitive. But Andy had other plans for the afternoon: the Big Wall.

Outside the Wells Fargo, Andy briefed me on technique. Then he sprinted straight for the wall, kicked hard against the bricks, and disappeared over the other side. As he trotted back, he was met with applause. An audience had formed, blocking the sidewalk.

'Impressive, isn't he?' I said to the guy beside me.

'I knew he'd make it,' the man responded. 'I'm waiting to see if *you* do.'

So what's your bet – did I get over the Big Wall? I could tell you, but as you'll learn from this amazing book, that's exactly the *wrong* way to approach Parkour. So read on, and once you've absorbed the story of the Yamakasi, throw on some baggy sweats and your scuffiest sneakers and follow them into a world you'll never want to leave.

Christopher McDougall,
author of *Natural Born Heroes* and *Born to Run*

Preface

There is something compelling about Parkour. It's almost impossible to be in close proximity to it or even just see it on TV without being tempted to emulate it. The movements often seem superhuman and the setting is always the everyday. Most will never climb Everest or ride a fifteen metre wave, but who hasn't wanted to skip across the rooftops of their neighbourhood? Who hasn't ever walked through their city or town and wondered, 'What if . . .?'

This is a story about how we see the world around us, how our bodies work and how they are capable of unbelievable feats even if we don't know it yet. It is a story of why as humans there is nothing more natural than to want to move, and what happens to us when we see others do so. It is about how one group of eccentrics distilled the simple joy of action into the twenty-first century's newest sport. They will make you believe that something as simple as a jump can change your life. Along the way they tempt fate on a daily basis, surprise all the firefighters in France, face avaricious agents and spiteful movie directors, find fame and walk away from it, overcome their demons and discover new ones, save each other's lives and almost destroy them. But they never stop moving and in doing so they inspire countless others worldwide through the elegance of their pursuit.

I first became aware of Parkour when I was 32 years old, living in Plymouth, England with an established career as an independent filmmaker. I wasn't particularly sporty or acrobatic, nor was I particularly interested in the outer limits of human physical capability. But when I saw Parkour – like many people around the world, on the Channel 4 documentary *Jump London* – I was immediately enthralled by the fact that these young men careening through the urban environment had brought the extraordinary into the realm of the everyday. It was clear that they were amazing physical specimens, but just as impressive to me was that they had seemingly developed a creative vision of singular beauty and power that infused their lives with movement. A dancer performs on stage and a gymnast in a gym, but the practitioner of Parkour brings their gift on to the street right outside your window and then dares you to follow.

I wanted to understand how these young people had come to do extraordinary things in ordinary places. So I went in search of the true story of Parkour.

I started by filming Parkour practitioners (known as 'traceurs') in London and went on to do a PhD on the meaning of the sport. But no matter how much I was able to explain its semiotics and methodology, the story of Parkour remained hidden until I started to practise it myself. Happily, when I began training I found that Parkour was as much use to intellectual, artistic types like me as it was to young men with dreams of sporting glory. I also asked myself why had I lost – or, perhaps, given up – the ability to move freely, as I had when I was young?

I want to explain Parkour to the world by telling its original story and showing it, not as disposable advertising, but as a tool for self-exploration and empowerment. Parkour represents what is possible – not just for a group of youths from the French suburbs, but for any ordinary person with the desire to move freely.

Introduction

Even if it's dangerous and we're putting our life at risk, as long as you enjoy what you do, it isn't a problem. You just need to be focused and ready, and to have trained enough to pass the obstacle. It's a bit like life, when you have problems ... Things happen, but it's your ability to react to a problem that will allow you to overcome it or not.

Malik Diouf

One by one the group of nine men followed the constantly changing leader of the pack. Silently they moved through the night as one did a move and then went to the back, rotating and replacing the one at the front. The slight scuffing sound made by the soles of their shoes was the only audible sound as their feet kissed the wall following each jump from one ledge to another. While others slept they roamed. When waiting for those at the rear to take their turns, the others stopped to do some push-ups, then held the plank position on their fingertips. There was always an opportunity to be working some body part or another. Keeping their bodies low to the ground as if creeping up on an imaginary enemy, they bear-crawled the length of street on their hands and feet. The branches rustled and leaves crackled in the cool night air with the weight of the bodies as one by one they swiftly scaled trees, skipped smoothly between the boughs before hanging and dropping several body lengths back to the ground. Instinctively everyone knew what had to be done. No instructions were shared; just a feeling and shared goals. Next on their journey were the railings at the subway underpass; each either lightly stepped over them or cleared it in one swift vault, dropping several metres to the concrete below. They landed in a squat position and then sprang back up as if the ground were made of rubber. In an instant they were ready to move on. Feral and alert, they scaled walls and lampposts, moving from one to the other. They dropped down from the tops of walls and landed using a martial arts-styled roll. They hadn't spoken a word to each other for hours.

The city was different at night. While others slept, it provided the perfect environment for playing probably the most imaginative, physically daring and greatest games of hide and seek, follow the leader and tag ever played. Their versions were games in which no one ever flinched and playfulness had escalated to the extent that constant, life-threatening danger became the new norm on the streets of Evry. It was one of the youngest towns in France with an average age of just 26.

To hide meant to go to places where you were not just invisible but also inaccessible. For this able bunch it meant that the parameters were quite wide. For four hours, they vaulted, ran, climbed and stayed in precarious positions. Residents normally didn't look up when passing by, missing the man bridged between two walls. The unusual placement of bodies was difficult to spy even if you knew where to look.

Next they moved on to the Bois Sauvage quarter of the city. The challenge was that they all had to stay clinging on to a lamppost for six painful minutes. None would drop down. They trusted and believed in themselves and each other. Their hands bled and their forearms burnt from the aching pain of hanging on for so long. However much it hurt, they would fight it. No one wanted to be the first to drop. Regardless of how many attempts it took, they all knew they would have to stay there all night until the task was completed successfully. No challenge was left unfinished.

Clad in rough stones, the three-metre-high lampposts bruised, cut and grazed their skin. There was only one way to climb and stay holding on to a lamppost for six minutes: a combination of good technique by exerting as little tension through your muscles as possible, and the sheer will to do so. Their minds and bodies were numb to the sensation of pain as each of them squeezed their feet into the sides of the lamppost. Their hands changed positions to find temporary relief but always held on tight. They fought. They were warriors without a war.

Whereas marathon runners need miles of slow burn to find their state of letting go, the friends achieved it more haphazardly, and often more fleetingly, but perhaps with an intensity equal to or greater than any other sport. As often as they laughed together, they cried together, from fear, anger, pain, fatigue, or more likely some combination of all of three.

Training was constant. It started before school, went on hiatus for a quick snooze through some history and maths classes, then resumed in the afternoon. It could, and often did go on all night – what the French call *une nuit blanche*. It had started as play but the more something scared them, the more they had to do it. Like children poking their own bruises, fear fascinated them and became a quantifiable and ultimately conquerable foe.

What they did happened because they were all different. A motley crew of active misfits with various sporting ambitions fed into a great adventure that would take them to the edge of lunacy as their backgrounds combined to create a new sporting milieu. The jump taken from basketball, the discipline and roll from martial arts, the overall perfectionist standards from gymnastics – to name a few. Why shouldn't such actions be performed outside and at any time? Wild spirits and intuitive movements led them to find a way.

1

Discovering Parkour

When you work with Parkour you can work simultaneously in the imagination and real world and that's quite a rare thing to find outside of the arts.

Alister O'Loughlin, Urban Playground Team

By the time I started filming the London Parkour scene in 2004, I still considered myself 'sporty'. The truth was that I hadn't done any kind of real exercise for ten years. What's more, I hadn't missed it. But as I watched members of the Urban Freeflow team training, it reminded me of the long-forgotten thrill of childhood adventures racing through the shadows and jumping from 'here to there' across the rock formations on Dartmoor, a National Park in the southwest of England. Suddenly, a decision I hadn't even been aware I had made – giving up the thrill of movement for movement's sake – seemed like a terrible mistake. I felt the same as if I had thrown out my entire music collection by accident.

'Julie, you need to try this,' said the little voice in my head which always starts whispering at me to do ill-advised things.

However, the voice of reason said something very different. There I was: a woman in her mid-thirties with a successful career, a stable, and happy life, all my teeth, and few noticeable scars, perfectly happy with life. Beneath all my excuses for not trying Parkour I was terrified. I was scared in the usual sense of not wanting to fall and hurt myself, but it went much deeper than scraped elbows and sprained ankles. My real fear, the fear that kept me from just going out and jumping around on a bench or trying to balance my way down a handrail, was the fear of what other people would think of me. Even more so, what would I think of me? I had unwittingly cultivated an impeccable facade of adulthood. Grown-ups aren't supposed to jump around on things in public. Any deviation from 'normal' is suspect. My fear of looking stupid trumped my desire to move, but all that changed when I met Forrest.

Forrest was born François Mahop to a Cameroonian father and French mother in the Paris suburb of Moissy-Cramayel not too far from Lisses, southeast of Paris. Like everyone involved with Parkour in the early years, he was a serious physical specimen: six feet, two inches and one hundred and eighty pounds of chiselled muscle. He was built like a NBA centre but moved like a dancer.

To say that Forrest has lived an active life would be an understatement. As a strong child with lots of energy, he was raised between the football pitch and the swimming pool. By the age of ten, he was the youngest swimmer in France to qualify for the national championships – an event he missed because he was playing in an international football tournament. By the age of fourteen he turned down a swimming and jazz dancing scholarship at a prestigious academy to play football.

After struggling to crack the professional scene and fighting injury, he retired from football at twenty-two, got a master's degree in sports science, competed at a national level in the four hundred-metre sprint, and stumbled across Parkour. A fellow athlete at his club, Sébastien

Foucan, introduced him to Stéphane Vigroux. At the time, Stéphane was injured and had given up on doctors and, whilst Forrest wasn't a medic, he did understand how his body worked. There would be an exchange: Stéphane would teach Forrest about Parkour and Forrest would rehabilitate Stéphane's knee. It worked.

At the time, the Parkour scene was exploding in London as the success of the documentaries *Jump London* and *Jump Britain* inspired many to take to the streets and start moving. The opportunity for Forrest to continue his Parkour training while learning English seemed like a good idea. He packed his bag and headed across the channel.

In those days, being one of 'the French guys' in London was a term spoken with awe and reverence. It was widely assumed the French guys had a level of understanding and experience far beyond anyone in London. It was true.

The more I got to know Forrest through the Parkour scene, the more I got comfortable with the idea of trying some basic training. Little did I know that this would lead to a new world of possibility, movement, fear and happiness; all in equal measure.

London's first indoor Parkour class – meaning the first gathering of traceurs that was more than a loose meeting on a random street corner at a vague and ever-changing time – was at the Europa Gymnastics Centre in Erith.

Compared to the buff, enthusiastic gymnasts tumbling around in their leotards, the would-be traceurs looked like a group of urban ramblers who had all wandered in off the street. 'Maybe it wasn't just for the elites like Forrest', I thought. I may not have been the oldest but I was certainly one of the more senior. Just as I was considering turning around and bolting for the door, a clear, beautiful laugh rang out and a single woman emerged from the group.

'Man, am I glad to see you. I thought I would be the only woman here,' she said with the kind of easy self-confidence that some very lucky people are born with. 'My name's Karen.'

Karen Palmer is a Jamaican British woman who was the creative director of a famous reggae record label, Jet Star. She had seen the documentary *Jump London* on TV and made up her mind then and there that she would learn Parkour. Once Karen had decided something, she had a knack for seeing it through.

'I've always been hyperactive – done zillions of sports – from kickboxing to squash, tennis, you name it,' she said, bouncing on the balls of her feet. 'But this . . . I've got a feeling that this is going to be better than all of them. What sports do you do, anyway?'

'Um, at the moment? None . . .' I replied.

She laughed and slapped me on the back. Despite my nerves, suddenly I was laughing too. Without preamble Forrest stood up and addressed the class. 'OK, we start.'

No explanation, no pep talk, no holding our hands. I automatically began to worry. From the looks on the other students' faces, I gathered that they shared my sentiments. Except Karen, of course. Karen looked even more determined than Forrest.

'And there is one more very important thing that you must always remember,' Forrest said, the grin creeping back across his face. 'You 'ave to smile!'

The first exercise was *quadrupedie*, the French way of saying, 'walking on all fours'.

Only our hands and feet could touch the ground so instead of being a comforting, baby-like crawl, it became a muscle-burning, animal lope. Perhaps it wouldn't have been so bad if it hadn't been for the second condition; we did it forever. For a 'rest' we would switch directions: forwards, backwards, sideways. My personal bane was the backwards duck walk – a sort of trudge performed from a squat that is specifically designed to make your thigh muscles feel like they are being rubbed with sandpaper.

When we were finally able to stand erect like normal human beings, I caught sight of myself in a mirror on the far wall and found that I had transformed into something that looked very much like a rabid dog. A red, puffy, rabid dog. I was dripping with sweat. Every muscle in my body, including a few I was previously unaware of, was tingling with exertion. I felt like I weighed three times my weight, and my breaths were coming in strangled gasps.

'It's good to warm up, no?' Forrest grinned and my heart sank. There was no way I was going to make it through this.

Forrest allowed us a little reprieve by having us walk across a wooden beam that was just a hand span or so off the ground. Then we moved up on to the proper balance beam just above waist level and I discovered a mild fear of heights. Or rather, a mild fear of falling from them.

Forrest interwove strenuous activities like jumping up on to a box and then back down numerous times with banal movements like walking backwards, squatting down and standing up. And jumping. Always jumping. At first all the movements seemed pointless, but slowly, through my sweaty delirium, I began to see a method to the madness. What Forrest was doing was not only making our muscles stronger; he was reintroducing them to the positions and movements that modern adult life had taken away. How often do you jog backwards? If you're like most people, the answer is very rarely. How often do you move on all four appendages? Unless you are a linebacker or a sumo wrestler, probably even less. All of these simple movements were completely foreign to me.

Also, I hated them. The pain and fatigue were one thing, but what really bothered me was how awkward and counter-intuitive much of it felt. I couldn't even squat properly. It was like I was an adolescent again just getting used to my body – only my adolescence had been a breeze compared to this.

'Juliiiieeee,' Forrest called in our third minute of a horse stance squat, which is a sort of position that you can imagine a cavewoman adopted while giving birth. During his days as a goalkeeper, Forrest had honed his voice until it boomed like a drill sergeant's. 'What's wrong? Is there something wrong?' He looked around the gym innocently.

'Me? I'm fine, see – I smile.' He smiled at me to prove it. 'You 'ave to smile.'

After a 'warm down' of the hardest abs exercises I had ever done, we all stood facing Forrest.

'Okay, now we make a round,' he said. No one moved, much less 'made a round'.

'You don't know how to make a round?' Forrest looked at us as if he had just asked us to do something very normal like clap our hands. 'OK, I show you.'

He crouched down and moved his torso and head forward until they curled over his knees. He wasn't exactly round, but he was about as close as you can get when you're six foot, two inches. Then slowly, ever so slowly, he began to stand up and uncurl, like those nature programs that show sped-up videos of seeds growing from the ground.

We all tried to emulate him, with varying degrees of success. When we regained our normal postures, Forrest thanked us for all of the effort we had put into the class. We thanked him in return as a group – a tradition borrowed from martial arts.

'Oh my god, that was amazing!' Karen gushed as we strolled out into the chilly night. 'I mean, do you remember jumping up on to that box? I swear, I thought I wouldn't make it on the tenth go, but I knuckled down. "Girl," I said to myself, "you just do this one more time and you'll be glad you did it tomorrow".'

Normally I couldn't care less about rehashing a workout, but this was different. For the first time in a very long time I had the sense that my body had really moved, and it felt great. Not only had I been pushed to my physical limit and not broken, or curled up into a snivelling ball of self-pity, I had enjoyed it.

As Karen and I walked back to our cars that night I felt an unusual sense of elation. Was this the fabled 'runner's high' of endorphins that my sporty friends so often pontificated on? Doubtful. The lactic acid had scorched any endorphins in my body to death at least an hour ago. It was, instead, a change of perspective: when I looked around the urban 'nowhere' of east London, it was suddenly somewhere. Low walls led off like paths in every direction, handrails beckoned like monkey bars, park benches begged to be vaulted. Every surface revealed itself as a step or a handle leading down untold routes of urban discovery that branched and interwove in an exciting hodgepodge of kinetic possibility. The city had not changed, but my mind had and nothing, not the highest wall, nor the nearest garden planter box, seemed outside my newfound realm of possibility.

2

Children of the Banlieue

The personal goal was a way to 'dress wounds' because in your quest, if you already had the answer, then you were already on a personal quest to overcome your being. But at the beginning you have to learn to know yourself, to reinforce yourself . . . you have to go through that way.

Yann Hnautra

So far, the summer of 1987 had been relatively uneventful. Yann Hnautra was fifteen and had just moved to Lisses, the Parisian suburb; a wild and free spirit doing whatever he wanted. He'd been hanging out with his new friend David Malgogne, who had just gone away on holiday. Ahead lay another day with time to kill. Yann set off for the local youth centre with the prospect of table tennis. Games were good. A skinny kid a year younger than him was happy to play. This guy was cool until he got angry, losing a shot, then another point here and there. Being a year older and at least double his body mass, Yann thought 'this bag of bones' can get as angry as he likes. He wasn't worried. The more Yann relaxed and laughed, the more it fuelled the rage simmering in his opponent. It was a good quality to be able to stand up to someone, to be firm, to not fear reacting, Yann told himself; if there was one thing that he respected it was strength, and a bit of rage. However, everyone had a limit and this kid was going too far. The volume in both their voices rose and their postures straightened like two snarling ridgebacks preparing for a fight as they circled one another. Every glance, gesture and accusation was a moment away from exactly what nobody was certain. Others in the room leant with their backs to the wall, taking refuge on the periphery as the young audience observed a teenage gladiatorial show of character. Yann's arms were larger than an average man's legs. They swung back, prepared to deliver the first blow and then somehow, in the midst of the angry testosterone-packed ramblings of two bickering teenagers, the name 'David Malgogne' was spoken.

'What! You're a friend of his?' Yann exclaimed as jubilantly as he could. 'The friends of my friends are my friends! I apologise.' With his arms by his side, a new and immediately different body language exuded from Yann. His enthusiasm for reconciliation was equal to that of fighting. Meeting a friend of a friend meant that the positive things found in your friend were also somewhere to be found in their friend; that was life according to Yann. The skinny angry kid was now a new friend. For the rest of the summer Yann Hnautra and David Belle were inseparable.

According to local legend Yann Hnautra had been roughly the size of a refrigerator since being born in a dirt-floored hut in New Caledonia. This was not entirely true – he was actually born in Dinan, a Breton village in the Côtes-d'Armor region of Brittany and travelled to and from to the Pacific islands depending on his father's military placement; staying one, two or three years at a time. His father was a Kanak – one of the indigenous peoples of New Caledonia – and an exemplary career soldier. In 1953 all New Caledonians were granted French citizenship regardless of ethnicity. Schooled up until age 15, he married his wife at 17, having met her on Réunion Island and by age twenty he owned a house with her in France. Yann's mixed ancestry resulted in a combination of brute strength and showmanship. Like his father and grandfather before him he was a fighter, coming from a line of warriors; in addition, he had inherited the joy, showmanship and sharp instincts of his mother.

'I was born in the sun, in the wind, in nature. I got up, I took a breath, I looked at the sky, and it made me want to sing. I sang. Then I wanted to run, and then I ran.' This was how Yann described his childhood. Regardless of the decades of social organisation imposed on the Kanak indigenous culture, children had the right to roam, to go where they pleased – and they did. Life on the reserve, on one of the outlying islands of the *Grande Terre* (Great Land) of New Caledonia, was financially poor, but kids growing up in an 'open door' society felt free and there was no segregation due to mixed race bloodlines. 'Where I come from, you're brothers or you're not. Even the word "cousin" didn't exist. We're family or we're not.' Yann's kinship bonds were that of a clan.

Things were hard for the Hnautra family in Nouméa, the capital of New Caledonia, but the streets of France were a different ballgame altogether. Entrenched more in the ways of Melanesian tribes and warriors than that of the French suburbs in the 1980s, the Hnautras were the first black family in their neighbourhood in Lisses. Soon more would follow but nobody was surprised when confusion and chaos ensued through their identities and customs being so intrinsically tied up in a group of tiny islands on the other side of the world.

Living a few doors down the road in Lisses was David Belle. He was intense, somewhat on edge and forever the odd one out. His parents were not together. His grandfather on his mother's side, Gilbert Kitten, had raised him from birth up until age fourteen in Fécamp, Normandy. He would see his mother at weekends and was in touch with his father, occasionally visiting, but it was David's grandfather who perhaps had the biggest impact on his upbringing initially. He was an authority figure and pillar of respectability, guiding and caring for David. He taught him the importance of manners and respectful behaviour towards others. He facilitated his grandson's sporting needs through gymnastics clubs and athletics, always instilling a sense of right and wrong, hoping he would one day become a firefighter as he had been. 'If you have to use your physical strength, do it for good reasons: rather than robbing a home, use this energy to help people,' he would tell him.

Although he was raising a child in his later years, his grandfather had 'few habits of an old man' according to David, who loved him dearly. He had been a Parisian fireman for 32 years and was a World War II veteran. The firefighters of Paris were not just your average firemen, either; they were part of the military rather than a civilian service. Their training and reputation went beyond rescuing cats from trees and putting out blazes. His grand-father had seen and known adventure; David, by contrast had not. He was lost, introverted and withdrawn; and coupled with an obstinate and stubborn streak he was also a poor student and failing at school. His mother's side of the family were academically successful, something that only reinforced his sense of alienation and lack of direction. His uncle was a headmaster, his aunt a teacher and David's cousins on his mother's side of the family were all doing well at school. David was the opposite.

David's father, Raymond Belle, was half-French half-Vietnamese and had gone to live in France in 1954. David was quarter-Vietnamese and neither looked like his father nor shared his character, sometimes leading him to think, 'I must have been adopted, there is no other way!' Raymond was charismatic, strong and bright; David was anything but. His father had been in the Vietnam War and then like his grandfather became a firefighter in Paris.

During his teenage years, on the cusp of manhood, David began to ask his family more questions about his father and his past. His grandfather shared many stories about his father's sporting accolades and rescues as well as his experiences during the Vietnam War. With a reputation larger than life, bigger and better than any superheroes he admired in his Marvel comics, David was desperate to know him better.

Other members of the Belle family had also left Vietnam after the war and were living in Sarcelles, north of the centre of Paris. David's father had gone to live with them, the 'Belles of Sarcelles'. Soon David would be living with his mother full-time in Lisses, almost thirty miles away. He was fourteen years old and it was an opportunity for David to be reunited with his father and get to know the Vietnamese side of his family.

Like many cities on the outskirts of Paris during the 1950s and 1960s, the population of Sarcelles was growing due to a combination of French residents moving from the countryside to the city seeking work, colonial settlers returning after decolonisation and migrants from abroad looking to fill labour shortages. The *pieds noirs* from Algeria, Morocco and Tunisia; Sephardic Jews escaping persecution from the newly empowered Muslim majorities in North Africa; Caribbeans, sub-Saharan Africans and southern and southeastern Asians; all of these made up the milieu of Sarcelles. Within a few decades it had quickly become a suburb with a population of less than 10,000 to one with about 50,000. Sarcelles was one of the most ethnically diverse cities in the Île-de-France region.

The early years following the Vietnamese Belle family's arrival in Sarcelles were alienating. They had to overcome obstacles including the language, the legalities of labour and cultural variations as they began their new life in a two-bedroomed flat in Villiers-le-Bel. Things improved when they moved to a large detached house in 'the village', the quiet old part of the city. Their new home was less than ten minutes' walk from the edge of the Ecouen forest, a vast expanse dating back to the days when the area had been a small village surrounded by farmland and the castle, the Château d'Ecouen, built in the mid-sixteenth century.

The Belle family house was a great place to gather, eat, drink and, as was custom in their family, rehearse at the weekend. Performers, musicians, comedians, painters and artists had reconnected after immigrating, creating an informal 'Vietnamese society', a theatre company. The older teenage sons, Phung and Chau, weren't so interested or enamoured by the gatherings, but the youngest, Williams, sat enthralled on his mother's knee, taking it all in for hours on end. Their father was a singer and president of the company. Their mother stayed out of the spotlight but created the costumes for the shows as well as relying on her sewing skills for work. Rehearsals could start on Friday and last throughout the weekend but Sundays were always the loudest as their Vietnamese guests maintained the tradition for Sunday drinking. Although none earned a living through their artistry, instead relying on labouring or sewing, theatre was their passion.

The house was full, but soon there was another guest. In 1988 when Williams was six, David's father, Raymond, moved in with members of his family from Vietnam.

'He's come to live with us from now on,' Williams's mother announced. It was after a three-week school holiday on the coast with his sister Nelly that Williams met the 'Very Big Great Uncle' Raymond when he came to pick them up from school. As was customary in Vietnamese culture, when the parents were busy working, the grand-parents took on the role of bringing up the children, passing on their education and values. As the brother of their grandfather, Raymond Belle would be looking after Phung, Chau and Williams.

With Great Uncle Raymond's arrival came the introduc-tion to his fifteen-year-old son, who would frequently go to visit him: their older cousin David. David was welcomed with open arms in Sarcelles. Although David was three years older than Phung, the most senior of the boys, they all became friends and Williams was always eager to tag along. Soon the cousins were regularly making the journey across Paris from Sarcelles to Lisses, accompanying various family members, aunts and uncles, to visit David in return. His friends were their friends.

3

The Artist
and the Alpinist

It seems to me to express visually the challenge accepted by
humans to strive to attain the limits of the possible.

Pierre Székely

'I've done all the passages, all the ascents, there's nothing left to do,' thought Yann as they waited for David's cousins Phung and Chau whilst staring up at the structure in front of them. The harsh, concrete urban training environments in Lisses and Evry were so different to the tranquil and luscious forest of Ecouen that the cousins had next to them in Sarcelles.

Whilst Sarcelles had expanded and become absorbed as a Parisian suburb, different forces were at play in Evry. Evry-Petit-Bourg, as it was previously known, had been a small village with a population of no more than a few thousand. A new era of urban planning policy had changed the landscaped by pursuing two goals. Firstly, to protect Paris from *urbanisme sauvage*, whereby rapid population growth led to uncontrolled urbanisation and threatened the city's balance and beauty. Secondly, to create new autonomous towns that would absorb this growth, with hubs of housing, commerce and industry, served by preconceived rather than organic infrastructure. The heart of Paris would be preserved culturally and historically while the *banlieues* or suburbs would absorb the projected population growth and become towns in their own right.

The project continued the economic and aesthetic separation of the suburbs that had begun one hundred years earlier when George-Eugene Haussmann reshaped the city at the behest of Napoléon III. Haussmann had transformed the centre of Paris, creating the wide leafy boulevards, sewers, aqueducts, fountains and green spaces that remain characteristic of the city. The number of trees almost doubled from fifty thousand to ninety-five thousand and the 'two great lungs of the city' were created: the Bois de Boulogne and the Bois de Vincennes. The suburbs were annexed as part of the transformation. The new project continued the separation of the suburbs economically and aesthetically while simultaneously offering a solution to the processes of gentrification.

With Parisians unafraid to repeat such grand architectural experiments, the *Schéma Directeur* project was undertaken in 1965 on a similar scale to Haussmann's. In a seven-year period its director, Paul Delouvrier, set in motion five new towns, three circumferential motorways and five regional express *Réseau Express Regional* train lines – the R.E.R. The new towns were: Cergy-Pontoise, Melun-Senart, St. Quentin-en-Yvelines, Marne-la-Vallée and Evry. Of all the plans, none were as bold and ambitious as those for Evry, situated twenty-five miles to the south-east of central Paris. The aim was to balance affordable housing for the working class with areas designated for social and cultural 'animators' to mix and cast a new character on to their autonomous urban locale. It was an experiment of daring vision that would allow a new population to live a unique social existence, architecturally and experientially.

The look of Evry was a return to a traditional sense of urbanism but with a modern look: the home, the workplace and the mall. The high housing density meant that the public spaces were geared towards pedestrians. Everything was side by side. Schools were placed below the houses, integrating the schoolyard without boundaries so that they were also next to offices and parking lots. The freshly cast concrete edges demonstrated perfect angles and lines. The striking, repetitive and varied angular geometries created buildings that looked like enormous terraced blocks or stepping stones waiting for mystical giants to cross. The spaces were new ideas reminiscent of the Brutalist architectural philosophy, a socialist utopian dream matching *béton brut* (raw concrete) with a young population who were ready to test it and be tested. The idiosyncrasies of these dense, concrete designs meant that walkways and passages didn't always connect and places could often be seen but not easily found or accessed by conventional means.

In contrast to the natural growth of cities, towns and villages that occur and evolve over decades and centuries through multiple layers of interactions between citizens and enterprises, the new towns were mapped out and created from a central political authority. The prefecture (government building) was built first followed by economically efficient implanted infrastructure; next came the residential areas, then commerce. The metropolitan area of Evry would include the villages of Lisses, Courcouronnes and Bondoufle.

Transport links were kept to the periphery, allowing for a mélange of civic activities to occur within public spaces made up of squares and walkways. Underground car parks kept cars out of sight. A separate road for local buses to take residents quickly and efficiently to the train station didn't intercut with any of the car or pedestrian routes, making links to Paris or elsewhere possible and accessible for all. The city had to be built quickly. The Pyramides quarter would provide seven thousand new homes within five years, with two thousand, five hundred in the first year alone. The *Habitations à Loyer Modéré* were high-rise social housing projects and again Evry's would look like no other. According to one of the architects 'there are three groups of pyramids and they were designed according to three things: diversity, integration (different social classes and populations), integration also means non-segregation, all of the different classes will be mixed, and the third one is animation.'

There were also 'unidentified spaces', areas deliberately left without a defined purpose. The planners were flexible and open to adapting to the needs and feedback of the residents. Although Evry had a political and commercial centre, some inhabitants felt it was still lacking something. It was overwhelmingly artificial and in need of 'renaturalising'. In response, more developments were added after the initial phase, and the biggest and most interesting part of the renaturalisation of Evry was the creation of the artificial park-lake of Courcouronnes in 1975.

As part of its design, the mayor of Evry proposed a structure that would mirror the famous boulders of Fontainebleau and be the first climbing wall of its kind in France. In 1970 Pierre Székely, the celebrated Hungarian sculptor, was invited to submit his ideas. Five years later, in collaboration with the decorated Italian alpinist mountaineer Guido Magnone, he told the residents that 'the mountain will come to you'. The resulting structure, the Dame du Lac, was a bizarre, characteristically French, somewhat surreal, modernist-infused monolith, south-facing and almost fifteen metres tall. It conceptualised the sculpted reflection of a female body in the lake and offered one hundred and fifty grips, appealing to adventurous new urbanites who felt the pull of the mountains but lacked the means of reaching them. The artificial mountain was a short walk from the shopping centre and accessible to all of the citizens of Evry.

The sculpture was intended for people to be able to learn how to climb and experience the activity's different techniques. The school of Evry would have an 'in-service' instructor and the wall would be open to the public – school groups, climbers, associations and anyone else with the will to scale it.

Interviewed in the magazine *Leonardo* a few years after its completion, Székely described his work: 'I have constructed a large sculpture for alpinists, whom I call *piétons de l'espace* [walkers in space], at the edge of a lake in a "new city" development south of Paris. Sculptors and alpinists, in their particular ways, contend with space. Their physique is guided more by imagination than mechanical devices and tools.'

Yann, David, Phung and Chau didn't consider themselves artists or climbers but the imagination of the young group of friends went wild on the structure. Away from any formal climbing instruction they tried and tested their ever-changing limits and loved it. The Dame du Lac was a place almost created for their motivations. A place where sport meets art.

The structure curved upwards from a broad solid base, gently at first and then more and more steeply to give the feeling of a forceful thrust skywards. Towards the top it bends slightly backward, producing a slight concavity. It was embellished with a central chimney, ledges and hand-holds and according to Székely 'leads to nowhere in particular'.

Guido Magnone, his alpinist collaborator, had described it as a 'vertical sports field'.

Phung and Chau had not waited long to make their first visit. They began by exploring the bottom of the structure, a reasonable approach, testing distances and ways to move. They were active, strong and able. Then they moved on to a new route going from the passage to the triangle. Phung and Chau were the first to go from the triangle to the first hole, an act that caused Yann and David to look on in disbelief. 'It was incredible. You think you've seen all of what can be extreme and then someone comes and does that, that and that – I never imagined that. It was unthinkable . . .' remembered Yann. He was inspired to try the new routes the others had found. He wanted to learn to become as strong as those he watched. 'To be strong you have to get closer to strong people. It's logical!' he thought.

Inspired by the new town's architecture, some of the young immigrant populations that explored Evry brought with them a wealth of ideas that would create a new type of beauty and interpretation of the landscape. However imaginative the planners were, none could have foreseen how unique some of the ideas and actions that would play out on their predetermined routes would be. Like-minded young people continued to move into the neighbourhoods. Those from Lisses and Evry met one another at school, college or as neighbours. David's visits to his father in Sarcelles brought his friends from Evry into contact with Phung, Chau and Williams in Sarcelles. Alone, nobody knew what were his limits and possibilities, but together, a convergence of personalities and pasts created a catalyst; the embryonic stages of an alchemy involving individual abilities that collectively could create, copy, inspire, challenge and create again. Their research had begun.

4

The Boy Who Wasn't There

You must be capable of doing it; you must become stronger because if you want to be capable of doing great things, you must be capable here and now of doing this.

Williams Belle talking to himself, aged nine

I t wasn't unusual for Williams to find sitting in a classroom a challenge, but this one morning, when he was just six years old, taking a seat at his desk was simply too painful. Seeing his discomfort, his teacher asked Williams to step outside the classroom, fearing that her suspicions might be right. At her request, Williams pulled down his trousers to reveal a backside that was black and blue with bruises – and not simply from a hand, but from a stick. Leading the small child back into the room, she addressed the class, Williams stood nervously alongside. 'Children, sometimes things turn out this way. Children get beaten up by their parents,' she explained as Williams longed to be anywhere but there. He felt ashamed and embarrassed but as he looked round he realised no one was smirking or laughing; the potential cruelty of children hadn't shown its ugly face. They all looked as upset as he felt. Maybe some of them are in the same boat as me, he thought. They'll understand. His father was summoned to the school where in front of the class he was told simply that in France it was not acceptable to beat children.

Williams was moved by his teacher's approach; her actions had provoked change and for that she was a hero. The war had taken its toll on his father and he still bore the traumas and emotional scars, but from that day onwards, Williams's father would beat his children much less. Although the internal effects of the beatings weren't obvious to others, the external manifestation of the beatings were clear: Williams had trouble speaking and stuttered a lot as a result of the violence he had experienced.

Being strong was a family thing. A Belle thing. His father, uncles and aunts had always been physically active and able. Confrontations needed to be overcome and challenges were there to be faced, no matter how insurmountable the size or fierce the foe. Nobody revealed their weaknesses. Even before his training began Williams had always sought out challenge and hardship. Sleeping on the floor with no blanket in the winter, forcing himself to endure the cold, not drinking or eating for a day – anything to gain more confidence, to reassure himself that one day he could face the violence and injustices he had suffered. He was scared of being beaten up and needed to change. He wanted to be the person who wasn't scared.

Great Uncle Raymond, their cousin David's father, was a strong presence in the household and not just physically. He was an authoritarian, military-like character who scared the hell out of all of Williams's friends. He had been an accomplished and celebrated firefighter and athlete. If they called for him during lunch, they would receive a blank stare and a door slammed in their faces regardless of any pressing information that needed to be conveyed or previous arrangements that had been made. A wrong glance and your face would be slapped, immediately followed up with a full explanation as to why you received such treatment. For all his harshness, however, there was an equal measure of love. Williams never excused the violence but never dismissed the love either.

Although extremely shy, Williams was also hyperactive and crazy about any sport or games he could try. Add a splash of mischief and he would take on anything. From the age of five at their small two-bedroom apartment in Villiers-le-Bel, he would climb the railings instead of walking up the stairs. In the park nearby he would see a tree and knew he must be able to catch the branch. Whatever it took, he needed to be able. Internally Williams had been asking questions and looking for answers for as long as he could remember. Setting goals was a way out of the violence of his early years.

While others thought Williams was gifted when he started training, no one knew he had been training by himself beforehand. In the park or forest, when no one else was around, every jump, every climb, every action became a test of strength, a little answer to a much bigger question.

Williams admired and aspired to the strength of those around him. Over time, he realised that it wasn't just the Belles who had such an appetite for all things challenging and strength-related. His family was definitely strong – his brothers, his cousin, his great uncle, his other uncles and aunts – but so were his cousin's friends. Sébastien Foucan was a big guy with huge muscles. If any of his brothers and cousin's friends could keep up with them, then Williams wanted to stay close to them too. He felt Sébastien was like something out of *Dragon Ball*, the action-packed TV manga show. Williams was always so happy to see them; they were special, but it was all so normal.

Setting out for the woods one summer afternoon in 1991, Williams was nine years old and had no idea that the events that were about to unfold would dramatically change the course of his life. His oldest brother Phung led the way as the youngest Belle sibling happily jogged along with his two brothers: Phung was fifteen, Chau nearly fourteen, his cousin David eighteen and David's best friend Sébastien, sixteen. From their house in the quiet cul-de-sac it was a stone's throw to the entrance to the Ecouen forest.

Their feet percussioned the earth as they ran along the gravel path, heading deeper into the woods. They passed the ghostly abandoned houses and trees replaced concrete as traffic and cars became a distant memory and nature enveloped them. Before they could get to the *parcours de santé* (fitness trail), there was just the small matter of a two-and-a-half-metre stone wall. The older ones all ran up the wall as though they had been doing it their entire lives. A quick burst of pace and a carefully judged foot placement fluidly transferred their horizontal run into an ascent, both hands catching the top of the wall with their body quick to follow. The ascent for Williams was more laboured, crawling up a slanted section Chau would then throw down a hand to pull his younger brother up to join the rest of the group. Williams was a pain but everyone always kept an eye on him. Looking down it felt high for Williams but he didn't want to stay low in front of the others so walked tall along the top of the uneven stones and narrow edge, which at times was only a little wider than his slender shoulders.

The slippery emerald landscape of moss- and ivy-covered sections on top of the wall was tricky to navigate. Branches brushed and bristled their arms and legs, leaving spikes and marks, nature's reminder of who was there first. The smooth, concreted section provided a welcome respite from the overhanging foliage. 'Are you able to jump above someone?' they asked. Williams smiled and nodded enthusiastically, not really knowing the answer. One by one they took it in turn to crouch and curl into a ball. The next one in line would jump over and take up the crouched position. Soon four human stones provided the landscape for one person to jump. Williams had played similar games at ground level with friends his own age but here were his older brothers and their friends, on the cusp of manhood but still playing. It took courage, but Williams loved it. The crouch became a squat and the jump needed was higher. Little challenges could always be made into more. When the Belles had first moved to Sarcelles their first visits to the forest started simply with friends walking, climbing trees and collecting chestnuts, but now their ventures had changed. As they carried along the wall they passed the castle cemetery jump; a gap in the wall that meant you either leaped across or climbed down and back up. It had been the first 'real' jump for the Sarcelles locals to conquer and the older ones flew across with ease, before helping Williams down and back up the wall.

Next up were the drop jumps – the *sauts de fond* – from the wall to the ground. Two metres was too far for Williams. He gazed in amazement as the wall rained men like paratroopers without a chute. Some landed on their feet on the muddy leafed path while others dropped and rolled to help absorb the impact. Williams squatted down to lessen the distance and tried to imagine dropping down, but still he knew it wasn't for him yet. They continued running until the lines of trees opened up to reveal the playground, whose main feature was a large wooden ship and cabin. It was a perfect hideaway with no-one around to see them or question their version of play.

Giant crossed logs created the skeletal frame with solid planks making up the bow. Inside there was a small ladder leading to a platform which provided good opportunities for jumping down on to another platform at the helm or to cross from one side of the boat to the other at different levels. Walking on the edges, crawling and balancing along the logs, jumping up on to or down from things: they were simply big, fun-loving kids. Williams had seen children his own age jumping and didn't find it special, but this was much better – it was grander, more impressive. And there was one jump in particular that he'd seen the others do. It was different.

'I want to do it,' insisted Williams, with a confidence nobody could mistake. It may not have looked much to a fourteen- or fifteen-year-old, but for the body of a nine-year-old it would be demanding.

'No, it's impossible for you. It's too far,' Phung replied, aware of the irony in someone like him saying such a thing. Who really knew what was possible? He knew he didn't want to see Williams get hurt. He was young and should just be having fun. Phung and Chau worried that if Williams got into training too soon it could stunt his growth. There was no rush. But Williams insisted, so they knew what to do. Phung, Chau, David and Sébastien took a stick and created two lines in the earth marking out the same distance as the jump. 'OK, try it.' He only just made it – but he was so happy. 'I did it! I did it!' There was no room for error, however: it had been that tight.

'OK, so now you can do it for real,' said David. 'If you can do it on the floor, then you can do it in the air' was the simple logic that they all seemed to agree on and abide by.

Invigorated by his success, Williams climbed up on to the structure. As quickly as the ground level jump had given him confidence, the real jump and its height froze him. Why had he been so quick to want to do it? He should have just kept his mouth shut. Avoiding eye contact with the others, he silently climbed down. He didn't know what to say and, even if he did, his debilitating stutter probably wouldn't have let the sounds out. 'Why was I born this way?' he thought.

'Repeat the jump,' Phung told him. 'Again and again and again. You need to build up your confidence, then you'll know if you are really strong enough to do it "for real". Once, twice, three times, five times, ten times . . . Williams completed the jump more than thirty times, each repetition reinforcing his will and self-belief. 'Go Williams, you can do it, you're a Belle!' David added.

As Williams climbed back up to take another look, the others collectively took off their T-shirts and placed them around what would be his fall zone if he didn't make it. The soft fabrics wouldn't help break his landing or soften the blow if he missed but this simple gesture of support, love and compassion meant everything to Williams. He wasn't jumping alone. 'Imagine you have to jump over there to save our mother,' Chau added, creating even more motivation for Williams to let go of his fear. He would do anything for his mother; he had to save her. 'I must be strong, I must be able to protect her,' he thought. He jumped.

Despite much celebration, the jump wasn't over: he had to do it again. Once was maybe luck, a chance encounter. Once was never. It didn't count. The others put their T-shirts back on and stood by as Williams completed the jump again for validation. No problem. He had always seen the others do three jumps, dedicating the last one to someone else. The third time, nobody was next to the jump 'just in case'. He had succeeded. 'I really did it,' he thought, but now, as was ritual for the older ones, he had to dedicate it to someone. There was only one choice: his mother.

Leaving the others for dust, Williams ran back home in a state of ecstasy. He had to share his revelation. 'I need to show you something, you need to come and break this jump!' Halis, his best friend, wasn't entirely convinced, but the next day the two young boys headed into the woods. It wasn't magic or chance. Williams happily completed the jump again. Halis looked but was too scared to try. As the others had done for him, Williams helped, supported and showed his friend the way. He jumped and made it but to Williams's shock and horror there was no revelation, no conscious reflection. It was just a jump. With an insight and wisdom beyond his years, Williams asked himself, 'How could he not feel something more? Is it just me? Am I the only one to have this "conscience", to understand that by breaking jumps you can face and overcome your fears and improve yourself in life, outside and inside?' That day he decided that if he had to train on his own then he would; but if someone needed help then he would always give a hand. He believed that to be strong involved more than physical strength. He had grown a deep, almost innate, sense that whatever questions he had in life this would help him find answers.

Training with his brothers made him feel good but, because Williams was considerably younger, he continued to drive them crazy. He was upset not to be always invited to go with them, so he trained alone in the dark in the middle of the woods, breaking jumps and fears.

Every evening after school – and sometimes in the middle of the night – Williams headed to his ship, his playground: it became his own symbol and ritual. Training was his journey. 'If you took your boat, your practice, you'll get to the other side,' he thought. The 'haunted houses' en route scared him like hell but, shaking, he peered in through the cobwebbed misty windows. He must confront his fears.

It wasn't for lack of love or concern but, a lot of the time, no one really knew what Williams was up to. His younger sister Audrey had just been born and his mother was working from 7 a.m. to 11 p.m. He was happy and loved, but the brutality and violent experiences of the older generation continually seeped its way in, inflicting new wounds for members of the family.

For the next two to three years, Williams trained hard and watched his brothers, cousin and their friends whenever he could. He considered what he witnessed to be a sort of question-and-answer session, individuals asking something new of themselves, and answering it. It was the most beautiful and honest thing he had ever seen. 'Where did they come from?' he thought. They were really something else. By the early 1990s the type of things they did didn't compare to anything he had seen in films or TV. It was better. His favourite martial arts movies included impressive scenes filmed with wires and safety nets but what he witnessed from them was real.

They moved subconsciously, reacting with reflexes that appeared from nowhere. Their bodies somehow knew the right thing to do. If they fell, they would reach out. They were open to every possibility and in harmony with everything around them. He could feel something of this as he watched and absorbed the most animated death-defying acts of play. There was never anything to win or lose and they gave their all each and every time. Whenever

Williams was with them, he felt their encounters had meaning. He could feel their compassion and love for each other and what they were doing. Alongside the physical strength there was so much respect shared between them. How each of them moved was somehow innately tied up in who they were and the result of what they were all individually as well as collectively searching for.

Climbing the water tower encompassed all these feelings for Williams, and indeed the others. It was a challenge beyond what could be practised on the ground. Situated in the heart of the forest, the tower was at least twelve metres tall, looming high against the canopy of trees. A solid, gigantic, grey and concrete structure, it was round at the top, supported on giant stilts and contrasted with the swaying leaves and natural surroundings. Phung's tiny figure at the top seemed out of place, juxtaposing man in both nature and the built landscape.

Those at the bottom – Williams, Chau, David and a few friends from the neighbourhood – were scared to watch, let alone able to relate to the mental state of the one at the top. There was no reference for such a thing being done before, no example to follow or reassuring knowledge of 'Yes, it's possible'. It was no longer a game. 'How,' thought Williams, 'do I transition from being scared down here to being like Phung up there?'

Even in climbing terms, the route to get to the jump was tricky with a challenging ascent towards the top that even seasoned climbers might struggle with. It was technical as well as high. Phung was a man of few words but his mind was always present, his mental strength enabling the physical to follow. If he thought 'I'm going to make it', then he would. The cemetery jump across the wall had provided a sound basis for jumping at height but this one was more than the next level up. They had jumped koala-like from the wall to trees, catching and grabbing with their hands, their feet landing firmly placed against the trunk, but nothing compared to the height of the water tower and the jump across into the top of a tree. Nothing could be measured or calculated, just felt, a pure instinctual sense of one's own capabilities in that moment. If he could see it, the energy was right, the feeling was there then he'd go.

The friends looked on in amazement as they saw Phung leap 1.5 metres from the side of the tower into the adjacent tree. Phung's arm-jump was unbelievable but real. Flying squirrels and monkeys made such leaps and now Phung had proven men could fly.

On first impressions, the older Yann and David seemed the strongest, but if there was a risky jump or new ground to take on, Phung was the one to complete it. He was the man of 'firsts', yet for a young man with the ability to impress, he was extremely cool. When Phung completed a new jump there was 'no Hollywood', their friend Laurent Piemontesi would say later. He liked to keep things simple. He was a naturally generous man of few words. Phung was the *example*. Especially for the impressionable and eager Williams.

'Of course Phung would make it,' thought Williams. It was normal. It was Phung.

Phung had offered to help Williams train and, in true Phung style, he kept it simple and with few words. 'Do this maybe more like this.' Williams liked the simplicity and mindset of his approach. If you're capable of doing something, you do it, otherwise go and train peacefully. There was a calm strength and inner rage contained beneath the surface. Phung, Yann and David all shared this aptitude for both the physical and mental side of their training – it seemed harnessed to who they were and provided a focus that they needed to stay on the right side of risk. They were confident at height and always looked to go higher.

According to his uncles, Phung's character was already formed by the age of three. He had spent the first three years of his life in Vietnam, born in 1976 amidst the chaotic aftermath of the war. He had always been athletic, always running and always training hard, even in their bedroom. Williams wanted to be able to do the same things, right now, but he knew there would be training to get there.

By the age of eleven, Williams's friends his own age had lost interest in simply jumping or playing in playgrounds for 'children'. At twelve years old he realised, 'I'm doing something that not everyone wants to do, but I want to keep it up because it gives me answers, and that's it . . .' He had invited his good friends to come and train in the woods with him. It was open to them all. 'What's the point? What's the point of jumping from up there to down there,' they asked. 'But you don't realise, if you can jump down there . . .' There was no point: they didn't care and their PlayStation was calling.

5

The Left-Hand Path

Everything was a game because in a game it doesn't matter who is the strongest one. There are no weak people. Everybody's strong: there's no weakness, just new experiences to live.

Yann Hnautra

Everyone remembers where they were the first time they met Yann. For David it was a fateful ping pong match; for Chau, Yann was up a tree playing his guitar. For Laurent Piemontesi it was 1989; he was sixteen years old and it was at Le L.A.C, the Lisses Athletic Club.

Basketball and athletics were Laurent's first sporting loves and they cost him nothing. The public basketball courts played host to many mornings, afternoons and evenings. You could run anywhere and Laurent did but that afternoon it was formal and structured. The pace of the five-kilometre felt brutal; his legs burnt and eyes stung with sweat. 'Hey, go faster!' the voice from behind boomed as the largest body on the track sailed up next to him, smiling, sweating and talking with the ease of someone on a conveyor belt rather than engaged in a physical act. Whoever this man was, he wasn't out of breath. 'I can't, I can't, I'm dying!' exclaimed Laurent, too exasperated to question anything. 'No, go up with your knees, up! Up!' he instructed while demonstrating a higher knee raise in his own technique. 'OK, sorry I have to leave you now, my brother is at the starting line, I have to go and see him.' With a smile as broad as his face he ran on ahead, disappearing as quickly as he had appeared.

A few minutes later Laurent crossed the finish line, relieved, panting and exhausted. There was the man again, as fresh-faced as could be. 'OK, so how was it?' he asked. Before Laurent had a chance to reply the voice over the tannoy announced, 'Would all participants for the eight-kilometre race please proceed to the start line.'

'Ah, sorry I have to go!' He beamed and he was off again. This time Laurent noticed something else about him. They had completed the same race but, unlike the other participants, he wore no medal and his race number looked somewhat homemade. Yann Hnautra ran for the love of running. He had never been a member of the L.A.C. He needed no medal, certificate or number. He just needed to run.

The first time Yann came to Sarcelles with David, Williams couldn't believe his eyes. He had never met a man who was stronger than his cousin but here he was. 'Yeah, let me introduce you to this dude, he is just breathtaking, he showed me loads of stuff,' David told Williams. 'Yann is *balèèèèze*,' Williams thought – a term used for the strong and skilled. 'Wow!' He was an incredible force of nature. He was . . . He was beyond everyone, beyond the norm . . . He had arms like legs! He was a crazy mass of energy, jumping everywhere. He'd do pull-ups with his friend Laurent on his back. He was so powerful, it was abnormal. He had so much energy, so much 'potato' – for Williams, Yann was 'potato-man', a clumsy raw energy with a good heart, but wild. Really wild.

Williams had been watching his older brothers, cousin and their friends move for the past three years and thought

David was the most gifted technically and would always go further. But Yann, despite his lack of technique, could go as far as David – who was more of a gymnast – just with the strength of his arms.

For Yann, being strong meant applying few limits. He chose not to believe in being tired. At the back of his mind he always felt that someone, somewhere in the world would be capable of doing more, so why not him too? His constant quest for strength was partially a means of escaping the harsh realities of his environment. He was an outsider in many ways; he looked different and was frequently the focus of racism. All this was exacerbated by the fact that he found it difficult to speak French. Discrimination was rife on the streets of Evry.

Since that meeting on the tracks, Laurent and Yann had become close friends, with Yann taking on the role of leader and trainer. Laurent arrived at Yann's house and as usual was welcomed with a plate of food. Then they ran. Then push-ups, 'OK, the first set,' said Yann, '101.' 'What? Yann, this is too much. It's bizarre,' said Laurent, questioning the number.

'It's not important, just do 101.' Yann had a certain way with words and repetitions.

Under Yann's creative (if occasionally sadistic) eye, training was founded on a simple paradigm of doing normal exercises an abnormal number of times. You could not, for instance, just do twenty push-ups if you were working out with Yann. You started at fifty-one – always an odd number – and worked your way up as you got stronger. By the time they were in their late teens, it was common to do 201 or 301 push-ups at a time, multiple times a day, every day. Sit-ups required at least 1,001 reps, no questions asked. When pull-ups became too easy, everyone moved on to muscle-ups, where you lift your entire torso above the chin-up bar as an Olympic gymnast lifts himself up above the rings. Next it was punching stones and the wall outside, bam, bam, bam! Before more running and then jumping over the waist-high bollards next to the bus stops, twenty-one in a row. Always repeating. Always having more to do.

Like the others, they had only one thing on their mind. 'We have to train.' Every conversation was fixed around this simple goal and every conversation evoked the same afterthought: 'It's not enough.' If they hadn't trained until they were exhausted then they hadn't really trained.

'OK, before we start training let's try and get tired,' suggested Yann the next day. 'Let's go and play football with our friends.' Laurent compliantly ran after him, always happy to oblige every idea that this unstoppable force of a man proposed. They ran up and down the field as they played, even when it was irrelevant to the play, but always sprinting up and down the pitch. Ninety minutes later they started their training. Yann didn't just run; he found time to talk, joke and laugh with every player on the pitch. He was a social creature. Whether being the heart and soul of the party or at a sporting event, he thrived off other people; it was always about the tribe. Laurent would have been happier 'training with the wolves', tucked away in the woods out of sight, without the distraction of curious eyes and conversation. However, together they were close and Laurent happily followed Yann's long training sessions and never complained.

It wasn't that Laurent didn't want to see other friends, it was just that there wasn't much time when all you did was train and all you wanted to talk about was wanting to train, what you had just trained and what you intended to train next. It was somewhat limiting. He wasn't the only one to feel this. 'We loved our families and friends, but this was just for us,' remembered Chau Belle.

The group of friends didn't drink or smoke, always pure to their training. Any form of sports drinks was considered cheating. 'Ah, you drink Gatorade? You are not strong enough. You need Gatorade? You can't have just water?' Such weaknesses were never tolerated. Step by step, other friends who didn't share this obsession felt a difference and distance as they no longer fitted in with the mono-maniacs. However, the counterweight to these somewhat exclusive behaviours in Lisses and Evry was the open house of Yann's family and the apartment of Laurent's grand-mother. There was always something to eat or drink, day or night. Everyone was welcome.

Going to Yann's house was, Laurent remembered, 'a kind of vacation because outside we were in a hard context'. 'It was tough," he added, 'but you go inside Yann's house and it's ahhhhhhh . . . exhale. You can feel all these good things about sharing.' The Hnautra house was filled with warmth and love from a mixture of conversation, guitar playing and songs that dissipated the tensions of life on the streets. Meanwhile, at Laurent's grandmother's there was always a plate of pasta chorizo. Likewise, in Sarcelles, although quieter than the Hnautras, the Belle's house was a communal home. The Belle's parents' friends would stay over, as would the younger generation of friends from the neighbourhood and those from further away. 'Your friends, really . . . ah, it doesn't matter. If there's food for one, there's food for ten!' their mother would say. 'You just make smaller portions.' They were a family with a big heart and a deep-seated sense of what it meant to share.

For Phung, Chau and Williams's parents it was normal

to see their children physically training and working out. Their father had trained in martial arts and so did they. Tapping into a disciplined mindset seemed natural. This sense was exaggerated for the brothers after their father left home when Phung was fifteen, Chau fourteen and Williams ten, having had an affair with a fellow member of the amateur theatre group. They saw their mother work hard. She was alone, fighting for her children, and they would fight for her. They wanted to be strong and able to protect their family. Without instruction or guidance, they were all serious about their physical preparation. Training at every given moment was just a part of who they were.

For each of them there was an individual need to be the strongest they could, which went above their love for training with each other. Just like the younger Williams, Chau knew he had some catching up to do to be as prepared as his older brother, cousin and their friends. Growing up in a household of athletes and firefighters as well as being surrounded by the older Yann (twenty), David (nineteen), Sébastien (eighteen), and Phung (seventeen) normalised the levels of activity and pushed him even more. Chau was determined. He was the *précis carré*, the precise perfectionist.

School started at 8 a.m. so he was up at six; pull-ups, push-ups, lifting weights, chairs, anything that was available. He knew he had things to do. Five thousand abdominal crunches throughout the day, or maybe all in one go. His training was efficient: if he had to go to the woods to do his exercises, he ran instead of walking. He climbed and traversed anything and everything he could find and completed a lot of small jumps. When he crawled his core muscles were sore afterwards, so he did more of that. The friends moved on all fours, an adult monkey-looking crawl, as a way to go up the sides of walls and bridges. If it worked and felt like it did something then Chau would do it.

It was an all-encompassing mindset. Even at school, where Chau proved an excellent student, the focus would be on the next training session. The next physical improvement. During class he would work on his handgrip as he tried at least to train something through the sedentary hours. His hands were sore. Everything was sore. Yann had always encouraged a sense of physical reinforcement, so with this idea and the influence of every martial arts flick he'd seen, he began punching trees with the flat part of his fist. If it was good enough for Bruce Lee, it would work for him too. He broke glass coke bottles against his shins and sucked it up.

Bruce Lee was the unofficial president of the friends' non-existent club. If he said something then it must be true and they should live their lives accordingly. Alongside Lee, the other unspoken mentors influencing the young minds were Jackie Chan, Jean-Claude Van Damme and the characters of *Dragon Ball*, which had popularised manga and anime in Europe. For the friends, who divulged every martial arts film available, Chan's movements and use of the environment was creative, unique, daring and unbelievably co-ordinated. He brought a new style and vision – his vision – to the realms of possibility because his stunts were real. As for Van Damme, his flexibility was legendary. *Dragon Ball* had it all, though. The Japanese TV series was a serious dose of martial arts comedy, drawing on every classic martial arts film with stories of epic quests and mythic structures.

Goku, the main protagonist and hero in *Dragon Ball*, was in training for the 21st World Martial Arts Tournament, and as life imitates art, his training wasn't far off that of the real-world strength training happening in various Parisian suburbs. There were no Fireballs, but pushing rocks, lifting heavy things and training for the possibility of some insurmountable foe all seemed relatable. The friends all had their heroes. The criteria: whoever projected a constant reference of strength and protection. Training tirelessly with a warrior mindset, they wanted to fight and test their skills because they had prepared themselves for it. They could see their progression through hardcore training. *Dragon Ball* was of its time.

While most young people indulged in the ideas put forward by their animated heroes, for the group of friends the concept of above-normal strength, astronomical levels of effort and attaining the unattainable were not a flight of fantasy. Even as they aged, such ideas never faded. Instead they manifested into something real. Alone each of them would have been the odd one out but together none of them were. The collective reinforcement of what they spent their time doing gave their actions meaning and normalised what for others was anything but normal.

'Hey Yann, there's this here . . .' David said. 'Mmm, are you sure?' Yann could be enticed into trying anything once an idea had been put in his head. Yann was crazy but not crazy crazy, and then he would do it, rising to the challenge regardless of how tired he was and what he had already achieved that day. You had to be ready at all times. Yann's approach was simple; he would see something and think 'Can we do it?' quickly followed by, 'OK, I'll try it!' Yann and David led the 'You can do this jump here' school of training that progressed to 'OK, now let's do the jump at height'.

David had always had a competitive streak and the games were starting to change as play and contest merged.

Friendly encounters had the potential to become antagonistic whereas, when it was play, no one felt defeated and everyone left feeling victorious. When they were games, there was no prize or recognition of the strongest, bravest or most skilled.

The purpose of play is to play, to experience the 'encounter' of it. The psychological benefits are manifold. Social play only works when everyone wants to continue to play; while some games can be played non-competitively, individuals may choose to play them competitively, depending on the attitude. There was one thing that was certain among the group, though: you had to keep up. And for some, being better mattered more than having fun.

To challenge oneself was to test your limits, an ever-changing goal of what could be achieved. With combative instincts Yann saw little distinction between warrior-like behaviour and playing games. Play was an important part of a person's education, not the conventional style used at school, but something that allowed you to test yourself in your environment. But the thin line between testing each other and competing against one other was starting to merge. For many of the friends, it stayed as play no matter how big the risks being taken. 'We had completely different mindsets,' explained Sébastien. 'David had a completely different journey related to his father, but my mindset was more I wanted to have fun, to enjoy and to play. The fuel of the practice, the core of it for me was the mindset of play, having fun and the freedom of it.'

David had always looked for how to optimise everything, to make his training and movements more efficient. He did his homework. Hungry for recognition and out of the sight of others – with the exception of his best friend Sébastien – David prepared for many of the jumps he'd spied, quietly working up to them until they were perfected. This was the kind of homework he liked. 'Ah, have you seen this one?' he said, feigning innocence as if it was a first, then boom, he'd jump. He wanted to impress and did.

'David just needed somebody close to him to go outside. He always needed somebody with him to push him because I really think he could do things very easily, so maybe he didn't feel the need of training. So when there was someone close to him, with him, I'm sure it was easier,' said Laurent of their early days. 'David was competitive, he was in competition all the time.'

It was this competitive need within David that introduced the idea of the three-month challenge. David's idea was simple and effective: they should all train all day, every day for three months and see what everyone could do. Like everything else, the 'three months' trainings', as it would be known, was a challenge. They could work towards breaking a jump or just see how they developed. Occasionally there was a day off, maybe one or two in total during the three-month period, but a day off for all of them meant perhaps just three or four hours of movement. The three months' training would become a staple part of their diet. By the time the oldest were in their early twenties, collectively, they were all obsessed.

The friends Charles Perrière and Malik Diouf trained with David. They had barely seen their other friends for a while but everyone knew that David would still somehow find the time to do his own secret training on top of that.

Chau ran up a hill a hundred times, then repeated 'flutter' kicks for the abs two thousand times, left side, right side. Traversed across walls in a plank position, back and forth, back and forth. Then, of course, there were the 'Yann push-ups' where the movement goes only halfway down instead of the full range of motion. Five sets of one hundred, then more abs, more push-ups and pull-ups, repeating drop jumps, then back to the hill runs – and so the combo of combos continued. Their range of exercises wasn't vast so whatever they knew worked, they simply repeated, a lot. When it became apparent that a new idea would help them to get stronger, they would train that almost exclusively for a month until it became absorbed into the normal part of what they did. From 9 a.m. to 6 p.m., this was the life of a sixteen-year old. If you didn't wake up with the sensation that everything hurt, then it meant the training wasn't hard enough.

To an outsider, it certainly looked a mad and intense lifestyle. It captivated the friends from the moment they woke up and could go on through the night. Sharing their homes and their towns for training meant they often got to try something new.

On one occasion Yann, Charles, Laurent and Malik had spent the afternoon in Sarcelles with Phung and Chau. Ecouen was a natural sanctuary away from the everyday tensions of Evry, and each visit felt like a holiday. They'd spent the afternoon traversing on logs, fighting a balance battle on them across the river. Like the video game *Frogger* they jumped repeatedly from one log to the next when to miss meant getting wet.

They finished the day with noodles at the Belle house and said their farewells as it got late. Tap tap tap went the pebbles against Chau's window at around midnight. The friends had missed the last train home. 'OK, OK, come in,' Chau whispered, trying not to wake the rest of the house. The small bedroom that Phung, Chau and Williams shared had one bunk bed and another small bed. From morning until evening when they were there they would do push-ups, lift the chair to strengthen their forearms and hang out of the window when no one was around. A fully equipped gym was nothing compared to what their room offered. A gym or sports club would have required money, of which they had none, so in true Vietnamese style it was about being resourceful and they worked with what they had.

Whatever ideas Phung and Chau had, Williams copied. When David and Sébastien came to stay, Williams would give up his bed, sleeping on the floor. Rarely did they all sleep. 'Look, we've done that, we've climbed that, we've done that and we trained there.' They talked all night, concocting plans and ideas. 'You have to be able to train at all times, you have to be ready at all times!' Williams heard them say as they shook him awake with the instruction, 'Williams, you need to do twenty push-ups right now!' He did the push-ups, then went back to sleep. 'There, you have to be ready at all times!' They were madmen but happy men.

After their full day of training, the friends were happy to relax and talk, apart from Yann – if he could talk, he could train. He constantly lifted weights and nothing seemed to wear him out while the others struggled. He was big, and whilst his weight had increased, he seemed as agile and light as ever. He may have looked bulky but he could sit and talk in the box splits all night, his flexibility and range of motion never hindered. He continued to set numbers of repetitions: fifties, hundreds, thousands – and so it went on all night. There was no point in counting the hours. Training was never over.

6

Hardcore Games

What I do is not really something that can be explained. It can just be practised.

David Belle

Malik Diouf's alarm clock went off at 3.45 a.m. and the first thing he felt was pain. Every muscle in his body was sore to the bone from overuse. A few hours before, he had been invincible, performing superhuman feats on the rooftops of Evry. Now he was just another sixteen-year-old who had school in a few hours and still hadn't done his homework.

'Malik! Turn the damn alarm off!' his brother growled from the bed on the other side of the room. Malik was the second youngest of five, all living in a small flat. If anyone's alarm sounded, everyone heard it.

He slapped the alarm and rolled over, but tired as he was, sleep refused to come. A few blocks away, Charles Perrière was already out of bed. In Lisses, David and Sébastien were stretching. On the other side of the city, in Sarcelles, Phung and Chau had already finished their push-ups and were on to sit-ups. Even their little brother, Williams, would be up already, off somewhere by himself, swinging through the trees in the dark forest of Ecouen. Yann, well, nobody was sure that Yann even slept.

Malik's pulse quickened at the thought of his friends training as he lay in bed feeling sorry for himself. It was all the motivation he needed. Kicking the covers off, he rolled on to the floor and started into his first set of one hundred and one push-ups of the day. After seventy-five, his triceps and shoulders felt like they were on fire. On the bright side, he no longer felt sore. Every time he thought about stopping, the thought of the others spurred him on. For the last twenty-six push-ups, he levered himself up on to his fingertips.

On his way out of the house Malik passed his father sitting at the kitchen table preparing for another day at another construction site.

'You're up early.' His father said. Malik could feel his eyes following him.

'I'm going to go train with Charles, Dad.'

'Training – again? What do you boys get up to anyway?'

Malik shrugged. "You know, just normal stuff."

His father chuckled and set down his mug. 'Normal stuff, huh? At four in the morning? Well, if Charles is there, I suppose it can't be anything too bad. But do me a favour whatever this training is, be safe.' Malik had known Charles since he was fourteen, through practising martial arts together. Malik bristled. 'I can take care of myself, Dad.' 'Of course you can,' his father said. 'But your mother is worried about you. Promise not to do anything dangerous.'

'Come on, Dad . . .' Malik began to leave. But when he got to the door he paused. Once he passed through the threshold he would enter another world – a secret world of incredible possibilities and immense dangers, a world that neither his family nor even many of his friends knew existed. Malik turned back and gave his father a clumsy hug. 'I promise I won't hurt myself,' he said, relieved that it was still too dark to make out his face. If his father had seen it, he would have known that Malik was lying.

Malik met Charles in front of his apartment and together they jogged towards the cathedral. The neighbourhoods they passed through had been crawling with gangs just a few hours before but now the only people awake were the bakers. The smell of fresh bread wafted through the streets and made Malik's stomach growl.

In ten minutes they stood on the roof of an empty parking garage set back from the main commercial street watching three young men balancing across a narrow wall that ran around its perimeter. On one side of the wall was a metre drop into the parking lot. On the other was a four-storey plunge off the side of the building. The three unlikely adventurers made an odd trio against the back-drop of the brightening sky. The first was giant and dark-skinned with arms and legs like tree trunks. The second was smaller and sallow-skinned with twiggy legs and a tiny waist but a chest and shoulders muscles so well-defined they could have been drawn by a comic book artist. The third had a body somewhere in between the two but exuded the quiet, catlike grace of a dancer.

'Morning!' called Yann, the largest of the three, without breaking stride. He looked pretty comfortable for a guy balancing between life and death on a strip of concrete no wider than his foot.

'Who wants to play "follow the leader"?'

Training had begun.

Yann finished his circuit and hopped down from the wall, followed by David and Chau.

'How did you guys get here so early?' Charles asked.

Chau chuckled and looked at David and Yann.

'We never went home,' Chau said. 'Brought three kilograms

of pasta with us and have been training since last night when they closed the garage.'

Malik had trained with Charles only until eleven at the gymnasium staircase in Lisses. Silently berating himself for having missed all the fun, he walked to the wall and peered over the edge. The view alone was enough to make his palms prickle with sweat.

Sitting out was exactly what Malik wanted to do; which was exactly why he couldn't do it. No one got strong by sitting out.

'You guys have been here all night, huh?' Malik said, summoning a smile that he hoped looked more confident than he felt. 'Guess we've got to make up for lost time then . . .'

He hopped up on to the wall and, just like that, life went from being safe and predictable to being utterly dependent on every ounce of his physical ability. One misstep and he was dead. The terror surged through Malik's body and made him feel weak and clumsy. He took another deep breath and called upon the focus he had honed through countless days and nights of doing exactly these sorts of weird, homemade exercises. Everything but the thin strip of concrete beneath his feet receded from his mind and he took a step. Then another. Mouth dry, sweat running down the small of his back, he began to walk. Instead of fighting the fear, he channelled it into steely control. After what seemed like a week of walking he completed one circuit of the roof. Then he did another. Yann insisted they all do eleven.

After Malik's final circuit he hopped down and the rest of the world came flooding back to him. The sun had peeked over the horizon and was casting weak rays over the awakening city. Malik savoured its warmth as he clenched and unclenched his fists to hide the tremors in his hands.

David completed his eleven circuits. He had dark eyes half-hidden behind heavy lids, but they didn't miss a thing. He said nothing, but the others knew what he was thinking. 'But . . . if you were being chased by a wild animal and you had to do it fast, like really fast, could you? It doesn't matter what time it is. If a wild animal attacked you when you were just waking up, you wouldn't have time to warm up.' They had heard it many times.

'Of course I could do it,' thought Malik. Do it, do it well, do it faster had been a favourite theme of late. 'I can run that wall as fast as walk it,' said Malik.

That got everyone's attention.

'Ho ho!' Yann liked crazy ideas. 'So let's go!'

Malik looked from Yann to Charles to Chau, and finally to David. He didn't have to do it. No one would hold it against him if he didn't. Now was the time to go home, take a shower, get a fresh croissant, maybe even crawl back into bed and forget he had ever come up here in the first place.

He turned back to the ledge and hopped up again. This was why he woke up when the rest of the world slept, why he did push-ups until he couldn't lift his arms, why he ran marathon distances for the fun of it – to find moments like these that were so intractable, the only place to go was beyond himself. There was a saying for it in French, *lâcher prise*, when you let everything go to find exactly what you're looking for. He began to walk, then accelerated into a jog. This time the fear did not recede, it peaked, then melted away entirely, replaced by a wild, primal urge to move that threatened to burst from his chest. The street no longer seemed so far below, the ledge no longer so narrow. Like a child riding his bike for the first time, he realised he could have done it all along.

'In order to do what we were doing, you had to be ready

to die,' Malik says today. 'Every morning you wake up, take your bag and maybe you don't have time to say goodbye to your parents and that sticks in the back of your mind all day because you know you might not come back. That was part of the training that nobody really talks about much anymore because now it's all about safety and fluidity. But back then, during those really intense years, you trained hard and you trained to be ready for everything. We lost some of the fun then, but it was OK because we were all there for our own reasons, searching for the extreme limit of what the body could do.'

Through this obsessive regimen the boys unwittingly honed their minds as much as their bodies. What they thought was learning to be 'courageous' was, in fact, something more complex.

When we expose ourselves to risk – be it financial, social, sporting, or in this case life-threatening – we are twanging our fight or flight response, a primal physiological reaction in which the brain releases specialised hormones that allow the body to react better to a perceived threat. As Malik stood on the edge of the parking garage contemplating his next step, his body was also getting ready to do something incredible. One of the most primitive parts of his brain, the locus coeruleus, fired up, lowering his sensory thresholds and making him hyperalert to sounds and movements. As he was mentally tracing his line, his nervous system was deciding which parts of his body were most important for the task at hand and restricting blood flow to all the rest, giving him butterflies in his stomach and a warble in his voice while priming the muscles in his legs, arms, lungs, heart and brain. Meanwhile his testosterone levels were climbing, boosting his blood's oxygen-carrying capacity and even his own self-confidence. Just before he started moving, adrenaline flooded out of his adrenal glands to supercharge his metabolism.

These physiological responses evolved to make people react to danger without having to think too hard about it. Today, since we are generally not fighting or fleeing danger in the course of our nine to five, we are instead unnerved by the unique intertwining of mind and body produced by the fight or flight response. Instead of understanding it for what it is, we experience it as fear or panic. If it goes unchecked, it can even become self-loathing and depression.

But what if you could harness your fight or flight response to help you perform incredible feats on demand? To some degree all athletes tap into their most primal physiological responses, but they do so through elaborate ruses – sports – made to simulate more stressful situations. Even extreme-sports athletes often shy away from overt risk, instead minimising it through preparation and safety equipment. Outliers like free-soloists (people who climb at height without ropes) and wingsuit pilots represent a tiny minority that make even their own peers nervous.

What the friends had stumbled on in the mid-1990s was the simple but elegant art of risk-taking. Why simulate risk with elaborate sporting rules or expensive equipment when all you really had to do to tango with death was jump off an overpass? Although it's easy to look at this sort of behaviour as a regression, there is incredible genius in the way it distils elements of form, movement, identity and plain old danger into a single, explosive act of self-expression.

As their training progressed and the climbs got higher, the jumps farther, and the exercises more intense, the dividends it yielded became apparent. Heights were no longer high. Pain no longer hurt. Fear no longer crippled. The boys had discovered something long understood by elite fighting units like the US Navy SEALS: you can habituate people to almost anything if you make them do it enough.

From the first day of SEAL training, candidates are relentlessly put into situations beyond their comfort zones, like hypothermia-inducing swims through freezing water in the middle of the night, or gruelling endurance exercises accompanied by constant verbal abuse after weeks of sleep deprivation. One of the most fabled SEAL tests is having to tread water in the deep end of a pool for twenty minutes, with your hands tied behind your back and your ankles tied together. Physically, most candidates can handle this, or anything else thrown at them, but what is really being tested is their mental toughness and fear of drowning.

The incredible thing about the young group in Evry, Lisses and Sarcelles is how closely their training mirrored the intensity and abusiveness of SEAL training in its long hours, its strange, mind- and body-destroying games, and its insistence on drawing strength from a core group. The salient difference was that nobody was screening them for anything. There were no drill sergeants waking them up in the middle of the night or forcing them to bang out another fifty push-ups when they didn't meet their times in the obstacle course. Instead, they were pushing each other, relentlessly, night and day, for weeks, months and years at a time, all before any of them had turned twenty.

SEAL training revolves around subordination, but theirs was a form of self-actualisation. Even the simple regimentation of training times or exercises violated some deeply ingrained sense of freedom of expression in all of its founders. They trained when the mood struck them and however they wanted. This was not, after all, training for a job or even training for enjoyment, it was training for a way of life in which the physical and the mental were inextricably linked.

Just how much this relentless conditioning had affected them became apparent one night.

When Malik showed up at Le Damier meeting point in Lisses, most of the group was already there. Chau had come down from Sarcelles, leaving Williams at home despite his younger brother's protests. It would not be a night for young boys. Of the Evry and Lisses collective, David, Yann, Sébastien, Guylain and Charles were there. Training started with some goofing around and plenty of trash talk. But the mood never stayed playful for long anymore. Gradually they started moving. Not just exercising, but doing *their* movements.

They had no words for these yet, so they spoke in an improvised onomatopoeia: 'Tac tac tac brrrrraa!' might describe kicking off a wall, catching a railing, muscling up on it and spinning around, then vaulting back off. Each chain of movements completed by one person was a challenge to all the rest, whether it was a certain line, move or a certain number of repetitions. As usual, they broke up their games with round after round of high-rep exercises, including the normal push-ups, pull-ups and sit-ups, as well as spicier things like dropping off roofs, running up walls or doing tricky jumps.

They continued like that all afternoon, moving from spot to spot in constant flow. Malik forgot himself, forgot everything but his friends and the training. By the time they got to the Train – an old, disused, playground opposite the gymnasium staircase in Lisses – talking had ceased completely, replaced by the steady percussion of hands and feet slapping steel, wood and concrete. A compulsive energy took hold of the group and reality was reduced to the crystalline ebb and flow of the action. The time to go home came and went unnoticed, the last trains stopped running, the stores closed and the streetlights flickered on. Now, like the early mornings, was when training really began. When the rest of the world was tucked up in their homes going about normal lives, the boys entered their own, private world of movement.

Sometime after midnight – no one ever bothered to keep track of time – the playground was used up and Malik felt the hectic, sublime energy that had possessed him all evening begin to wane. He should have called it a day – they all should have – but they couldn't. A new challenge was needed: something bigger, something scarier, something that would redefine that sharp end they were all searching for.

Yann was the first to move. He turned north and set off back towards the housing estate, the others falling in step behind him. No one had to ask where they were heading.

They loped through the quiet walkways, breaking apart intermittently to vault walls, balance on ledges, and leap between buildings then coalescing again, as if attracted by some sixth sense. Their course deviated only when they caught wind of a resident peering out from behind their curtains at the strange sounds and movements outside. Without pausing they stealthily made their way to the edge of the estate where the concrete stops and the grass starts.

When they reached the Parc du Lac the 2.5-metre metal gates were locked. Without breaking stride, they each vaulted the measly barrier and set off around the perimeter of the lake. Its inky surface reflected the stars above their heads. On the far side, in deep shadows, stood the thing they had all come for: the Dame du Lac.

Weather-beaten and crumbling, the Lady seemed to mirror the decay of the post-war dream. She had been closed to the public after several accidents and was increasingly disused by anyone who valued their safety.

This did not include Malik and his friends. When they reached her base, they slowed and then stopped completely for the first time all night. Malik peered up at her pinnacle and relished the familiar flutter in his stomach.

The group split and went scampering up either of her curved sides. David and Yann chose to take the middle route – the hardest. As they climbed they could feel the entire structure tremble under their movements. Malik trembled with her, but pushed the fear away and continued up towards the stars.

On the top of the Dame there was a small platform originally built to secure the belay ropes of aspiring alpinists. It was on this little platform, suspended in the sky, that the crew reconvened. While some sat and caught their breath, dangling their legs into the void, David walked to within a few paces of the edge and crouched down. Slowly, carefully, he lifted himself into a handstand. All eyes watched him, no one spoke or even dared to breath. One wobble would mean a fifteen-metre fall on to his face. The seconds ticked by and still he balanced, statue-still, in that all-consuming state of utter terror and complete control that comes with confronting a fear head on. Finally, he lowered his legs back to the platform and exchanged places with Sébastien, who did the same.

When Sébastien was 'safely' back on two legs, Yann stepped up to the edge. But he was thinking of something a little more interesting than handstands. He turned to David and smiled. *'Bon, c'est l'heure. On y va.'* It's time. Let's do it.

Malik and Charles looked at each other. Chau smiled in that mysterious way of his and simply nodded. Sébastien took a deep, steadying breath. David made no outward response at all but he looked like he had been waiting for this all night, maybe all his life.

He walked to the edge of the platform again and dropped on to his stomach. Sliding along the rough cement, he manoeuvred his torso over the edge and out into space. Sébastien and Yann each took one of his ankles and pushed him forward, farther and farther until suddenly, they each held the life of one of their best friends in the palms of their hands. Everybody had to take a turn holding and being held out over the abyss. When it came time for Malik to hang, he knew two things: he was ready to die and he trusted his friends more than anything else in the world. The Rubicon had been crossed. From that night on there was no turning back.

7

A Way Out: Yamakasi

I can't stop because this is what I like. Instead of doing bad things on the street like stealing a bike or a scooter like my other friends did, I preferred to train and do something good with my body.

Malik Diouf

Although Evry was only a fifteen-minute walk from the calm, quiet and open green spaces of Lisses, growing up there was tough. The dense concrete architecture was the backdrop for a city at war; there was a turf conflict with gangs from the nearby town of Corbeil-Essonnes. Being in the wrong place at any time could have serious consequences. The police patrolled and people stayed home. Wary and afraid, families and children weren't seen on the streets after dark, yet a certain group of young men still went out to train.

Against this tense antisocial backdrop, 'being strong' was a personal mantra-cum-obsession to the friends. More than any established sport, their 'training' with its focus on utilitarianism and an ever-present state of mental readiness for risk and danger allowed them to create an armour to shield them from the constant menace of life on the peripheries of French society.

It wasn't just the turf wars; gangs of teenaged youths who were searching for a defining identity were exposed to high rates of criminality and racism on a daily basis. According to Yann, in Evry 'you had to be of the right skin tone, or strong enough, or ready to face what could come your way. You had to be a man with a capital M.'

The group of friends, including Malik Diouf, Charles Perrière, Sébastien Foucan, Guylain N'guba Boyeke and Laurent Piemontese, were all second generation immigrants (from Senegal, Central African Republic, Martinique, the Republic of Congo and Italy respectively). 'So where could we open up and feel included? At the church? At the mosque? Even there they don't accept each other; so where? At school?' asked Yann. Training was their own form of multicultural utopia, a way to turn lost, searching boys into men.

Hardship was a familiar theme for the group even before they met and started training. The journeys and experiences their families had endured to be able to start a new life in France had not been simple. Their parents' struggles and pain influenced how they viewed the world around them; the children respected and admired their family's attitude towards effort and determination. As Charles recalled in *Le Parkour* the book he wrote with David Belle, 'I often thought about my mother when I was faced with an obstacle, when I was about to jump. She has given me a strength that has stayed with me through Parkour and in all areas of my life.' She had been forced to flee Cameroon aged twelve: her siblings had died and her father had left for Chad. She was alone and, after being taken in by a family, went to look for her mother in Sudan. Many of their families came from very hard contexts; for some the simple fact that they had made it to France was a miracle.

While immigrants were seen as an economic success for

France once they became part of the workforce, socially they were often seen as the cause of many problems. The multicultural friends were often discriminated against and they had their own ideas and approach to inclusivity. They created their own social microcosm based on a culture of sharing, effort and physical achievement.

Charles and Malik knew every corner of Evry's mean streets; there was no route untouched and they were comfortable with training anywhere. When the police saw them repeating their drills it looked unusual and this was reason enough to stop and question them. Being angry people protecting volatile streets, the cops could make trouble. 'OK, you are not doing anything bad, but you must leave and if you don't want to leave we're going to arrest you,' the police often remarked. The friends had already made a conscious decision not to run when confronted. Firstly, why take such an easy option? They could outrun them if they wanted to, but then where was the challenge? It was a simple choice to make, so they would do as the police asked and move on even though they knew they weren't doing anything wrong – running just wouldn't be smart. There were always more places where they could train. They were looking for respect and acceptance, not to start a riot.

One night, much like any other in Evry, after endless hours of running, conditioning, talking about nothing in particular, Malik and Charles were at Parc de Lodge near the university. They were chilling out, but as always it was never one hundred per cent relaxed. This was Evry and their instincts were always on standby. A mass of about fifty men suddenly appeared around a corner. Charles and Malik knew nothing good could come of it. Recently a friend of Malik's had died from a gunshot wound having been ambushed by a gang of twenty near the cinema. So the two ran for their lives. With the gang hot on their heels, they sprinted away with an idea of how to escape.

Within moments they reached the overpass. Their hands grabbed the rail at the top and with one swift rotation their bodies turned and they were on the other side of the wall. The only thing they had to do next was let go and drop down; it was what they had trained for. The brutality of landing five metres below was absorbed by a finely honed combination of muscles, tendons and technique, allowing the pair to bounce back up and sprint off. No one followed; even thugs and criminals knew when they were outcrazed. As a result, word on the street was that the guys like Charles and Malik were extreme and not to be messed with. That night, the gang had seen something abnormal – unnatural even – and it scared them. But above all they respected and admired what they had seen. It took courage to jump.

It's not hard to imagine bones cracking and joints exploding under the kind of stress and impact of the drop Malik and Charles had taken, but their training had paid off. The creation of their natural body armour had involved graduating from climbing on walls and trees to climbing on water towers and rooftops. They had begun going higher, to locations such as overpasses, where they hung from the bottom ledge and dropped down. They then progressively increased the impact by standing up on the ledge and dropping down, incrementally increasing the height and impact. They dropped off eleven, twenty-one, thirty-one times a day to adapt their bodies to the shock of hitting the ground from height. The longer they did it, the tougher they became until they could drop from incredible heights onto hard concrete as easily as if they were stepping off a bus.

For all of their apparently body-ruining exercises, no one was ever seriously hurt. Instead, they got stronger.

Yann was already well known in Evry. He was twenty-four and scared of nothing. The city had always been 'access all areas' as far as he was concerned. Combative in both spirit and action, he always won his fights. Even his friends never knew when he was going to start one. Their training ethic meant they had to be fit to fight as well as move. It was a test, another challenge. Could you? Would you? What were you made of? A professional career in fighting had been a potential option for Yann and, if urban legends were to be believed, he had also been offered a career as a stuntman and had tried to join the Foreign Legion. Yann's mere presence allowed the friends to go in areas they otherwise wouldn't dare to explore.

With Malik and Charles' impressive escape and Yann's influence on the streets, the group of friends' reputation had built into that of the 'crazy guys'. The gangs never bothered any of them again, especially when there were more of them. At times the group could have been from twelve to twenty men, with many joining along the years as their night-time antics and training became well known. Tinaro, Rodrigue, Karim Mouhous, David Malgone, Rudy Duong. They were all prepared to jump.

As with all young adults, moving into their early twenties meant that they were faced with questions of the future – of jobs, housing and paying their way but career options were always uncertain and antisocial temptations were never far away. As Yann and Laurent trained in Yann's garage, the kids nearby smoked weed whilst planning the next burglary or dividing up the proceeds from the last. If you wanted a scooter or gun, someone was always buying or selling. If they had ever been that way inclined, the friends were in great shape for breaking and entry. To the untrained eye their training was simply mastering the art of escape. Despite this, however tempted or lost they were, to use their skills for such an easy way out never appealed. They were warriors and pioneers. They didn't just have to overcome their physical limits; they had to continue to believe in their dreams and the possibility of change.

No longer in the free abandon of their teenage years, they were adults responsible for their own lives and choices. There had never been an option of living at their parents' expense. They all loved sport but their ideas about what sport was, and had the potential to be, differed from any mainstream definition. Military service was in many ways the natural step for some and made more available due to the obligatory ten months of military service that young men faced in early 1990s France.

In 1993 when David was twenty, he joined the Paris military fire brigade, hoping to follow in his father's and grandfather's footsteps. He injured his wrist during training and while recovering decided that there wasn't enough action within the fire brigade to suit his needs. He transferred to the marines based in Vannes where it quickly became apparent that his physical prowess was above and beyond the other recruits.

The challenges David and his friends had experienced at the top of Dame du Lac, balancing and moving at height, gave them skills that were similar to if not better than the circuits performed by the marines completing the *parcours d'audace* (the audacious routes) at the commando school at Mont-Luis in the Pyrenees. It was generally understood that the commandos needed to have balls of steel to do what they did. Their training focused on techniques that were both physically demanding and performed whilst under extreme stress to simulate a combat situation. It involved climbing drainage pipes, performing accurate jumps at height from one platform to the next, pulling their bodies along the *tyrolienne* steel cables and going down ziplines. Unlike what the group of friends had been doing for years, the commandos were clipped in with a harness. There was no need for extra risk.

For the modern, alternative version that played out on the streets of the Parisian suburbs, the friends also trained to be ready, but for exactly what they didn't know. Their training shared similarities with the *parcours du combattant* used to train infantrymen to tackle different obstacles that might be found on a battlefield. A course typically consisted of a high ladder, a wall to climb, a deep jump, a *planche* (a plank of wood on two poles, two metres high and passed using either a muscle-up or leg-swing technique), some balancing on an elevated beam, crawling under barbed wire, beams to go over and under, and stepping stones. Depending on the location, although it had been standardised in general, there were slightly different versions of the course to facilitate competitions between regiments.

However, while some of the military training actions may have looked the same and required similar focus, the mentality and motivation was different. David's personality wasn't suited to taking orders. His reasons for training were personal. He felt no call to duty or to serve for his country on a combative level, yet he knew his actions and style of training had the potential to help others.

What David and the others had been doing for so many years didn't fit into any existing structure or category. There was a huge void that existed between the military training of commandos, the mandatory sports young people did at school, professional competitive sporting environments and the kind of physical preparation they had explored. Their aim, as well as to become strong, was to live a happy, healthy, strong and free life that could help and protect others. 'Compared to my Parkour training, the army felt like an amusement park. I couldn't feel proud about crawling in a pipe under a road because compared to what I had been doing back home, it was nothing,' wrote David in 2009 in his first book, *Parkour*.

Although during his experiences David had gained a gymnastic agility certificate of honour, and like his father had held the record for regimental rope-climbing and the Essonne obstacle course, in military life someone else dictated what you did and when. David thrived on autonomy and it would never work. 'Unlike in the military, here we could develop in our own way,' wrote David in his 2014 book *Parkour: From the Origins to the Practice*. Although the friends' training shared with the army some values regarding elements of risk, David said they did not 'brain wash'. He completed his obligations and left. He took various part-time jobs and travelled to India to study kung fu for several months.

Many of the friends completed their military service. Sébastien was twenty-three and had spent two years completing his firefighter training in Paris but was forced to leave after breaking his arm. Laurent had chosen to join the army and signed up for five years to escape the limited options he felt were available to him in Evry.

When the group of friends came of age they had all completed their national service and various part-time jobs had come and gone, anything from warehouse worker to security guard or furniture salesman. Peacetime military conscription ended in 1996 by which time Yann was twenty-four and worked on construction sites, Charles was twenty-one and worked for the army having completed his national service, Guylain was twenty and a painter-decorator, Malik was twenty and studying marketing and brands, and Chau was eighteen and working as a waiter.

Williams was now fourteen and had been doing his own training for the past five years. He had instinctively moved over, under and around obstacles, constantly looking for challenges to complete. There had never been any structure to his training but he had become a lot stronger and done a lot of work on his musculature. The others could see that he was progressing and felt he was ready to join them. For the first time Williams was introduced to structured training. He did squats to help with the spring in his jump and push-ups to make his arm-jumps more comfortable.

Keeping up with the others was tough – he was ten years younger than Yann – but the requirements were the same for everyone. Nobody was allowed to complain or speak negatively about the training. As the youngest, Williams always complied and did what they asked. It was hard and he suffered. They all suffered. 'Each time I trained with them it was . . . it was super hard! You can say we suffer, yeah . . . It was something very, very, very, very, very, very, very hard,' recounted Williams years later.

None of them had studied any form of pedagogy, but their methods and extreme games continued to further their progress. They didn't seek out any sports science books, instead relying on their empirical, intuitive and counter-scientific methods. Traditional styles of performance training dictated programmes that worked on strength, power, agility and endurance by working certain muscle groups together – i.e. 'leg day', or the 'posterior chain' of muscles – but the way the friends approached their training was far simpler; you used your whole body in everything you did, as often as you could, for as long as you could. They were generalists, not specialists. Through the seasons and years, as their environments constantly changed so did they; adapting to every surface and sensation.

They continually strived to pursue new limits and that meant going through some extreme experiences. Battles between determination and physical ability constantly played out in everyone's minds. Unknowingly, the activities and innate instincts of the young Parisians from Sarcelles, Lisses and Evry reflected the arguments of some of the most influential thinkers and pioneering physical educators from continental Europe. During the seventeenth and eighteenth centuries, their predecessors had promoted a wide range of activities, training outdoors in nature to create strong, resilient bodies and minds for the greater social good.

French philosopher Jean-Jacques Rousseau (whose books had been both burnt and banned at the time) had promoted the educational and social benefits of engaging with nature from a young age as a way to encourage free thinking and enquiry away from the constrictive rules of cities and religion. Rousseau was a major influence on key educational reformers such as Johann Heinrich Pestalozzi and Johann Christoph Friedrich GutsMuths. In 1793, GutsMuths created outdoor gymnastics training that involved running, leaping, wrestling, climbing, balancing, lifting, carrying, pulling, dancing, walking, military exercises, bathing, swimming, manual labour, public speaking and fasting – which he presented as altruistic, civilian and educational tools. Pestalozzi's teachings were characterised by an egalitarian and altruistic ethos.

However, while some saw the benefits of such programmes, others saw a different potential; if you could be strong for yourself, you could be strong for your country. Physical education was further developed and utilised as a way to prepare civilian populations for military activities. A passive population could be taught how to become strong, brave and active when motivated by patriotic behaviour.

This was not the first group to utilise the concept of the warrior as a form of outdoor physical training and preparedness. The Prussian Friederich Ludwig Jahn created *Turnen*, a term based on the word *torner* meaning 'warrior'. Jahn used GutsMuth's methods – omitting the more obviously military exercises – as a covert way to train and change a passive civilian population into an army capable of revolting against Napoleon. Whether for educational, social or revolutionary motivations, the ideas of body culture and physical education can be traced back to the Ancient Greeks, and since then the dissemination and acceptability of training outdoors has been dependent on the dominant political motivations and ideological context of the times. The militarisation of physical education went through numerous shifts throughout the turbulent eighteenth and nineteenth centuries. By the middle of the twentieth century the ideas and methods for civilian physical educational training had been diluted, tamed, domesticated and taken inside.

Regardless of what was deemed normal, there were always the outliers, renegades and mavericks who would never feel satisfied with the comfort levels and expectations that the physical education system had to offer. The young collective of masochists busy forging their bodies in the streets and forests of the Parisian banlieues of the 1990s were such renegades. Their exercise was their own philosophy, art and education.

* * *

All the group wanted to do was train, but for that to be possible, they had to somehow make a living out of it. There was no guarantee that it would work, but it was a risk they wanted to take; they had to go public. In 1996, the initial plans were put in place.

'Hi Williams, is Chau home?' asked David on the telephone one evening.

'No.'

'OK, can you pass a message on to him please? We are going to create a new group called "Yamakasi" with Yann and Charles and the others. It's about *L'Art du Déplacement*. We want him to be in it."

'What's "Yamakasi?"'

'I can't remember exactly, but it's good, it means something like "coming from the school of life, a school for hard people". You can be in it too.'

'OK, thanks, cool. I'll pass the message.'

With that Williams put the phone down and realised that this was an opportunity. Somehow he could realise his goal – to train! Who needed school when you could live off your passion?

David had doubts about bringing his cousins into the project, but at Yann's insistence they were included. Phung and Chau's level was very good and Williams's lack of vertigo made his acrobatics at height impressive, but David felt that their training in Sarcelles was different from the brutal raw concrete landscape of Lisses and Evry. Yann told him that they would be stronger together. It wasn't just about the time they had shared training, he explained; it was as much about all of their experiences; sharing, eating, sleeping and living together.

School wasn't as enthused by Williams's new vigour for non-stop training. His absence was noted and many letters sent home. His father, although absent from the house, was still the authority figure and accompanied Williams into the headmaster's office, determined to put his son back on track. The school wanted to suspend him. His father was hoping for compliance – a commitment from Williams to returning and attending school. It wasn't to be.

Although his father hadn't been living with them for the past four years following his affair, Williams still feared his potential for violence. Would he get beaten if he went against his father's wishes? He didn't know. It was the final chance, insisted the headmaster. They would keep Williams, but he must attend and change his behaviour.

Clearly and calmly Williams told them, 'I don't want to go back to school.' He knew exactly what he wanted to do, what he wanted from life and why. His father pleaded with him. How could his son not see how important school was for him?

Williams's father and great-uncle had always been role models for him, embodiments of masculinity and all the violence that accompanied it. Traditional patriarchy meant they were simply entitled to a better place in the hierarchy of things. When they returned home Williams was sure his behaviour would result in a beating, but he did not regret making his decision. His mother sat in the kitchen awaiting the conclusion of the school meeting. With freshly empowered eyes, Williams saw things in a new light.

Even though his father and great-uncle had gone very far on their path of life, his mother had reached even further. She was the total opposite of them. She had suffered and endured everything that life had thrown at her and was bringing up six kids on her own, selflessly with love and generosity. It's a strength very few people have, Williams thought, but she has confidence in life and the future. These were the qualities he wanted to emulate.

Williams's father didn't beat him after the school office scenario. Williams knew that in the headmaster's office that day, he had begun to break away from the cycle of violence. He had the confidence to believe in his own future and would continue to do so by training hard, not with fear or anger in his heart, but love and sharing whenever possible. He believed in his potential for change and that it was possible for him to grow up in a way that meant he was no longer afraid.

8

The Cat Jumps
Out of the Bag

*When we saw that jump, we reasoned that anyone who could do
it would be the best in the world. But this kind of jump – you can't
just go and think or hope you can do it. You must be ready in your
head and your body.*

Malik Diouf

The city was their playground and they'd never stopped seeking new terrain. From the ship playground in the Ecouen forest they had progressed to the cemetery wall gap and then to the water tower. High walls at the school in Lisses and the Dame du Lac all contributed to the progression from childish weakness towards an all-important ideal of strength. Where next?

The Manpower jump seems to have existed in Yann and David's minds for as long as they had been walking the streets of Lisses and Evry. Neither remembers noticing it per se, just that it was always there. The gap between the two rooftops looked approximately twelve metres across and the jump down was at least eight metres. To see the possibility was one thing, but to train for it and do it was another. On some level, the jump itself was actually secondary. It was what it *meant* to do a jump like that, to wager everything you had on one beautiful, insane movement and know that you were going to hit the jackpot because you were too good to lose – that was the point of the Manpower jump.

Their heroes had experienced the transcendental beauty of jumping between buildings, going rooftop to rooftop, since they could remember. Spider-Man, Batman and real-life hero, Jackie Chan had all made a leap of faith at some point. The Manpower jump, as it was known, so named due to the ubiquitous *Manpower* job placement offices below, held legendary status. Whoever could do it would ink their name in some imagined ledger of strong men that only the friends knew about. They had jumped from the footbridge and dropped five metres, but this was different. This jump went from the corner of a vocational school to the opposing corner of a mixed block of apartments and offices. If you missed the landing zone, the fall would be fatal, dropping thirty metres on to the pavement.

If someone did a big jump then everybody had to do it, but this jump wasn't something you could just do, even with a single or even two of the three-month training sessions to prepare specifically for it. Standing at the top looking at it, you had to feel if you could do it. 'It's not large,' thought Williams, 'it's really, really high.'

The making of the Yamakasi video was the group's first step towards going public and the final motivation David needed. He was ready. The video would showcase everyone's skills. How David had transformed himself physically from the skinny kid who started a fight with Yann over ping pong a decade ago was impressive. His level of ability was incredible. 'Everything was beyond the norm,' remembered Williams. 'At the time I thought it was normal but actually it wasn't.'

Williams's main influences among his family were still

his mother and two brothers. David was someone he saw as being strong. 'I could just see someone who had a certain state of mind; he was my cousin, I was proud of him because he was always doing incredible things. I could see him jumping and all. But then he would go home and I would get on with my day. I could see him asking himself many questions. And I was thinking: "I hope he'll find his answers,"' recalled Williams.

David warmed up on the roof as Williams and Sébastien waited below. Everyone in the group knew that if one of them jumped, it was because they were ready for everything, even ready to die. Williams was only fourteen but had been on the rooftop and looked. He knew and felt he could do it but was told to let David do it. Disappointed, he watched on as a new reference was set and, unlike so many previous magical moments, this time it was captured on video.

At street level a passer-by would never have imagined the possibility of seeing a man take off from one edge and land across on the other. The hang-time in the air was enough to make shapes, with the body passing across the width of three apartments of the building in the background before hitting the gravelled ground, then rolling to disperse the impact. As soon as the jump between the two buildings had been made, you had to return to ground level as quickly as possible. To get to the street, three more massive drops on to concrete were needed. However, after the roof-jump the impacts felt light.

Despite their apparent lack of fear the group weren't immune to the idea of danger and injury. One day when training at the Dame du Lac, a local fireman had fallen from halfway up. The group called for help and tried to keep the man alert and conscious as he lay injured on the ground. They never spoke of it again.

Big jumps like the Manpower jump that led to a heavy impact on landing could, then, be 'broken' – or completed – and the three-month training regime had given them the way to prepare their 'body armour'. To match David's achievement, Malik sequestered himself with Yann for three months of preparation that included doing six big jumps and bridge drops on some days and thousands of repeated small jumps on others, seven days a week. This was how you got your body armour.

When he came to do the Manpower jump, the force of hitting the rooftop was so strong that gravel stuck to the back of his head when he rolled. Down on the ground, Yann hugged and congratulated him, then grew serious. There was, after all, a protocol for these things. The first time you're lucky. The second time you do it for yourself, as confirmation. The third time you do it for someone else. Once is never.

'The second time was even scarier,' remembered Malik, explaining that he knew then the amount of force he would need to take. When it came time for the third go, he couldn't do it. It was just too much. There were limits that were unwise to cross and, just as an all-important level of self-awareness and knowledge had kept them safe until now, so it would again. Despite external appearances, they weren't reckless.

Jean-François Belle, David's older half-brother was a firefighter and had seen what his younger sibling, half-cousins and their friends had been up to. It was impressive. He wasn't alone in thinking there must be a way for them to shine, a way they could do something with this. David's father thought it was a good idea for them all to form an elite group of strong men. Nobody else in the world was doing what they did.

Jean-François had spent time getting to know David once he moved to Lisses and could see that now, a decade later, he had no real direction in life other than a passion for his training. He had worked in a warehouse, as a part-time security guard and even a furniture salesman. 'With your skills you could be a super-policeman or something above special forces, but you can't earn your living, because there's no championship. What if we film what you're doing?' asked Jean-François.

Yann's father was also separately encouraging them and saw great value and potential in the group. They were stronger together. David's father Raymond offered a gymnastics coaching session for the group – the one and only time he offered to train them – but acrobatics wasn't their thing. They didn't go.

Jean-François put together a demo tape of the most impressive moments of his brother and friends, and presented it to his superiors at the fire station. It was the first time that the spectacular movements of the friends' everyday training had been captured. The idea of taking a camera along to a training session would have been bizarre had any of the group suggested it. To care about capturing images would have meant not giving everything to the act of training.

The 1997 open day and performance of the special gymnastics unit of the Paris Firefighters would be an ideal opportunity to showcase the group's skills. Jean-François had seen them but, apart from a few curious neighbours twitching their curtains late at night, the rest of the world had no idea. For the Yamakasi it was their first chance to share their talent, a gift to inspire others and to show what was possible.

Following the example of his father Raymond Belle,

Jean-François Belle was a sergeant at Villeneuve-Saint-Georges, the military branch of the fire brigade. The firefighters' unit had been set up by Napoléon I in 1811. Initially a battalion belonging to the engineers corps, it was the first professional firefighters' unit in France. Napoléon had been attending a ball at the Austrian Embassy when a fire broke out which led to more than a hundred fatalities. A professional and efficient fire service was deemed necessary. Prior to this, public water pumps had been spread across Paris, and civilians made responsible for putting out fires, while landlords and tenants were required to have a bucket of water at the ready in their apartments.

Sauver ou Périr, Save or Die, was the unit's motto. Training had been the same as for the rest of the military until the arrival of Don Francisco Amóros y Ondeano, a Spanish nobleman and physical educator who had previously been a director at a Pestalozzi Institute in Spain. Forced to take residence in France as a political exile, he dedicated himself to introducing physical training in his new homeland. He started training firemen in 1817 and by 1819 had established a gymnasium especially for them.

Gymnastics training in Europe at that time included running, crawling, jumping, climbing, throwing, catching, lifting, carrying, swimming and combatives. Amóros changed the direction of academic and military gymnastics, creating a revised form of physical education in France. Later he would train gymnastics teachers for the army.

Within the military firefighters' unit there was a 'special gymnastics' team, an elite group who would be called upon for some of the most daring rescues. They were also used for public demonstrations and performances, such as the 1997 open day in the southeastern suburb of Paris where the crowd of more than a thousand were now taking to their seats for the much-anticipated show, with families fidgeting and staring out on to the open ground of the Villeneuve-Saint-Georges fire station. The tall, metal water tower loomed above them, part giant ladder, part crane. Amongst the crowd were friends of the Yamakasi, many of whom had supported them through the years of relentless training despite never having really understood its purpose. For the Yamakasi it was the best day of their lives. The friends were together.

A high-pitched sound sung out as, without warning, two men ziplined in from the top-right corner of the square. Dressed like a modern, special forces ninja, four more men ran out and dived over the top of a car and then rolled on the ground as they landed on the other side. Next they climbed on top of a fire truck and then, cat-like, managed to jump and pass over it. The two who had ziplined in then climbed to the top of the tower, although it looked more like vertical running. Meanwhile, the others performed perfect handstands. No sooner were the two at the top of the tower than they scrambled back down even more quickly, jumping from a great height to hit the ground sooner than anyone expected. What had just happened, the crowd asked themselves?

The tight-fitting black tracksuit pants weren't the friends' normal style of clothing, but they needed a uniform of some sort. If the elite firemen were in uniform, then so would they be. White sweatshirts had the Yamakasi name and logo that Sébastien Foucan had designed, with the words *L'Art du Déplacement* underneath. Like all ninjas, they hid their identities under black hoods. David and Sébastien felt on top of the world as they flew down the zipline. Chau had sprained his ankle during rehearsals the day before when doing a *passe-muraille,* or wall climb.

He put the pressure of his leg on an open car door, thinking it was closed, and his ankle rolled with nothing solid to land on. No one in the crowd would have had any idea that there was an injury amongst them.

'Yeah we did it, crazy!' the group said to each other as they celebrated afterwards with hugs and excitement all round. Knowing it was a chance to showcase briefly their potential, the friends had had a very clear goal that day: whatever they did, it would be better than the firefighters. The special gymnastics team were impressive; they were the crème de la crème of probably the most respected fire-fighting unit in all of France, with a reputation for excellence. Big muscles, uniforms, matching haircuts and a consummate air of discipline and ability. But whatever they jumped over or under, the Yamakasis would surpass their achievements. However fast the firefighters' special gymnastics unit got up the tower, the friends had wanted to do it faster. The special gymnastics team could climb the tower in one minute. The Yamakasi made it in thirty-five seconds. The rest of their performance involved a simple zipline, climb, some dive-rolls over a car and arm-jumps across a fire engine. If these guys were faster and better than the special performance team, then that made them really special. The simple actions they choreographed for two scenes in the show had impressed. The local popula-tion had a new fascination: the Yamakasi.

The name Yamakasi in Lingala, the Bantu language from the Democratic Republic of Congo, means 'strong body, strong mind'. It was the idea of Guylain N'Guba-Boyeke. He was born in Kinshasa, the capital, but his family's story had lead him to Evry, where his life was transformed by his friends. He had kept up with the group and was a firm member of it. They had also needed a name for what they did. Sébastien suggested *L'Art du Déplacement*. *Déplacement* was 'the way of movement' and if there were martial arts then there could be 'arts' of movement as well.

Entry to the Yamakasi and continued membership was guaranteed to no one. 'It was very difficult to join our group of modern-day Samurais,' recalled David. The unspoken rules of performance dictated that you had to keep up with the training, extreme games and constant assessment. They believed that anyone who fell behind then had the potential to slow down the progress of others. There were no explicit leaders, they were simply together. Phung had declined the invitation to be in the group. He believed in sharing and the values of collective effort but had seen that the individualistic behaviour of some had become the norm. Whatever the project was going to be, it wasn't for him. He loved his brothers and cousin dearly and, after wishing them all the luck in the world, decided to join the army.

Jean-François's ambition for his brother went beyond the firefighters' performance. He gave the video compilation to a contact at the local television station. The call back came quickly – when could they start filming? 'At this time all of us were together, heading in the same direction, same vision, no money, no religion, no business, nothing,' remembered Malik. It was just a group of friends who had for many years shared some very unique experiences.

The Stade 2 TV crew followed the group (with the exception of Guylain, who was unavailable, and Laurent who was still away in the army) around all of their local spots in Lisses and Evry. Jean-François, the now de facto manager, put David at the front. He led the way through their local streets while the group did what they usually did; they moved. The show was broadcast live on a Sunday. Chau and

Sébastien were interviewed in the studio while the others did a demo. This was intercut with the pre-recorded report.

Across France on that Sunday afternoon the general public witnessed the seemingly impossible acts that the friends had perfected in their environments over the past decade. In various apartments in Lisses and Evry, certain parents began to ask questions of their children – is that what had they been doing all these years? On Monday morning, the phones started to ring.

9

Enter Stage Right

Everything that's an obstacle is part of our art. When we're walking and we encounter a challenge, that's what we work on. It's a way of saying: 'I'm breaking free, I'm free and I can go where I want.' No one can tell you: 'You have to go this way because that's the way it is.' I follow my own path.

David Belle on Stade 2

I t was a joke right? Claude Zidi, the director of the *Astérix et Obélix* film, wants to talk to the Yamakasi . . .. seriously? 'For us it was too much, it was like, "Yeah, c'mon. We are just jumping. We are not stars,"' recalled Malik. These bad jokes were getting to be a bit much so they never bothered to call back. Jean-François and David's friend Jocelyn were the group's de facto manager and agent, the gatekeepers to contacts and opportunities. Newspapers and TV reporters started to become fixtures in Lisses as the group shared and showed their skills.

Within the group there was no agreed direction in terms of their practice being orientated towards sports or its artistic potential for performance. It was just what it was. While Sébastien was definitely the dreamier and artistic one, many of the others also had a clear creative flair. However, no matter how creative their movements or unusual their context, they all related more to the mindset of athletes than artists. Theirs was a functional fitness and they were the hardest-working athletes on the most unconventional playing fields. Their discipline couldn't be restrained to sport or art and instead combined the two with a firm set of values.

What had begun as a collective experience was being individually carved up through media opportunities as some were given positions from which to shine more often than others. What should be shown and by whom was leading to rising tensions between the group. A swell of discontent replaced the initial tide of jubilation that had followed their first successful performance.

Several months after the Stade 2 broadcast, the French-Canadian musical theatre lyricist Luc Plamondon, producer Charles Talar and renowned choreographer Gilles Maheu were on a plane to Paris. The theatre world was crying out for new and more exciting choreographies to match the spectacle and success of musical shows such as the Irish production *Riverdance*. Plamondon was working on a new project and, after seeing the Stade 2 TV piece, had an idea. First he had to see them with his own eyes. As a man whose professional life played with the illusion of reality on stage, he needed to be sure that they were as impressive as they seemed.

The guided tour began just like many of the others for the media. They met at the Dame du Lac and the friends displayed their skills. Laurent had secured an early release from the army due to the success of the group and joined them. Throughout the afternoon they hit the other training hotspots to demonstrate their physical prowess. Big drop-jumps at the stone walls at le Van, arm-jumps in Evry and, of course, the Manpower jump. They ended the day back in Lisses at the ping pong tables, showing the director what was possible with just a table. Plamondon started to explain the opportunity and offered all of the Yamakasi a part.

The show was based on Victor Hugo's masterpiece, *The Hunchback of Notre-Dame*.

It had not been a standard audition, but the Yamakasi had nothing to compare it to and it promised to be an unconventional show anyway. The social context would intertwine asylum seekers, outlaws and pop culture, while mixing popular scores and styles with text from Hugo's novel. Plamondon's success with the rock-opera *Starmania* had prepared him for the next stage in the evolution of musical theatre. Even the costumes, the academic Rebecca-Anne C. Do Rozario wrote, would be '*couture* of the street, emphatic in how they symbolised counter-culture, with the *sans-papiers* [non-registered immigrants] wearing colourful braids and loose, tie-dyed and splattered clothing'.

Things were starting to get serious, but not all the group shared the same enthusiasm for the project. They would have to sign up for two years and so much could potentially happen in that time. It was a big commitment and, being associated with something for that long, could endanger their sense of identity. Should they wait for something bigger and better to come along? Should they hide the discipline? What about waiting for a film offer? Some were unsure of performing in front of a live audience even though they had all done that for the fire brigade. Theatre was a different type of stage.

One month after being offered the roles, there was still some indecision. The year 1997 had been amazing for the friends and they had at last begun to see the potential in finding a way to live from their art. As much as everyone in the group pushed themselves hard – or had a high level of 'self-competition' – and were all great athletes, opinions differed between them on what were the human values of the practice and, in particular, what aspects of it could be shared.

Individual recognition and a need for validation from those who had inspired them had created new divisions.

On a February morning in 1998, Williams arrived late for training with Yann, Charles and Malik. Chau couldn't make it that day. With little explanation, Williams was told that both Sébastien and David had independently left the group. Sébastien was David's best friend, so it felt normal that he would somehow follow David, but Sébastien had taken his own decision. Sébastien had always thought that education was the pathway they should take their discipline along. David was nearly 25 years old and wanted to be in films. Williams was sixteen and had spent so much of the past years growing up with David and Sébastien, sharing their experiences in Sarcelles, that nobody was sure which way Williams would decide to go, but he always had the feeling that his cousin David was a very individual person who would follow his own path.

Williams would stay with his older brother Chau and the group. Nobody asked him to do any different or tried to persuade him otherwise. He had spent most of his life training alone but Williams knew the others were there for him when he needed help and they had been happy to share their experiences. That mattered. 'If I'm here today, it's because I know I could always count on you,' he told the others.

Regardless of how the Belle family in Sarcelles had tried to make David feel welcome and how much they loved him, for him the discipline was only a family thing in regard to him and his father, not the other Belles. He believed that the origin of the practice had been passed only from father to son even though his father had lived with and brought up his cousins for ten years. David was on his own quest.

For Williams, however, it wasn't just the Belles; it was also the Hnautras, and Piemontesi; it was Guylain, Malik and Charles. He believed that it should never be closed down to one family name or person who would be put first. It wouldn't be easy for everyone to live together, but there was nothing Williams loved more than a challenge. Yamakasi was a multi-family tale. He felt that stronger than ever now.

Regardless of the split, they all shared the same story. The Yamakasi wanted to promote the human values of respect and courage alongside the physical aspects of the discipline. Even though the Yamakasi, Sébastien and David promoted the same message – that the practice could promote a sense of autonomy and bring about a sense of freedom and meaning to one's life – the way they lived their lives became very different. 'David likes to have the light on him. Yann and the others like it when the light is on everyone, and that makes a big difference,' said Laurent.

A friend of David's had sent a copy of the video of him in action to Hubert Koundé, a well-known actor from Evry who had played a lead role in the seminal Mathieu Kassovitz film *La Haine*. Koundé watched the tape. 'It's crazy what you're doing! I don't know if you realise!' he told David. They met up to discuss how they could put it on the big screen. Koundé would give David his first acting lessons.

Koundé also suggested that David create the word Parkour by changing the 'c' to a 'k' and losing the 's' from the word *parcours*. David had heard his father talk of the various *parcours* (courses) he had trained when he was younger, but a 'k' made what David did his own. With a specific name for it, there was the potential for it to lead to something. It was a simple way to differentiate it from the *parcours* of life. Rather than a normal *parcours*, it would be a new and improved one. David wanted Parkour to be known. Not only would it be a way to live life on his own terms but it would give his father the recognition that David felt he deserved. 'Raymond Belle is the foundation of it all – of my life, of the creation of Parkour and its development throughout the world. Without him, there would be no David Belle and no Parkour,' wrote David many years later in his book *Parkour*. But first, Kassovitz told David, they had to start work on his acting abilities. The play *Pygmalion* would be his first performance.

Before the Yamakasi embarked on the *Notre-Dame de Paris* show, another offer came their way. They had become urban legends across many of the *banlieues* of Paris and two brothers, Bruno and Patrick Girard, from Nanterre, a suburb northwest of the city, had created the company Pam Productions. They wanted to involve the Yamakasi in a short film project. Inspired by Grandmaster Flash's 1982 hit track 'The Message', they wanted the film to portray the suburbs in all of their multicultural urban glory and with a positive image, in contrast to the typically negative media representation. The film was self-funded and would showcase the capabilities of their production company.

The original plan had been to show various elements of street and hip-hop culture, including graffiti artists, breakdancers, capoeira and so on. However, as soon as Bruno and Patrick spent time with the Yamakasi, it was clear to them that the group was the link between all the other artists and should feature more heavily in the film. They also thought that what the friends were doing had the potential to become more well known, even internationally. Preproduction began in 1997 and the shoot would begin the following year.

Although the group had already met with the director of the *Notre-Dame de Paris* show, they were invited to attend the formal auditions. The 1970s venue the Palais des Congrès was the show's home and would provide the setting for the now seven-member Yamakasi group's first taste of treading the boards. Breakdancers, acrobats, dancers and a host of other performers gathered for the auditions in one of the large convention halls. The Yamakasi had already been invited to be on the cast so waited in the wings as quietly and as still as they could. Never an easy task for movers.

While the others limbered up and anxiously awaited to discover whether they would be given a role, the casual-looking group seemed to be there for no reason that was apparent to the other performers. 'Why aren't these guys moving? It's not fair for the dancers and acrobats,' grumbled Cyril Raffaeli, a disgruntled up-and-coming acrobat and performer. They didn't look anything special at first glance, he thought. Unless someone had seen the short Stade 2 report on TV or attended the firefighters display, nobody knew the Yamakasi. Why was there such special treatment for these guys?

The Yamakasi were unused to being around performers or jealous behaviour and weren't prepared for such animosity. They had never felt the need to prove themselves to anyone outside of their group before. What they were capable of was spectacular, but the spectacle itself held little to no interest during their training over the past five years. Their approach to it had bred a certain level of humility. It didn't matter how much they laughed and clowned around, when it came to knowing what they could and couldn't do they were deadly serious. If they said they could do something, then they could. If they had earned their place, then they didn't deserve to be questioned.

Luc Plamondon and the producer Gilles Maheu explained that they had already conducted a different type of casting and the guys were in the show. Dissatisfied by the explanation, Raffaeli continued to protest. Bored and tired, the Yamakasi took the situation into their own hands; they were always ready for action. If this guy needed to see something, no problem.

A seven-metre-long ladder leant against the wall leading to a raised platform above the stage. Without warning, Charles climbed the ladder and squatted on the platform. From there he dropped seven metres directly on to the wooden floorboards of the stage. Their critics were silenced, but a compromise was made: only two of the seven would be in the show, Charles and Chau.

The first month of rehearsals was as frustrating for Charles and Chau as the casting had been. Their foray into the world of storytelling, entertainment and illusion wasn't what they hoped for, and they were resigned to waiting in the wings while other performers went through their roles on stage. They would be performing against a fifteen-metre-high wall that was yet to be built. Actors, dancers and technicians, all with at least ten years of experience behind them, looked on with curiosity, wondering why these guys were there. Charles and Chau began to question it themselves. Chau was twenty and Charles twenty-two, the youngest of all the performers in the show. They were again the odd ones out, but took it all in, making the most of the opportunity by learning the rudiments of choreography. The importance of the physical elements and choreography of the show wasn't to be underestimated. In an unprecedented step, twenty-four dancers and ten acrobats and breakdancers were listed in the show's programme, giving them equal billing alongside the seven principal singing parts.

Everything changed for Charles and Chau as soon as the

wall was built. It gave them the props they needed to perform from. Like the rest of the show, there was an unconventional aesthetic to the stage setting. There was nothing gothic about the style of the cathedral wall of this theatrical Notre-Dame. There were footholds and grips that facilitated choreographed abseiling, and multiple levels of blocks that could move to form secondary walls and areas for both physical performers and singers. The battlements ten metres up on the wall allowed for precision jumps and, each night, Charles and Chau would drop at least five metres to the floor. They created all of their own choreography as nobody else knew or fully understood what they could do, including Martino Müller, the show's revered choreographer.

Once the pair started moving, some of the cast began to understand and appreciate their abilities. Now it made sense. Theirs was another form of physical yet artistic expression, but there were others who still didn't get it. It wasn't what they were doing but more the 'how' of it all. There was a level of agility to the movements that Chau and Charles performed which other cast members had never seen before. The extra spins and rolls that would allow movements to continue and carry their natural momentum from one obstacle to the next was different to the dancers performing at ground level. 'How can you be strong physically and have a mind stable enough to take such risks and still feel happy?' the perplexed and curious among them asked. The risk of a sprained ankle could ruin a dancer's career: the risk of injury was never far from their minds. But years of preparation had mitigated the risks for the Yamakasi. They had absolute clarity about what their bodies could and couldn't do at any given time. Fear was never shut out. Conversely, it was always attended to and weighed up alongside their agility and fitness to provide a precise self-knowledge.

Even the basics of jumping enthralled their fellow performers. Everyone wanted to jump high. The dancers, acrobats and even the tightrope walkers asked, 'How do you place your feet when you land? How do you control yourself in the air? How can you jump that high and that far?' 'It's about landing properly,' Chau replied. 'That's the basics.'

Two months before the *Notre Dame de Paris* opened, the group began filming on *Le Message*. The production followed the Yamakasi for three months. 'They were a bit secretive at the beginning, but when we started to shoot, everyone opened up. They didn't want to show everything; there was a lot of discussion around what they wanted to show and what they wanted to keep,' remembered Bruno. While they were keen to show what they were capable of, the group felt it was too early to start showing their methods. They filmed in Evry, Nanterre and Rueil-Malmaison. Yamakasi action sequences were mixed with other urban activities and examples of life from the suburbs.

It was up to the production company to fund the postproduction. The film wouldn't be ready for the world to see for a while, but Bruno and Patrick cut some action clips together to help make showreels for the Yamakasi to use.

Chau and Charles had been busy with final rehearsals for *Notre Dame de Paris*, so they featured less than the others in *Le Message*. *Notre Dame de Paris* opened to rave reviews on 16 September 1998, and whilst Charles and Chau were doing a great job, ten days after opening the producers thought it best to bring in Malik and Williams as their understudies; the positive reviews meant it could be a long run and, at some point, even these superhuman machines might need a rest. Malik and Williams loved it. The range of movement and artistry introduced them to another world and one they were open to. 'I had to change my way of moving,' remembered Williams. 'Because before there wasn't an aesthetic thing about my way of moving. It was impressive but it wasn't very beautiful. I had to change things. I started calling what I did "the dance in the air".'

Unlike performers who rest before and after a show, the four of them still trained all day before arriving at the theatre – and then they trained afterwards not that anyone knew. It felt like quite a lazy period because during the show they were supposed to remain still and rest back-stage. It was nothing like their previous, self-imposed training commitments.

'I'm gonna kill you! You killed my jumpers!' screamed the producer just a month into the show. In an artificial environment, one that relied on the timings and the actions of others and had been 'prepared for 'safety', the worst accident any of them had experienced had just occurred. The lighting technician, in particular, was in shock. During the scene *La Cour des Miracles*, Charles and Chau had to drop down from the wall. They'd started at about four and half metres but, as usual, they had been keen to make the movement bigger. The drop they performed that night was six metres. There had been technical problems with the lighting from the start and most had been ironed out, but nothing like this. The lights were cut *before* rather than after the landing, leaving the two Yamakasi in pitch black as they dropped through the air and depriving them of all visual cues as to when they were going to land and the position of the other performers. The mistimed flick of a switch meant they both suffered serious injuries, were ruled out of the show and left devastated.

Chau had shattered his heel and spent a month in a cast. For the next six months after that, he did between five and ten thousand calf raises a day, fighting the fear that his heel would be unable to withstand the force when he would need to land on it again. Doctors told him he wouldn't climb or jump properly again. 'But they didn't really know what we were capable of,' recalled Chau. 'Getting that kind of injury on a jump like this, it could've been worse. But I got hurt because I impacted, instead of landing on the ball of the foot. It was just that. Back then I was ultra-ready. If I wanted to avoid hitting the dancers, I had to land like that.' He was right: the doctors didn't know. Soon he would be back and could jump further and higher than before.

The night after the accident, Malik and Williams were on stage in three roles, as gargoyles, for 'the party of the craziest' and as French pirates. While only two Yamakasi were officially listed in the show, the reality was that the others were there all the time. The show became a new open house as Yann, Laurent and Guylain were always backstage or watching out front. Everything any of them learnt or experienced was shared with the others. There were seven shows per week, one per night five days a week and then twice on Saturdays with Mondays off. Each performance lasted an hour and fifteen minutes, but still Williams and Malik trained every spare moment they could find. Their behaviour didn't go unnoticed. 'You must calm down because, without you, they can't have a show,' the producer repeatedly told them. 'Look what happened to Chau and Charles. You need to be careful because you have a contract and need to be pro-fessional, not just like you were before you joined the company.' It was true, there were responsibilities – but it was hard to tame wild souls.

The Yamasaki's obsession hadn't allowed for the kind of reflection on their practice that the other performers on stage would most likely have gone through in their formal training. Dancers, actors and acrobats had a different type of schooling. The Yamakasi had written no dissertations nor had they created performances based on studying a lineage of masters of their craft, no matter how much Jackie Chan and *Dragon Ball* they'd consumed. The nature of performance was a different creature to that of getting up and going outside to do something. Their skills or 'tacit knowledge', an informal knowledge, was the result of vast, immersive and innovative experiences and of the emotions they had felt through years of dedicated training. They had matched a perfectionist mindset with relentless and endless trials of endurance. The practice had become part of their consciousness, their intuition and sense of being. It existed because they shared with one another the activities learnt and knowledge gained.

Every night an audience viewed what had been an introverted practice recreated as an extrovert, spectacular performance. The firefighters event had been a demonstration whereas now it was a conversation with an audience who had to believe in what they saw and be moved by it. Some interpreted the movements of the Yamasaki as akin to 'release technique' in contemporary dance whilst others saw it as a new form altogether. In some ways their stage performances were no different to that of the other physical artists on stage. They were present and in the moment. Every move was mindful and exact. There was no dilution in the act of doing it. However, the pacing of the performance processes was new to the Yamakasi. They never marked their movements. There was no 'going through the motions'. Whilst other performers paced their days and kept something in the tank for when the audience was seated, Malik and Williams maintained their timing, pace and intent by doing the full action every time.

They had to be at the theatre a couple of hours before the show, ideally around 6 p.m. for an 8.30 p.m. start. Williams was sixteen years old, the youngest in the company, always late and in trouble. Finishing at 10.30 p.m., he would then need to take the last train to Sarcelles, but rarely managed to catch it, so he could only go as far as another town nearby, entailing a thirty-minute jog before arriving home around midnight. It was training, so he didn't mind. After a while he moved to Paris with his girlfriend but would still go back to Sarcelles some nights.

They were learning new approaches and movements. They danced, lifted other performers, held poses, did acrobatic moves and choreographed climbing sequences in harnesses. To be in the show and stay in the company, they had to be complete artistic performers. It wasn't just about the Yamakasi way of moving, even if that was what got them there in the first place. Everyone they worked with was at the top of their individual fields and Williams and Malik absorbed everything, filling in the gaps in their own practice. They doubled for dancers, acrobats and for stuntmen who'd fall down the stairs as a drunk monk. They were ready for every task.

Even before opening, the show had been marketed on various billboards and in the press as something special. It went on to break box-office records in France and afterwards in Belgium, Canada and Switzerland. The French-Canadian production had moved the heart of musical theatre from Broadway to Paris. *The Guinness Book of World Records* listed the show as having the most successful first year in the history of musical theatre. The soundtrack album was released eight months before the show opened and the single *Belle* sold more than three million copies, staying at number one in the French charts for thirty-three weeks. Everyone in France could hum or whistle the tune.

For the next two years Malik and Williams – and the rest of the Yamakasi by default – were part of the show. After opening in France, the show went to Canada for six months. Chau and Malik spent three weeks in Quebec teaching their specific choreographies to their Canadian counterparts. The success continued and the show went on to Las Vegas. This time it was Yann and Laurent's turn as the flamboyant world of Las Vegas theatre temporarily replaced the streets of Evry. Their minds as well as their bodies were exposed to new ways of thinking and being.

Not only were they exposed to a new type of performance but Yann and Laurent's trip to Vegas put them in contact with people from the new, contemporary circus movement that was taking the American theatrical scene by storm: Cirque du Soleil. While it merged theatre and circus, the Yamakasi gave a performance that merged theatre with elements of their own art. There was a natural connection as the two groups started to talk.

The success of the *Notre Dame de Paris* show meant more press coverage and TV interviews. The executive film producer Virginie Silla saw one of them and was impressed. Charles was waiting in the wings of the theatre when he took the call from her. 'What, I don't believe it!' It had been their dream to work in films. Now apparently Luc Besson, the famous French director of the hit film *The Big Blue*, wanted to meet them.

10

Baby Steps

Work on your ability to grow, to open up, to trust more in yourself so that you may trust more in others as well. Work on your ability to reduce your fear, to know yourself better so that you may know how to react in life.

Williams Belle

There was very little 'delay' to the apparent 'Delayed Onset Muscle Soreness' after my first Parkour class. If eyelashes could ache mine would have done. I wasn't prepared for the extent of my absolute inability to do anything involving movement after being briefly reacquainted with Parkour twelve hours earlier at a gymnastic centre in east London.

To a whimpering soundtrack of moans and groans, I trudged around my apartment the next day. By 4 p.m. I couldn't walk down the stairs and getting up from a seated position was slow and painful. I continuously drank water thinking it would provide a miracle cure, but that meant certain seated positions just weren't that easy. Laughing at my self-imposed physical inadequacy and misfortune triggered more pain. I didn't have a six-pack; I had just one big sack and not a strong one at that. However, amongst the layers of discomfort, I had a deeply satisfying feeling, an invisible badge of honour signifying that I had done something. I had turned up. I had done what I had wanted to do for a long while but been too shy to try.

With the knowledge that I couldn't jump well, high or far; that I stepped up on to things as opposed to vaulting over them; that I definitely couldn't climb a rope or much else, Thursday nights at Erith became a fixture in my week. Forrest, the instructor, kept smiling and asked us how we felt. 'Angry!' one honest soul replied whilst sweating like a pig, legs shaking from the jumps and still holding that goddam horse stance and squat position.

No matter how much I intellectualised the reasons and justifications for hurting so much, the simple truth I couldn't ignore was that we get good at what we do a lot.

Like most of the British public I spent vast amounts of my day in a potentially damaging posture. I'd never read any glaring headlines with the mandate 'Stand up!' so I didn't. I sat while reading the newspaper in the morning, while attending to emails, watching footage I'd filmed, editing that footage, and then when my work was done I would relax by watching a film – not standing up. I worked from home and so couldn't even blame a long daily commute for my sedentary nature.

In 1953, a seminal British survey reported that bus drivers were nearly twice as likely to die from heart disease as bus conductors; yet schools, colleges, workplaces and Western society at large offered nothing but four-legged foes in some shape or form – a stool, bench or chair. While being elevated from the floor was originally for those of elevated status – nobility, statesmen and such like – for the commoner in a bygone age, the choice was to sit on the floor, squat or kneel.

Recent research has shown that sitting for more than four hours a day leads to increased health risks in the following conditions: heart/cardiovascular disease, diabetes, cancer, obesity, high blood pressure, muscle degeneration, back ache/neck pain and osteoporosis. Evidence also suggests a link to depression and dementia.

Four hours were nothing on my daily rituals. I had even invested in a stylish chair so I looked and felt good while slowly and silently allowing my potential for health and movement to deteriorate as I worked, relaxed and sat my days away. I conformed with convention and copied what I saw. Sitting was sophisticated, normal, intelligent and nothing to be ashamed of, as far as I knew.

How we learn to use our bodies is a way of becoming members of society. Tradition lets us know what is appropriate related to our status, age and gender. All of this is transmitted across generations to make these mechanisms seem 'normal', eventually entering the realm of 'natural', but they are not. Physiology meets psychology meets sociology. Menial and mundane physical habits are socially and culturally formed: we copy what we see, what we are told to do, and what we have learned by example and by order. Monkey see, monkey do. Bodily actions such as bleeding and vomiting are natural; the way we walk, sit, run and climb is not.

In 1934 Marcel Mauss, the French sociologist and anthropologist, wrote an essay entitled *Techniques of the Body*. Techniques, he argued, are actions that are effective and traditional. Efficiency and competence in them are the product of training. He compiled an index of how these actions had varied culturally and historically – the way people slept, walked, sat, squatted, and how they had been in motion: walking, running, jumping, climbing, swimming. Rather than people possessing an innate capacity for these actions, he argued that each society has its own special habits that are continually 'in process', changing and incorporating new influences – and so the social order is maintained. He studied a military march, for example, and found variations in the frequency of the soldier's stride. He noted how Parisian women changed their style of walking based on the influence of American films.

Our physical form, then, is continually changing and adapting to what we are doing or not doing. Children, for example, imitate the actions of those they have confidence in and those with authority over them. 'Cases of invention, of laying down principles, are rare,' Mauss wrote. 'Cases of adaptation are an individual psychological matter.'

For some of the youth in Evry, to be included within the group, to gain status and authority, you had to move in extraordinary and challenging ways. To be able to master your strength and confront your fears, certain very active young men adapted, invented and inspired those around them.

Forrest, my French Parkour coach, was still in touch with his friends who had set him on his own Parkour path. He had talked about Stéphane Vigroux with great fondness. 'What's he like?' I asked Forrest many times. 'Ah you'll see' was all Forrest was prepared to say, with a smile that meant it would be good.

Stéphane's movements and techniques had been emulated the world over. He was one of the most revered yet aloof and evasive early Parkour practitioners. Sometimes referred to as 'the ghost', he was at last willing to speak. He had agreed to be interviewed for the Parkour group Urban Freeflow's online video series *UFTV*. Forrest arranged for a group of us to travel to France to meet and interview him.

The crickets sang in the morning sunlight while I sat in

the back of the Urban Freeflow van, eager to meet Stéphane. We pulled up to the Vigroux family house in a quiet cul-de-sac in Bondoufle, a few miles from Lisses. Packed into the van was myself, Forrest, photographer Andy Day and writer Dan Edwardes.

Fresh off the plane from Thailand for a short family visit, Stéphane looked like something out of a kung fu film. Ponytailed dark hair tucked into his woolly hat, tall, skinny and androgynously beautiful, he looked cold and slightly unsure of what he was getting himself into. Ubiquitous cheap sports clothing of a sweatshirt and baggy grey sweat pants— the uniform for both the inactive and active – gave little away. The way he walked was loose, even uncoordinated, with his head slightly down. He was understated. His Vietnamese heritage lent itself to a sense of ninja mystique. He jumped in the van and, after a shyly spoken 'hello' to each of us, his focus was on Forrest. Stéphane was happy to see his old friend. The atmosphere was quiet and respectful. Nobody wanted to blow it. A rare pathway had been made available to a previously inaccessible and impenetrable level of Parkour understanding.

We made our way through the empty, quiet and green streets of Courcouronnes, arriving at the Long Rayage estate in Lisses ten minutes later. If these were the Parkour badlands, they didn't look so bad to me. Just dull, if anything. In my mind's eye, French ghettos involved densely populated high-rise buildings filled with rubbish and graffiti; here there were mixed level, four-storey and single-storey houses with neatly maintained window boxes with flowers. The white walls and contrasting pink edging of the supporting pillars in the estate felt welcoming and far from the social dystopia I'd imagined.

As we walked towards the heart of the estate I assured

Stéphane that nothing I filmed would be shared without him approving the final edit and, of course, he didn't have to answer any questions if he didn't want. A small smile, a nod of agreement, I pressed 'record'. For two days I watched, filmed and listened as Stéphane spoke of his past, present, hopes and dreams for the future. I never thought about Parkour the same way again. Parkour was a training methodology, one that required several key elements such as a certain physical condition and a sensitivity to every action executed – the touch. Stéphane paid homage and thanks to David Belle, his teacher who 'taught me everything I know about sport' and to Williams Belle, a 'very positive man'.

When Stéphane began Parkour in 1998 it was difficult to find out about, unless you were friends with someone 'in the know'. Stéphane had Ken Mayarde.

'Look, Steph, I've got this video you should watch.' Ken pushed the VHS tape into the machine and hit play.

'What the hell!' Stéphane was shocked. He couldn't believe what he'd just seen. It was real, but not. Raw. I mean, how? This man, this animal, this . . .

'You know what, this guy trains in Lisses at the gymnasium staircase. We could go there and train,' Ken added.

'OK! Of course, let's go and see that guy!'

Stéphane was eighteen years old, 'always acting crazy', and never listening. His physical outlets were Viet Vo Dao, a Vietnamese form of kung fu which he practised two hours twice a week, and breakdancing, which he did whenever and wherever possible. Ken Mayarde was Stéphane's 'big brother', partner in crime and local legend. He was good at everything he tried, a natural athlete and fighter, and always in the know. He had heard about some 'mad real ninja guys' training in the woods who were 'so, so strong'. If Ken was impressed, it meant something.

'Stéph, what are you doing? You're not going to school, you're not working, you just play monkey all day, and it doesn't make any sense for me.' Bernard Vigroux had said this to his son on many occasions. With the face of an angel, Stéphane had always been a problem with an insatiable appetite for trouble. Fighting, being escorted home by the police; how to piss your parents off was an almost full-time task. The eldest of three sons and a daughter, his father was a company guy. He'd started at the bottom, played by the rules and let discipline and convention play its role, working his way up to respectability, responsibility and a rigid sense of right and wrong. He had worked for IBM all his life. Stéphane's mother, a half-Vietnamese telephone receptionist for a phone company, was warm, kind and forgiving, good cop to his father's bad cop. Stéphane was given the kind of stable family home life many can only dream of for their children. What was a dream for his parents was a living nightmare for him. Rage brewed, against what? Everything!

Stéphane couldn't have foreseen that years later he would be living in London teaching a Parkour class to a group of women, one of whom he'd met a few years before and who had made a documentary about him, *Le Singe est de Retour* (The Monkey's Back).

In 2005 there were very few women in the world training at Parkour. I was one of them and I was rubbish at it. I was scared of everything and didn't spend much time training. What women were capable of in Parkour, nobody knew. There hadn't been many – if any – women who had the same level and years of training as the guys. Other sporting and athletic disciplines provided examples of how high or far women can jump, how they climbed and how they combined movements together in dance and gymnastics – there was something very original in how this outdoor body-centric discipline fused them all.

The Hammersmith & City Tube line rattled overhead at Latimer Road Station in west London as a small group of us waited outside the newsagents; backpacks, trainers, sweat-pants, ready for what, we never really knew. My stomach rumbled, not from hunger but from anticipation of what potentially lay ahead. In the past, I had avoided entering this situation on many occasions, whether through fear, or my own rationalisations and manipulations regarding the weather, public transport delay updates, the time I'd get home – *I'll be late in the first place so why bother?* or *I had just eaten so no point* – yet, even with an endless line of excuses, I was somehow here even though no one had actually asked me to do it.

You couldn't have pictured a better looking couple as Stéphane Vigroux and Katty Belle arrived, all smiles, looking somehow as amazed as the rest of us at what was actually happening. A group of women were meeting up to go and train Parkour. Katty Belle had grown up moving; her family all moved, including her older brothers Phung and Chau of course and younger brother Williams. They were all strong, it was a 'Belle family thing'. She had met Stéphane through her cousin David.

We started running. God, I hated running. The only thing that I enjoyed more about the indoor classes was the fact that there was simply no running beyond a few laps of the room at the start. But outside, we always ran. Whatever chance I had of doing anything diminished after having to run somewhere first. This basic human movement left me out of breath, way too hot, wobbly and nauseated. My feet were shod in Nike Airs with orthotics inside just to make sure I had no real feeling or feedback whatsoever, such was the wisdom of various doctors and podiatrists of the day. With brute force and no technique, I was barely effective in getting from A to B, let alone efficient, always bringing up the rear of the group with my long, heel-striking stride.

We didn't go far, but it was always a relief just to put down my bag and delay the inevitable by sipping water and tying my shoelaces yet again. We'd only gone just around the corner from the station. A three-metre brick wall divided a space between a walkway towards a bridge and a pedestrian, benched area leading to a playground in a residential estate.

'OK, how do you feel about that?' Stéphane asked our small group. Katty smiled and was up for it. No problems there, nor for the next to try. Amy Slevin was in her early twenties, physically strong from a dance background, and she spent her days working in fashion as a PA at Alexander McQueen.

A third lady bounced up the wall. Tracey Tiltman was a geology student in her final year at Kingston University and, although also very new to Parkour, this challenge wasn't going to be a problem for her either. I had seen Tracey do one-legged squats on a balance beam in her first class. Others included Layla Curtis, in her early thirties and physically in the same boat as me. She was a successful fine artist whose work involved mapping borders and boundaries both real and imagined, and her presence was appropriate. She had survived Antarctic expeditions and travelled through the jungles of Borneo, but here she was venturing into new terrain: west London residential estates.

To follow, Stéphane had proposed that we combine three movements into a short route, taking a short run-up, jumping across two obstacles and landing hanging against a wall. As light as a feather, he demonstrated with silent movements and explained that, firstly, we would step with one foot up on to a small, square, knee-high bollard, make the next step with a one-footed stride on to a low wooden bench, and then leap on to the side of the brick wall, catching the top of it with our hands and ending up with our feet against the wall in a hanging squat type of position. The last move was an arm-jump, or cat-leap, as some called it.

'No.' That was how I felt. Layla agreed.

'OK, well what about this?' Stéphane deconstructed the sequence down to just the first two elements.

'No.'

He continued to deconstruct and I continued to be negative.

'How about first stepping on to the small square bollard and then jumping off to the side? Then how about we mark out the distance on the ground from the bollard to the bench and see if you can make the distance with one leap? What if you find a spot on the wall where you can take a few steps and then take a small jump on to the wall, landing with your feet slightly before the hands and lifting and bending the knees so you don't slam your shins into the wall?'

I was capable of walking, so I was actually able to try all of the suggestions. I didn't like people who said 'I can't do that' without even trying, but there I was doing exactly that as I voiced the word 'no', followed silently by 'I can't do that'. Every cell in my body just didn't feel good about any of it. Eventually Stéphane's breakdown of the movements asked me to take one step on the ground. Like music to his ears, 'OK' came out of my mouth and I proceeded to try each individual action.

The arm-jump – jumping at a wall – was odd, fun and

hard. I didn't go through life wearing gloves, but the skin on my hands was as soft as could be. The bricks grazed the tips of my fingers and my fingernails made an uncomfortable grinding sound as they made contact with the wall.

We all had our strengths and weaknesses. I'd never run at a wall, but Amy was very comfortable with that. She hated doing the accurate precision jumps, but leaping from rock to rock on Dartmoor National Park as a child had made me very familiar with the movement. I'd done handstands against a wall, but jumping at a wall was a new idea.

Out of the corner of my eye, I could see the others succeeding and repeating the route. Katty, Tracey and Amy moved with grace, power and confidence. They were beautiful – Batgirl, Catwoman and Wonderwoman, real-world role models, products of their own imagination and not something out of DC Comics.

I tried, failed, laughed and felt frustrated. Jumping up onto something and then onto something else filled me with an irrational fear. Of what, I don't know, but I had no belief in my body's ability to see the movement through to the second step. An overactive imagination led to visions of me with fewer teeth, a broken neck and more injuries than even the bionic man had ever sustained. By the end of the session I had learnt that I didn't like jumping up onto things and going anywhere else afterwards probably wasn't going to happen.

'Follow me, let's go for a walk,' said Stéphane after patiently guiding us through the various progressions (or not) made by the group.

'Oh my god, oh my god, Jesus f***ing Christ,' I said silently. As a secular humanist I had no idea what I had any faith in, but it definitely wasn't in the ability of my own body to walk along the top of a wall three metres above the ground and rising. The top of the wall was a comfortable width to move along, but after a few metres the distance to the ground increased as the wall followed a path up towards a pedestrian bridge. There was always the option to jump down relatively safely to the left but, meanwhile, the drop increased to seven metres on the right, messing with my mind and therefore body.

I hadn't walked far when I suffered an emotional seizure and jumped down to the safety of the ground on my left. The others continued. My breathing was erratic, my nerves fried. I could have cried. We are born with only two innate fears: loud noises and the fear of falling. The rest of my issues were learnt behaviours, a product of what I didn't do rather than what I did. I hadn't walked far on the wall but I had taken my first steps. The next time I would go further.

11

Master and Grasshopper

If you hang out, two guys like this together, then you are going to end up doing very crazy stuff.

Stéphane Vigroux

It was an ordinary day in the summer of 1998 when Ken Mardaye and Stéphane Vigroux made their way from the car park in Lisses down towards the tall, tree-lined avenue. The school and children's playground were on the left, the gate to the lake on the right. Inside the large, plain yellow and brown walls of the gymnasium building, the metal staircase thundered. It sounded like a lion escaping from a cage. Landed on, taken off from, held and let go of by both hands and feet, the staircase vibrated to the movements made by one man. Stones on the ground percussioned as a figure jumped from above and landed on the concrete. Then he rolled across as if it were as soft as foam.

Ken introduced Stéphane, who made a humble martial arts bow as the man in front of him dripped with sweat, looking unimpressed at the next wannabe. Stéphane had seen and relished the SpeedAirMan video featuring David Belle. The posture that David held at the end of film, showing his tattooed torso, had tied into all of the ideas relating to quests and learning that Stéphane had drawn inspiration from. But to be here, to see him moving in the flesh was mesmerising. The action in the video had been the most impressive thing he had ever seen. Yet, standing at the staircase, he realised the gaps that David had jumped across, dropped down from and generally seemed to fly over were actually much larger in real life than they looked on video. He was a one-man whirlwind of action. His movements were powerful yet accurate, making him a blend of superhero and warrior superstar. He exemplified how to take a different path.

'Follow me if you can,' David said.

After a short jog through the residential part of the estate, they all ran up a small set of stairs and sat perched in a squat position on the top of a narrow, concrete wall two metres high. Parkour graffiti, the marks left behind from the soles of trainers making contact with the wall, marked the smooth white and grey concrete. Nobody looked up and saw it; residents were blissfully unaware of the untold epic night missions. Almost straightaway, David jumped one and half metres across to the opposite wall catching the top with his hands, legs tucked in, then he dropped to the ground with an elasticity that made the pavement seem like a sprung floor. Without any instruction, Stéphane somehow understood. Next it was his turn, heart beating, adrenaline flowing like never before. 'OK you can do it, Steph,' he said to himself. He wanted it. He wanted that jump so badly. He had just seen that it was possible, so it must be! This man was such an impressive reference, but now it was up to him. 'OK go, OK now, OK, fuck, go!' He jumped and caught the other wall with his hands, attempting to copy the style of what he had seen. Too shy to show it, he had never felt this good about anything in his life.

Stéphane was hooked. Every day twice a day Stéphane rode the six-kilometre journey from Bondoufle to Lisses. He looked ridiculous as his long limbs arched over the frame of his younger sister's bike, but it got him from A to B so he didn't care. David told him what to do.

'Jump a hundred times from this rock and back again, landing like this, perfectly, or it's not a jump, no bullshit. If you miss one, start again.'

Nothing was big in size; just quality and quantity, a disciplined approach to repetition.

'OK, done, give me one more,' Stéphane eagerly replied after every task.

A hundred drop jumps from there to there. Make your way from here to there without touching this or that. Hold this stress posture for this amount of time. Do this number of this exercise, this number of that, hang on that wall for this amount of time. Never an explanation of the what and why; just do. Stéphane obeyed unquestionably. He had low self-esteem but had never been so conscientious with anything. He'd cheated tests and lied to his parents and teachers but, with these actions and no one watching, he was honest and he cared. It was scary never knowing what the next challenge could be, but David continued to set them and Stéphane wasn't going to let him down. He had failed at traditional classroom education, but this extreme, experiential style felt good.

'Fuck, this guy keeps coming back,' thought David. 'Maybe he's worth something. He's committed.'

Challenge by challenge, Stéphane gradually qualified for entry into David's world. After four months of the training tasks being successfully completed, David occasionally invited Stéphane to join him in a training session. There were others who were also following and training under

David. They all had one thing in common; they had to be able to keep up. Many wanted to train with David, but his approach was elitist. Fifteen people had tried to follow at one point, but that was quickly whittled down to ten by the time the likes of eighteen-year-old Kazuma did his first training session with David. 'I didn't know what I wanted with my life, neither did David . . .' Kazuma remembered. 'But I knew I wanted to be ready in any circumstances.' Whatever background David's followers came from, they all they wanted to prove themselves and that happened at an extreme level of physicality.

Stéphane had seen other people on the early video that Ken had shown him, but he had never had the chance to meet the Yamakasi or Sébastien Foucan. According to David they were scared, too chicken and they sucked. After two more months of challenges, tasks, fear, discomfort, commitment, quality, control and hard training, Stéphane had earned the right to train with David full time.

In the dark, in the wet and snow, hands tied, or eyes shut, anything where the notion of a comfort zone was a distant memory, they trained together. They always met at David's. The Dame du Lac was a stone's throw from his front door. Stéphane had visited the structure as a child but never imagined he could stand on top of it. David had many things to show his new protégé. Stéphane followed David up the left side of the structure. He felt on top of the world at the windy summit. It was such an achievement, a mental challenge to keep steady as each hand and foot was accurately placed in the small indented holds and grips that were evenly placed along the side. It was a great feeling but not great enough. To get to the top via the middle route was far more difficult. At first it was just a straightforward climb up the zigzagged section in the middle, but as the wall's structure curved, different fears crept in as the surface in front of Stéphane became concave. Every move and hold pulled him back into a void, willing him to let go and drop to the ground. It felt wrong. A straight wall made sense. Gravity played its part, but you could always pull with your arms and push on your elbows and there would be a way. Near the top, the moves became much harder. 'Fuck, how to get to the platform?' Panic started to overwhelm Stéphane as he held an overhanging position. He tried to pull himself up on to the platform but failed. Whatever he tried was ineffective. He hung, helplessly. There were no options.

'Fuuuuuuuuuuuuuck.' He imagined his fall as the grip weakened the longer he held on. 'I'm not going to make it, I'm fucked. I can't climb up, I can't go down. Fuck, I'm going to die, if I lose the grip I'm going to fall off.'

'David, help! Help! David!' he screamed with all the force that his lungs could summon. He looked up, but the size of the wall only made him feel worse. Every breath was short and fast. He felt his body weakening as he tried to maintain the overhang position. Was this it? If he didn't do something, he was going to fall and most likely die. There must be a technique, a way to do it. Others had done it. He pulled himself together, replaced panic with calm and made the move. A split second later, David arrived and was there to help him, but Stéphane was safe. He had done it.

Speed and explosiveness; David had lightning reactions. Zero to hero, no warm-up required, cold starts were where David excelled. Nothing motivated him like a sense of urgency, something to test him or sometimes the potential of another's achievement.

The training days were long, but Stéphane and David were inseparable. Master and disciple; trainer, student; friends, brothers – a profound alchemy was forming. One talked, the other absorbed; one led, the other followed – and more importantly, Stéphane could keep up. The angry teenager and misfit had found a sense of belonging, and in David, someone who shared his dissatisfaction with life. 'We were often cultivating subtle anger in our discussions. We were antiestablishment and feeding our anger in each other in our long conversations after training. Our only reality was the action of Parkour every day. That anger and feeling of being superior was feeding our ego and acting as a fuel to be better at Parkour,' remembered Stéphane.

Stéphane trusted David more than he trusted himself. 'Do this, I'm here,' was all Stéphane needed to hear. He had blind faith. He let David dangle him from the top of the Dame du Lac by his hands, by his feet, and inverted. There was nothing Stéphane wouldn't do if David was there. David's endorsement made every jump seem more achievable.

'*C'est bien vrai*' – It's really true. David's message was one of simple humility. It wasn't about *Yeah, if I warm up I could do it* or *I can do it tomorrow* or *Yeah, but I don't want to do it now*. Even if you're drunk or tired or whatever, if you said you could do something, you had to be able to do it now. If not, shut up. Don't talk about it. *Pour de vrai* – Do it now. 'If you're true, then you don't say you do it; you do it, then I know you can do it.' David was crystal clear about what mattered.

Stéphane was in love with Parkour. His younger brother Johann needed to know about this.

Johann was fifteen years old and always looked up to his older brother, no matter how ludicrous his games and ideas. If Stéphane was doing it, he wanted to try it. Anything to be close. Stéphane had once suggested tying their karate belts together to make a rope so that Johann could climb out of the bedroom window. Cool, thought Johann! It had all been going so well until their mother saw him dangling outside the window as he came into view while she sat in the lounge.

Stéphane hadn't been around the house much lately. He was up to something, thought Johann, but then again he was always up to something. Unlike Stéphane, Johann excelled at school and had no problems with anyone. He didn't particularly like school, but it came easily to him. He was good at it and his parents liked that. Whatever was going on with Stéphane, at least their second child was turning out OK. The brothers arrived at Johann's first Parkour session and he recognised the man he'd seen flying around in the video. Standing next to four other people, David had a captive audience. They listened and then followed him as he set off.

The Sunday afternoon pace was light and easy. Luckily for Johann he'd joined in a 'discovery session'. They walked and then started moving over, under and through various obstacles in their path. David told them to look around and find a few jumps. Johann didn't see anything. 'What about this?' David asked, pointing out a gap between two walls.

'It's a jump if you say so, but not for me.' Johann wasn't scared of something he wasn't going to do. They moved on, arriving at the gymnasium stairs. David wanted them to jump from the top of the railings on to the opposite wall. Johann climbed on top of the railings and looked. That was as far as he'd go. He walked down the stairs and stood at the bottom of the wall. David pulled him up. They moved on to the grassy area near the bus stop. There were large stones dotted along the edge. The challenge was to make your way around the grassy area without touching the ground. You had to jump or position your body in some way to be always on the rocks using whatever trees were in your path. Crocodiles, lava, escaping pirates, whatever worked for you – stories were silently played out as the group jumped, stepped and balanced their way around the area. Nothing that day had really sparked Johann's interest yet, but this challenge was achievable and within his reach.

With no pressure, suggestion or nudge from anyone, Johann revisited the rocks alone on the grass every day for three months. He felt he could do it and he did. He said little to his older brother, who likewise continued to share little about what he was doing. They were two individuals, side by side, living parallel lives but rarely connecting. Three years' difference was a lot at fifteen and eighteen years old.

Stéphane became entrenched in the elite, the 'elders' of the Lisses Parkour scene. He had occasional part-time factory work, but in reality he was training full-time. His parents despaired of him. Was it worth kicking him out of the house? What good would that do? At least if he was there they could try to influence him and help him in some way. His father shouted, his mother stayed quiet.

With the confidence of his first route under his belt, Johann was curious and went to the Dame du Lac to see what was going on. He soon made friends with some of the others closer to his age: Seb Goudot, Michael Ramdani and Jérome LeBret. Johann was the rookie but keen. Every day after school he went to Lisses and found his new friends. In contrast to the first light afternoon of discovery and exploration, Johann had no idea how hard training was until he saw what these guys were doing. His four hours of gymnastics, hours of Viet Vo Dao and learning to spin on his back breakdancing on the living room floor each week hadn't really prepared him. Johann was determined to copy whatever his new friends were doing as well as Stéphane and David. His ambitions were simple and his appetite for Parkour insatiable. He wanted to be better at what he was doing. The jumps needed to be further apart and higher, his movements faster and more explosive. He dared for and wanted more.

Gradually, Johann worked at getting to the top of the Dame du Lac. It took a few weeks to get to the first level, then the second. The height training was intense. The sensations of going up brought some vertigo and fear, but getting down was even harder. On the way up you could at least see exactly where you were going. Soon Johann was completely ingrained in the same way Stephane had been.

Except there were no push-ups. No planning, no routine, no recovery, just tired bodies that said, 'Pfff, so what, let's go out, let's find challenges, look for trouble. Let's look at something we can't do and we want to do.' For Johann and his friends Seb, Mike and Jérome their cravings grew. Four or five jumps had to be broken on a weekly basis, or they hadn't achieved anything. Whatever anyone else saw on the surface, mentally they were in overdrive.

Together Johann, Mike and Seb, the young guns, were three wild kids in Lisses who kept themselves to themselves. They were of the same age and soon pretty much at the same level. Only occasionally did they mix with the elders, but somehow through the grapevine of local urban myths on the Parkour scene they were aware of what David and his group were up to. 'Hey, did you hear Stéphane and David did 100 muscle-ups?' They could take it. What was a bit of pain anyway? There was only one thing for it: there would be a lot of muscle-ups to do that day.

'Hey, you guys, have you done this jump?' David asked them one day when their paths crossed.

'Yes,' they replied, proudly.

'Oh and have you done this one?'

They felt confident, it was time to impress. They'd done all the jumps around there, he needn't worry.

'Oh, well have you done this one?' David pointed out a gap so large they had never been seen it let alone thought about it. There was always a very clear and distinct hierarchy of achievement and therefore status. David's abilities were in a different league, no matter how much progress the young guys thought they had made.

Unbeknown to their parents, Stéphane and Johann could have come home with a broken bone every day of the week, but didn't. They saw them lazing around the house, not so different from many their age. Stéphane was full of attitude and Johann was still a good kid doing well at school. One Sunday morning the two seemingly lazy teenagers were chilling out sipping hot chocolate in front of the TV.

'Hey, Johann, you know what, how about we do that jump?' Stéphane asked. It came from nowhere, but as usual Johann thought, *Why not?* 'OK, let's do it'.

With no more thought than that they picked up their bags and left. The jump was big. They had a short warm-up and no intention of doing anything else that day. Stéphane went first and Johann videoed the moment. From the rooftop of one building, it was a running jump across to the rooftop of a lower garage. It was far, tricky. You had to be really precise. Too long and you're fucked; too short and you're breaking bones. There was a lot of impact, with no opportunity to roll. The take-off was awkward with an odd surface that was neither soft nor hard. Everything messed with your mind. There was no option of missing, just committing. Stéphane flew through the air, the hang time was impressive. His body looked like a manga character and then – boom – he hit the landing of the roof. Another drop and he was on the ground. It was intense, but he had made it.

Stéphane had confidence in his younger brother, having seen him train hard for the last twelve months. If he made a decision to do something, it was because he knew he could do it. Despite how it looked from the outside, Johann was far from reckless. This time, however, Johann seemed to be taking his time as Stéphane watched him walk back and forth from the take-off point to the start of the run-up. This wasn't like him, thought Stéphane, this was rare. He had never seen such hesitation. 'This is my brother,' he thought. Suddenly the reality of the situation and potential consequences hit him. 'Oh shit.' There was nothing he could do but watch and trust in his brother's capacity to know his own abilities and not mess up. Johann too wasn't sure. This was big. Could he? Should he? He had to do it. Whatever the result, he had to try. He thought about it and looked one more time. He had made up his mind. He was ready to die for the jump. He started running.

Twenty minutes later the brothers were at home, reunited with hot chocolate and their Sunday dose of manga. Exhausted from the adrenaline, they looked and smiled at each other, their parents again none the wiser.

12

The Maddening
Diversity of Handrails

*We changed the relationship between human beings and the city.
We reminded people that you don't have to live in conflict with the
place you live; you can live in harmony with it. Maybe it's not the
best place, but you can make it more beautiful by just changing
how you use it.*

Laurent Piemontesi

Nestled in amongst some of London's most sought-after real estate in the borough of Kensington and Chelsea lies a fifty-four-acre oasis. Bought by the London County Council in 1952 from the 6th Earl of Ilchester, it is a sanctuary for the senses, with semi-wild woodlands that are soft underfoot and peacocks who roam free. Couples laze their sunny afternoons away on grassy banks overlooking the ruins of a Jacobean mansion, Holland House, cleverly converted into an orangery and home to the open air Holland Park Theatre and Holland Park Opera. During the summer months, those who don't pay to see the performances simply picnic on the grass as haunting voices serenade them. The setting could not be more splendid. An extensive children's play area, sports facilities (tennis, cricket, football), elegant youth hostel, cafeteria serving some of the most delicious cakes and a park within a park, the Kyoto Japanese garden, make up Holland Park. This was one of my chosen training grounds.

Whilst the London Underground station for Notting Hill is only a few minutes' walk, the walled and gated park is restorative once entered. The Kyoto garden welcomes you from the northwest side. Created in 1991 with sponsorship from the Kyoto Chamber of Commerce for the Japan Festival of London, the area includes a waterfall, pond, colourful koi, a small bridge to view it all from and benches for contemplation; you can't help but exhale.

The garden was originally designed by the revered Shoji Nakahara and later maintained and redesigned by Yasuo Kitayama. Beyond the 'Japanese-ness' of it lies a heritage layered in ancient philosophy, poetry and myth. Dominant features of the garden are water and 'mountains' – represented in miniature here in the form of rocks – two fundamental building blocks of the natural world. The tortoise-shaped pond symbolises longevity, good luck and support. There are no straight lines – 'evil thoughts travel in straight lines' – therefore the bridge crossing the pond is staggered.

On the side of the sloped pathway that winds its way up, parallel to the waterfall, unnoticed by most, stands my nemesis. Waist-high and rounded at the top, it is an unassuming rail. The less able hold it to guide their way up as it defines the border between the footpath on one side and an area of grass on the other. My hands held it but not to assist my walking. I shook it almost violently, the actions of a mad woman to the uneducated eye. It seemed sturdy enough as I continued to walk along shaking and pushing at regular intervals. I'd seen wobbly rails before and, whilst other people may have been able to manage them, a rounded top and going uphill were new variables for me to encounter.

I waited until there was no one walking in and I attempted to get on top of the rail. This was often harder than actually staying on it afterwards. Facing the rail, I placed two hands on it and tried to place my right foot on the outside of my right hand. Flexibility prevailed; so far, so good. I pushed down on my hands for support, slightly leaning my body weight over the rail. My other foot left the ground, moving all my weight onto the right foot on the rail. The only thing I had to do was push myself up and move my weight on to my right foot and let go of the rail. It was all so much easier when someone stood next to you with a steady hand of support. My hands liked the rail. I felt safe when holding the rail and was reluctant to let go. The slower everything happened, the less chance there was of it working. My arms flailed and my ankle felt stressed; standing on a narrow rounded surface wasn't familiar.

Positive and negative forces played out in my mind as I repeated the drill over and over. I knew many of my friends would get on and walk along it to the top of the slope. They inspired and annoyed me. I didn't feel very Zen about it all. I was standing at the edge of a beautiful Japanese garden, battling balance with a metal boundary. There should have been a simplicity, naturalness and refined elegance to the task. I had imperfect form on a perfectly formed and standardised structure. Inspired by my teachers, I set a goal to hold my balance for eleven seconds, rather than ten. However, nothing was to be forced. Unlike the garden that evoked a sense of stillness, quiet and tranquillity, my thoughts were active, loud and full of frustration. My movements were far from minimal; instead my body deployed every ounce of energy available.

'In order to reach the essence of things, all non-essential elements must be eliminated.' I didn't know whether it came from a marketing campaign that played on ancient wisdom or actually was a Buddhist teaching, but my inefficient movements felt essential at the time. There was a lot of room for improvement, but Parkour wasn't going anywhere and I had all the time in the world. There was no race, competition or deadline, just me, the railings and a lot of training to be done.

This rail to me was not 'just another rail', and likewise the garden was for some not just another garden, it was a Japanese garden . My imagination was aroused. I hadn't been striving for spiritual awareness, but I was aware of an absolute truth – that on that day, at that moment I wasn't walking on that rail. I was transcending the conventional use of the structure and the experience wasn't subtle. I could have cried. As more people entered the garden they glanced over at me – they just didn't understand.

As I walked up the pathway towards the woodland area, I reflected on my failings on railings. It was so much harder than it looked. Waist height might not bring much fear into the hearts of some but for mine it did. I would have enjoyed an ideally somewhat lower rail. However, I couldn't adapt the environment to suit me: the work to be done was mine and mine alone. People talked about training for rail-balancing as part of their 'active recovery' as though it provided a sense of calm and stillness. I grumpily knew the only way to get better at balancing on rails was to spend time balancing on rails.

They were everywhere: outside the supermarket, next

to grass, in the subways, curved variations that facilitated locking bicycles. Some were guarding a thing or a place, some gave a clear message of which way or direction to keep moving in. According to the Cambridge dictionary, a railing is 'a vertical post, usually metal or wooden, that is used together with other such posts to form a fence'. A new definition had emerged for me. A railing was a way for me to see who I was: scared, brave, able, deluded, all form and no function. To see what kind of stuff I was made of. It exposed layers of fear that had been lying dormant but were now glaringly present in my daily choices.

There was a 'simple' task at hand and I yearned for improvement. There had been moments where it had all come together but then instantly fallen apart, a brief glimpse into the elusive feelings of stillness, balance and calm, enough to realise that success may one day be possible.

Squirrels darted in and out of my path as I headed towards the cafeteria. The grassy area wasn't yet busy. A small tai chi group trained in a corner under the shade of the trees. There were some small wooden fencing posts with pointed tops on the edge of the wooded area and a few peacocks wandered. Neither interested me. As I passed through the formal gardens, suddenly I discovered exactly what I needed. Majestic, solid, green iron: a rare species of knee-high, flat-topped rails.

The Iris Garden consisted of four quadrants surrounding a circular pool and a William Pye-designed fountain. Each of the quadrants had a set of truly perfect beginner rails standing guard on the blooms within. Flowers on one side and pavement on the other; as long as I *never* came down on the floral side I wouldn't, I decided, be damaging anything. Wooden benches nearby made me feel the most exposed I'd ever been, but the opportunity was too good to ignore. I'd gone public and I was hungry for rails.

The comfort and security in being able to simply step up on to the rail was immense. The skinny width of the top made it appropriately challenging. Standing on one foot felt good. I took another step. Yep, that was OK too. Now to remember to breathe; such a basic function was always ignored when physical concentration came into play. I tried to relax my neck, arms and shoulders, and off I went. My aim was to be able to walk around each quadrant five consecutive times without falling off.

Having never before found rails that I could so confidently walk along, I had not experienced the mental exhaustion involved in maintaining such balance. The challenge turned out to be a strange endurance event. Too focused and I fell; too relaxed and I fell. There was only one thing left to try.

Abbey Road is known for many things. Everyone knows of the recording studios and their musical heritage. Few know of the rather fat, tall, rounded blue rails situated at the entrance to the residential estate. My introduction to them was through Gogoly Yao, another talented French athlete and character on the London Parkour scene, who had been kind enough to say I was welcome to tag along when he was out training.

'What's wrong? Are you drunk?' he would say of my lack of balance, following up with the biggest laugh possible. 'Try singing. You'll see, anything, a nursery rhyme, any song, try it.'

'Are you serious?' I asked.

'Think of a song you know really well. I mean really well, anything. And don't worry, you don't have to sing very loudly. I won't be able to hear you. No one will hear you.'

My mind was both numb and blank and then from the depths of somewhere it came. I still don't know why it was this song; I never liked it and still don't.

'Go on, go for it, try it, you'll see!' Yao's enthusiasm was contagious.

My lips started to move and quietly I began to mumble . . . With a sound only barely audible to nearby dogs, my breath allowed me to make sounds, small subtle soft sounds.

'Old MacDonald had a farm E I E I O. And on that farm he had some . . .'

I paused and fell. 'Oh shit!' What did he have on that farm goddamit! Why did I start thinking? OK, try again and up on the rail. This time there were ducks, pigs, dinosaurs and Parkour people. The more ridiculous the creatures, the better and longer the balance. I excelled when happy. Meanwhile Yao danced on the rail.

I had perfected the art of almost silent singing. It couldn't be completely silent, as it seemed to void the effect but was just enough to help me balance. Neuroscience could no doubt make sense of it, but I had all I needed to know: it worked. I took this methodology to the Japanese Gardens.

For the next hour I sang, wobbled and walked on the low rails of Holland Park as an imaginary farm was filled with all manner of exotic and ridiculous creatures. I loved and respected these rails. People may have been watching and asking, 'What is she doing?' Some may have thought, 'Why?' I neither knew nor cared. I had railings and my soundtrack and I wasn't afraid to try.

In a society of more spectators than sportsmen, people revel in sitting and watching others be active, regardless of their success. There are also those who enjoy being seen. There is a long cultural tradition of physical spectacles: everything from the barbaric gladiators to non-competitive festivities, rites of passage, to the original Olympic Games. Movement cultures and physical education were around long before sport ever, was but now sport is everywhere in some shape or form in almost every culture. Sometimes it looks more like play, in others it's more like a battle. It can be beautiful and charming as well as brutal and competitive.

There are currently three generally accepted characteristics that define what makes something a 'sport' according to the academics, committees, federations and various experts in their fields. Whilst all sports are a form of play, not all play is a form of sport. To be a sport currently, it must: 1. Be competitive. 2. Be organised or conform to a set of rules. 3. Be physical and use the body. Chess, for example, is a game not a sport. So what is Parkour?

Parkour didn't fit into the conventional sporting norms. Was it a risky dance, an art form, a cultural form of identification and heritage? Other activities that defied such categorisations had come before, such as capoeira, a discipline combining martial art and dance. Its definition had sparked debates in Brazil, where they tried to 'sportify' it but failed. Sportification meant insurance. Insurance meant all capoeira masters needed to be some sort of physical education instructor. But what about the older Brazilian masters who'd been training and teaching for the past fifty years? Their agility was testimony to their experience and knowledge. They fought back and capoeira is currently safeguarded as a cultural activity.

What would become of Parkour? Its heritage was widely unknown beyond 'It came from Paris in the 1980s' and many of its practitioners simply didn't care about its roots anyway. Currently, the Parkour practitioners of Brazil want Parkour to go down the same route as cultural capoeira, but in America it's about insurance and competitions. Even those who encourage Parkour as a non-competitive sport host Parkour competitions stateside.

A lot comes back to the C word. That's competition, rather than co-operation or community, connection or cohesion. Society in general celebrates the winning athletes, not the act of participation. Are the winners predisposed genetic freaks or was there ever an even playing field of opportunity for the masses? Being self-competitive is no longer enough for those whose worldview is so deeply entrenched in an aggressive neo-liberal model of capitalism, with its highly competitive behaviour and consumerism. Parkour has its own money politics like all sporting cultures. Should you or shouldn't you pay for coaching? What brand of shoes and T-shirts? But beyond the latest fashion trends set by those doing the biggest jumps in the videos with the most hits, the reality is you don't need anything. Even shoes become questionable when the barefoot trendsetters join in.

Parkour has it all: spectacle, skill, daring feats and, yes, the hero could potentially die. Debates and tensions have stirred between traditionalists, purists, competitors and founders over the duality of sport and non-sport, between those with a chance of a professional career with all the trappings of prize money and celebrity, versus those who value the unmediated version stripped of consumerism, logos and the desire to sell the brand. These are the Parkour equivalent of the soul surfers who wouldn't be seen dead in a Quiksilver shirt. It seemed such an unlikely debate when my slow walks on rails were always rewarding. Was it easy to be anti-competition because I saw no glory in it for me or were others on a similar journey?

I had enjoyed competitive team sports in my youth, but

here I was engaged in such a simple act that took me back to a time of opportunity and possibility, when life had yet to be defined or laid out. Everything was open. The railings returned me to a time and feeling that allowed me to regain that which is authentic, that which is functional, and it felt great.

13

The Guard Dies
But Does Not Surrender

*Like most former soldier children, he had troubles adapting, and
drives he had to learn to control. I saw in him a man fighting his
own instincts all his life. He had accepted to be part of the system
at some point but, sometimes, the rebel within him was coming
back to the surface.*

David Belle, *Parkour*

By the time Stéphane Vigroux started to know David
Belle's father, Raymond Belle, the man was well past
his prime and out of shape, despite the many stories and
reputation that preceded him. He was the man who could
punch through a car window to get at a man he was fighting
with. During his time as a firefighter, he had somersaulted
through a window two storeys high and landed on the
ground just to demonstrate to his colleagues there was no
problem with moving or falling from height. While others
tested their resilience by holding a burning cigarette close
to their skin, Raymond let his rest on his arm. If there was
someone who could go further or be stronger and braver, it
was Raymond. You couldn't beat Raymond Belle.

The aging Vietnamese man stood in his flip-flops, arms
crossed atop his pot belly in front of the Dame du Lac,

looking on as his son, David, performed his current repertoire of moves for a new promo video. Raymond had an
idea. 'Hey, David, why not try this?' he asked, suggesting
his son run along the hammer section, then cat-pass with
split legs – a sort of high leapfrog – then drop and roll to
the floor. 'Really?' replied David. 'Yeah, you can do it, don't
worry,' his father reassured him. David wasn't sure but
wanted to please. It was a classically gymnastic and dynamic
'Raymond' move that David executed perfectly.

However severe or extreme David's self-imposed actions
were, they never could or would compare to the tragic circumstances of his father's early life. If David fell and was
severely injured when trying something he himself chose
and wanted to do, he would be cared for. Raymond never
had such luxuries. David always had the choice to step
away from his personal journey of mental and physical discovery. No one was pointing a gun at his head. By contrast,
Raymond had been forced to stand at the end of a barrel,
fighting to save his life from a young age. To choose to take
risks and suffer cannot be compared to enforced cruelty,
violence, abuse and the darkest sides of humanity. Lack of
choice creates a different set of references.

There was generally only one type of feedback that David
received from his father, no matter what he performed:
'Could be better.' Or 'I could do that when I was nine.' A
misguided attempt at tough love and encouragement, or
simply stating a fact? With Raymond's past, anything was
possible. It was very hard to impress him.

Raymond was born in 1939 in Vietnam to a French
father, a doctor, and a Vietnamese mother. At the age of
seven, a life of comfort and privilege was turned on its
head with the outbreak of the First Indochina War in
December 1946. What began as a rural insurgency against

French authority soon became a full-blown conflict. The country was torn apart, with geographical lines drawn between north and south Vietnam. The French Far East Expeditionary Force aligned with the Vietnamese National Army to protect and defend the borders of the French union, fighting against the communist Viet Minh troops led by Ho Chi Minh, who occupied the north.

In one of the rare interviews he has given that discusses his father, David said that when the conflict broke out, seven-year-old Raymond had been visiting an uncle and was subsequently unable to return to his family. He was taken to the military school and orphanage in Dalat in the south of Vietnam.

For the next nine years, Raymond Belle was trained to be a soldier. In addition to the *parcours du combattant*, or assault courses, used for his military training, he would sneak out in the middle of the night to train on courses that he had created: courses to test and train his endurance, agility, resilience and stealth, mastering every move until he had reached the point of perfection. He decided he would not be a victim.

In 1954, after nearly eight years of fighting and the United States' refusal to send air support, the French forces were defeated at Dien Bien Phu, resulting in the Geneva Accords that established the 17th parallel as the temporary geographical and political dividing line between the ruling powers of north and south Vietnam. Aged sixteen, Raymond was sent to France and was based in Lyon, where he continued his military education until 1958. Aged nineteen, he had maintained his impressive mental and physical condition. It was suggested that he join the military firefighters of Paris due to his physical prowess. A life previously devoted to cultivating skills that were designed to kill could instead channel them into saving lives.

Raymond was a man of firsts. His physical skills and the many competences he had mastered through years of brutal mental and physical training, coupled with a personality shaped and hardened through the horrors of war experienced at such a young age, resulted in heroic acts and record-breaking sporting endeavours whilst with the firefighters. He was an outstanding athlete and his achievements did not go unnoticed. He joined the special team of gymnastics coaches who assisted in the most difficult or perilous operations. When the Paris fire brigade started using helicopters for rescue missions, Sergeant Raymond Belle was selected to be the first firefighter involved in an airborne mission, on 19 January 1969. The call to headquarters stated the following: 'A Viet Cong flag is at the summit of the spire of Notre Dame, approximately ninety metres high. The access to the cross at the summit of the tower is usually done via the outside with the use of rungs spread apart by ninety centimetres, more or less. Using the traditional pathway is very dangerous, as the culprits have cut off four rungs. The special police team have attempted the climb but to no avail. The removal would be possible by skilled mountain climbers with the use of a helicopter.' Sergeant Belle successfully removed the flag.

His peers gave him the nickname Kamikaze. In 1975, following an illustrious career that gained him the exceptional bronze Medal of Honour, he retired from the fire brigade, heralded as an 'exceptional rescuer'.

Raymond then worked as a security guard in various prominent establishments across Paris. Like many who were looking for a new life and opportunities for their family, one of his brothers had moved from Vietnam with his wife to France in 1969. Their son's family (Raymond's nephew), followed suit in 1979, moving to Sarcelles with their sons Phung and Chau Belle. It was this connection, of course, that finally increased Raymond's contact with his son David who was in Lisses, and linked him to his cousins.

Raymond had fathered three sons – Daniel, Jean-François, and David – but raised none of them. He lived with his nephews and nieces for ten years. He picked them up from school, took them to the Ecouen forest and encouraged them to move and test their limits, to explore that feeling of being on the top of the castle's surrounding wall. Whereas most guardians and parents might say 'stay away from the edge', the young Belles in Sarcelles were encouraged to go there, see what they could do and gradually explore their movements.

Despite having left the fire brigade over a decade earlier, Raymond was still in excellent physical condition. With his nephews Phung and Chau, and son David, who would visit with Sébastien, they would play 'stick'. Raymond versus four young guys who would try to pull a stick away from him. He wouldn't budge, instead staying solid as a rock. They couldn't move him. Whilst in his fifties, he could still perform the 'flag', a gymnastic move where the hands are placed around a pole or similar edge and the body is lifted to be parallel with the ground. It is a move that many young gymnasts and athletes struggle with, requiring a huge amount of upper body and core strength. Raymond was impressive. As David and Sébastien often said, Raymond didn't do sport, 'he *was* sport'.

For the young Belle siblings, Raymond was only one of several references for masculinity and strength, along with their other uncles and father. As well as demonstrating his physical abilities, Raymond would leave letters for his nephews around the house; notes of guidance on the virtues of sport, outlining thoughts on courage and will-power. He wanted to share the values that he had been taught in the army and with the fire brigade. It was important to be strong so that you could be of use and help others. He was also a talented artist and enjoyed cooking.

The Belles' home in Sarcelles was a French household still entrenched in Vietnamese culture. They lived with the effects and aftermath of families torn apart through the war, bringing both the good and bad of the older generation's experiences. As well as the virtuous writings, there were uncontrollable moments of violence and examples of great resourcefulness. For a while Raymond lived in a tent in the garden. It could have easily have been a small military shack. He would make slingshots and bows to hunt, even if it was only pigeons that were available. Such things were commonplace and natural for both Raymond, Phung, Chau and William's father. Food could be found and foraged, therefore trees had to be climbed. Shelters and houses could be built, therefore not bought.

Williams was shocked when he arrived home one day to be told that Great Uncle Raymond had been thrown out of the house after ten years of living with them. The reason remained private, but suffice to say Raymond's behaviour meant he would never set foot in the house again. Whatever his previous hardships, rescues and other brave acts, what happened meant the Belles in Sarcelles could no longer hold him in high esteem. He would be acknowledged as many things – the extraordinary athlete, the exemplary employee, a hard-working professional and responsible man – but he was not a hero.

However, Raymond stayed in contact with Phung, Chau and Williams, telephoning all the time, encouraging his nephews to train and supporting the idea of the Yamakasi group. Raymond believed that they were stronger together, an elite group who could really do something with their physical skills. If they wanted, he would help them. He followed, watched and took extensive notes about their Stade 2 TV piece, for example. As always, his feedback was direct and straight to the point.

Raymond went to watch the group train. It was the last time he would have the opportunity to see them all together. The next day his son David chose to the leave the group.

David chose to hold a grudge against those who wouldn't speak of Raymond as a founding influence of what they trained. 'If my friends had been fair and honest, if there had been some recognition of my father's input, then it could have worked,' he told the journalist Sabine Gros La Faige years later. 'My father was the word and I was the action.' For David it was easy to ignore his father's negative acts, but for his cousins and the rest of the family in Sarcelles it was impossible.

On New Year's Eve, 1999, David received a phone message from his father: '*La garde meurt mais ne se rend pas!*' – The guard dies but does not surrender! David played the message to Stéphane but, by the time they reached his father's apartment, it was too late. David's older brother Jean-François and fellow firefighters had already broken down the door and removed the body. David and Stéphane entered to see the pool of blood left behind after Raymond had shot himself in the head with a shotgun.

Forever of the military mindset, Raymond chose as his last words to his son the famous words cried out by General Count Etienne Cambronne, the head of Napoléon's Old Guard and an elite veteran with the iconic military leader's 'immortal' Imperial Guard, at their last stand at the Battle of Waterloo.

David suffered three losses in a short period of time. His oldest brother Daniel had recently died from a drug overdose and his grandfather died within two weeks of his father. At the end of his life, Raymond had fallen far from his glory days of celebrated rescuer and family patriarch.

14

The Trials of Hollywood

I think we embarked on something we weren't ready for. We hadn't done anything prior; we didn't know how to handle money. We thought everyone was nice and friendly; we thought they were all people of their word.

Yann Hnautra

Dressed as ninjas on the tops of several stationary trucks, Yann, Laurent, Charles, Malik, Guylain, Chau and Williams all had roles in the action-packed, high-octane car-chasing sequel to *Taxi*. The Yamakasi proceeded to wow the audience as they assisted in the kidnapping of one of the main protagonists and evaded an incompetent, bumbling police officer. They ran and jumped from the tops of one vehicle to the next as below them an officer struggled to keep up. The ninjas artfully wove their way through the traffic; vaulting, jumping and rolling across the tops of cars while in the officer tried and failed to emulate their moves. They made an impressive jump over a rail and dropped down from the top of a bridge to a truck at least eight metres below, then dropped and rolled on to the street disappearing from sight. It wasn't all over, though: against all odds the officer managed to catch up and thought he had them cornered until they unleashed their grand finale, scaling walls in various directions and gaining access to more rooftops, finally shaking off their tail. The determined yet athletically challenged policeman then faced the final humiliation of falling into a skip full of rubbish after once again failing with an attempt to copy their movements.

The Yamasaki had never thought of what they did as stunts, but others like Luc Besson did. Performing their particular style of 'stunts' was what had opened the door to filmmaking opportunities. When Besson first met the group he had wanted them to perform their moves in the next film he would produce, *Taxi 2*, which Gérard Krawczyk would direct. Stunt work wasn't exactly what they were looking for, but they would all be in the project together and wanted to be in the movies. It was time to move on from *Notre Dame de Paris* and start a new project.

Regardless of the success of their theatrical and TV achievements, filmmaking was a different deal and there were only so many risks that a production would take with a relatively unknown cast. If they performed well in *Taxi 2*, then they could discuss making a film of their own. 'Don't challenge the Yamakasi!' thought Malik; they would be the most amazing stunt ninjas an audience had ever seen.

Taxi 2 was shot in 1999 and released in 2000. With an audience of more than 10.5 million, it was the biggest box office success in France in 2000. The Yamasaki may have been masked but they were starting to gain more recognition as the press drew attention to their stunts. Besson kept his word and within a year they were working on their own film, *Yamakasi – Les samouraïs des temps modernes* (*Yamakasi: The Samurai of Modern Times*).

Besson wanted to work on the story with all of them and asked them to write their ideas. A few weeks later, retaining some of Charles's ideas, he put a story together and Charles was given a writing credit for his original concept.

The film played with the semi-sociopolitical context of the marginalised youth and subculture of the banlieues. Even if the film wasn't their life story, it blurred the lines between fact and fiction. Their assigned nicknames in the story were somewhat ridiculous and even derogatory, but they went along with it.

The story followed the antics of a multicultural group from the suburbs who moved and explored their city in unique, interesting and gravity-defying ways. A young, inspired fan tried to copy their movements, fell from a tree and was left in need of a heart operation that his family couldn't afford. Going against the law, the group endeavoured to put things right by finding the funds to pay for the child's operation. Chaos and comedy ensue. The group's good intentions involved breaking and entering, chases and more action. In true Besson style, it had to entertain and be a feel-good family movie. There would be a few heart-stopping moments and raw action, paving the way for a new era of stunts, the likes of which French cinema had rarely seen.

While the script was being fine-tuned, the producers received some worrying news that one of the Yamakasi might not be able to perform. Yann and Laurent had been performing in Las Vegas, finishing their turn in the run of *Notre Dame de Paris*. Apart from being unsure of how to act and perform on stage as opposed to turning up and jumping from here to there, they were settling into their roles, annoying the cast with a non-stop level of action, and the show was well-received. 'Bastard Yamakasi! Bastards jumping in the morning! It's 9 a.m., I want to sleep!' shouted one of their fellow cast members from their hotel window as Yann and Laurent went about their business on the reverberating iron fire escape. Not everyone shared their schedule or enthusiasm for such early active starts to the day.

One evening back at the hotel, Laurent suddenly started to feel really warm. He opened the window and the cool, evening air floated in, but he continued to feel his temperature rise. When unsure of something there was only one solution . . . push-ups. If you were Laurent, large amounts of push-ups were the cure-all approach to pretty much everything life had to throw at you. They did little to cool him down. He went outside and took some deep breaths, but his body was on fire. More push-ups. His head hurt and the pain felt unlike anything he'd experienced before. Whatever was happening to him wasn't normal. 'Yann, I need to go to the doctor,' Laurent said with a sense of rare seriousness and urgency.

He had suffered a brain aneurysm and the doctors told him they needed to operate.

Nobody was sure what the damage was or what the future held for a man who hours before had been an example of supreme health and fitness. He had kissed death more closely than ever.

Laurent dealt with the news and his recovery the only way he knew how: a brain aneurysm was a life obstacle to be overcome. The mentality he had towards his training crossed over. 'If you are a warrior, you are a real warrior. A warrior everywhere! It's not a costume. Now I'm a warrior, I'm going to do sport! And when I stop doing sport, I remove my costume and I forget everything,' Laurent told interviewers years later.

'When I went back to training, it was strange. Sometimes I thought, perhaps I won't come back alive from this training. If I had said that to Yann or to Chau or to Williams it would have been: "stay home, are you crazy? Don't go training!"' he remembered. He could have lived a life being grateful for what he had experienced before the aneurysmn but that wouldn't be a life well lived for him.

'I was surrounded by strong men! I could only become strong!' thought Laurent.

The kindness of the other performers touched Laurent, as the most flamboyant characters – the kind that he would not have been associated with on the highly masculine streets of Evry – were the ones to whom he now owed everything. They watched over him, never leaving his side, making sure he was OK.

On hearing the news, the producers of *Yamakasi – Les samouraïs des temps modernes* wondered if there was anyone who could replace him. They found there was. A meeting was set. David Belle wanted to be in the film. Even though he had gained a lot of media attention over the previous two years, he was yet to be offered a film role. David had never wanted to share the limelight, but now that the light was being shone on others, he was asking for his share, two years on from leaving the group.

Meanwhile, the Yamakasi had all worked hard at promoting, sharing and communicating the positive values of their discipline the best ways they knew how. They spoke of its values during interviews to journalists and received rave reviews for their work live on stage as well as on film. David's talent was undeniable and the effort and years he had put in made him worthy of the opportunity. Of course he should have recognition and a chance to shine, but like this? Replacing Laurent? It had to be discussed. If anyone had the right mindset to make a full recovery it was Laurent, and the rest of the Yamakasi knew it.

'This is just not possible,' thought Williams. 'We started

together with Laurent, so we'll finish with Laurent.' Leaving him out was not an option. One by one as they went around the table at the production office they each had to provide a simple yes or no answer as to whether they were happy for David to be in the film. Like a dog with his tail between his legs, David awaited the results. It wasn't looking good in general, but an interesting point was made. If David deserved the opportunity to be in the film, then surely the same should be offered to Sébastien? He too had been a big part of everything at the start. David disagreed; he was there to ask for himself alone. The final vote was no, but Besson committed to making another film with David in the future. It seemed like a reasonable and fair conclusion; David would get his chance but not right now.

To come back, ask, and be refused by the group stirred bad feelings in David towards the Yamakasi. They had grown distant after *Notre-Dame de Paris*, and the relationship was relatively cool. Now they were frozen solid as David drew his battle lines. Hurt and angry, he would tell the world his own version of the Yamakasi story.

When filming began on what the Yamakasi thought would be a dream project, not everything was how they would have imagined. To passers-by, the seven bodies sleeping on the pavement looked like homeless bums. Their heads rested against small sports backpacks and T-shirts covered their eyes from the afternoon sunlight in the Choisy-le-Roi area of Paris. 'It was our first film, and we thought it was all normal, but a lot of things were actually not,' remembered Chau.

The opening sequence of *Yamakasi: Les samouraïs des temps modernes* required them to climb a twenty-six-storey building. Due to practical logistics and the need to stay away from the prying eyes of local residents and the public, the action had to be filmed in the early hours of the morning. The group were on set at 2 a.m. and climbing by four. Filming had begun on 3 July 2000, two years after David had left the group and they had begun work on the *Notre-Dame* show. For the first few weeks of filming, the seven lead actors had no dressing room of their own and instead shared one with the costume department and extras which was busy and noisy all day. They had come a long way since their first media interview in 1998.

'We need to keep them fresh because it's physically demanding,' said the director Julien Seri. Even he questioned the wisdom of the production's treatment of their lead roles, along with some of the other actors on the set who were equally confused at how the Yamakasi were being treated. It made no sense. Although the Yamakasi were happy to have the opportunity to be in the film, the group soon realised that saying yes and keeping things simple wasn't the way to earn respect in the film industry. They were a group of friends who were always laughing and training, but they were not actors and therefore didn't get treated as such.

'You don't have your own dressing room?' a friend of Williams asked in disbelief when he tried to explain why they were sleeping on the streets. She had worked on films and knew how things should be. 'No, why?' Williams asked naively. 'You're the main actors, you should!' she told him. 'Go and demand one!'

They realised she was right. 'Maybe they think that since we do so many dangerous things, they can leave us outside because we'll do anything. Why would people do this to someone?' Williams wondered, upset by the basic lack of respect implied by treating anyone like that. It was a big production with a lot of money invested in it. It seemed to

Left: The Yamakasi group (except Malik Diouf) prior to the first Stade 2 TV report in 1997. © Malik Diouf

Above: Yann Hnautra at La Défense filming for *Le Message* in 1998. © Bruno Girard

Right: Chau Belle training on the wall of the Ecouen Forest, 2008. © Andy Day

Above: Chau Belle in the Ecouen Forest, France, 2008. © Andy Day

Above: The Dame du Lac, 2014. © Julie Angel

Above: The architecture of Evry. © Julie Angel

Top: David Belle during the filming of *Rush Hour* for the BBC channel ident, 2002. © Moviestore Collection/REX/Shutterstock

Left: Sébastien Foucan during the filming of *Jump London* in 2003. © Mike Christie

Below: Sébastien Foucan on the Forth Bridge during the filming of *Jump London* © Mike Christie

Above: The stage set for *Notre Dame de Paris*, 2009. © MARKA / Alamy Stock Photo

Above: David Belle and Cyril Raffaelli during the filming of *Distric 13 Ultimatum* in 2009. © Magnolia/Everett/REX/Shutterstock

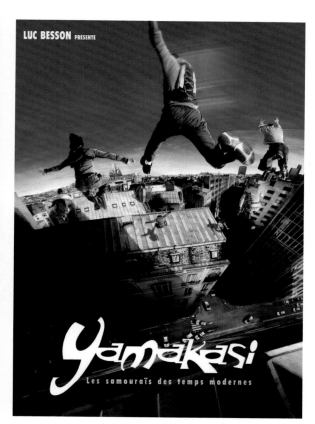

Left: Promotional film poster for *Yamakasi: Les samouraïs des temps modernes.* © REX/ Shutterstock

Below: The Yamakasi at a photocall for their second film, *Yamakasi 2: les Fils du Vent*, in Paris, 2004.

Above: Malik Diouf taking a break from rehearsals with the Urban Playground in Brighton, UK, 2014. © Julie Angel

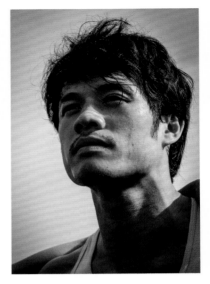

Above Williams Belle at the International Parkour Gathering in Gerlev, Denmark, 2011. © Julie Angel

Left: The Cathedral of the Resurrection, Evry. © Julie Angel

Below: The Long Rayage Estate, Lisses. © Julie Angel

Above: Yann Hnautra doing the Manpower jump for the film
Le Message in 1998 . © Bruno Girard

Above: The Manpower rooftop jump, Evry. © Julie Angel

Above: Stéphane Vigroux, Williams Belle, Katty Belle & Thomas Couetdic in Koln, Germany, 2004. © Johann Vigroux

Above: David Belle in action for *Distric 13 Ultimatum*, 2009. © Everett Collection/REX/Shutterstock

Above: Yann Hnautra at the Parkour Generations Rendezvous event in London, 2009. © Jö Holmes

Above: Sébastien Foucan and Williams Belle at the Parkour Generations 7th Rendezvous event in London, 2011. © Julie Angel

...ane Vigroux, Johann Vigroux & Williams Belle at
...Generatinos Rendezvous event in London, 2011.
...el

Left: Sami Saula doing a drop jump behind the post office in Evry. © Sami Saula

Left: The gymnasium staircase in Lisses. © Julie Angel

Right: Johann Vigroux & Michael Ramdani at the Gymnasium staircase in Lisses, 2002. © Johann Vigroux

Above: Yann Hnautra during the SKOCHYPSTIKS Motion Tour in Pag, Croatia, 2014. © Saša Ševo

Above: After training at the Dame du Lac, from left to right: David Terrien, Yves Bozec, Franck Vinchon, Sami Saula, Brahim Meslem, Serika Kingmen, Fabrice Lusukarnu © Sami Saula

Above: Stéphane & Johann Vigroux performing in Koln, Germany, 2004. © Johann Vigroux

Above: Stéphane Vigroux on the Dame du Lac in 2005. © Andy Day

Right: Stéphane Vigroux in Distric 13 performing for Nike in the Sacry Cat commercial. © Thomas Couetdic

Below: Stéphane Vigroux in London, 2007. © Andy Day

Right: Stéphane Vigroux at the Cathedral in Evry, 2008. © Andy Day

Below: Thomas Couetdic at Hampi, India 2011. © Andy Day

Above: Police removing two traceurs on their parkour pilgrimage from the Dame du Lac in 2014. © Julie Angel

Above: The North American Womens Parkour Jam in Seattle, USA 2015. © Julie Angel

him that just because they were strong mentally and had the ability to create something from nothing, it was assumed that they wouldn't expect to be given very much. The cold reality of their treatment detracted from the earlier joy and excitement at being involved in the project. After they protested, things improved; two weeks later they got a dressing room, better food and even massages.

'I risk my life when I do something, and I don't put a price on my life,' Williams recalled of his time on the film. 'If you ask me to give you a price, I'll ask you to give all you have, because I'm giving all I have. If you ask for a small price, I'll say it's worth much more. It's taught me to respect what I do, the art I practise and the person I am.'

They minimised the risks they took on the film by working closely with the stunt co-ordinator. The Yamakasi skill set was different than the standard repertoire of stuntmen who had learnt the art of falling. Theirs was based on not falling. Like all good stunt co-ordinators, theirs had been preoccupied with safety and wanted to place thick crash mats down for their landings. The group explained they preferred hard surfaces; they knew their skills and what to expect from solid surfaces. They had trained their craft outside and there would be occasions when using mats would be more dangerous than not. Compromises were reached and thinner mats were found.

For the opening building climb, the Yamakasi had to wear harnesses despite being more than capable of making the ascent unsecured. Doing it in 'the stunt safe way' with wires was new. They wanted all of the film's action to focus on the realistic and less showy side of what they could do, whilst the production wanted more acrobatics. Against the group's wishes, acrobat doubles were brought in to perform the flips.

Work on the film for the Yamakasi began and it required

more than just action from the group; they had to learn lines that had to be 'felt' not just memorised, as their acting and voice coach Harmel Sbraire insisted. She wanted them to bring their life experiences into the role. While everyone benefitted from the coaching sessions, this was particularly true for the man who had problems getting his words out in the first place.

The film was more than a career opportunity for Williams. His encounter with Harmel moved his life forward. Externally his body moved and flowed but internally he was still blocked, having locked emotions away that stopped words from coming out.

He stammered badly, but Harmel's job was as much about figuring people out to understand what was holding them back as it was about vocal exercises, diction, rhythm, breathing and concentrating on how to express emotions. For two months she worked with Williams, deciphering and reading his barriers, helping to heal the trauma and wounds that had held him back. 'Harmel gave us the keys to the film that we will never lose,' Williams was quoted as saying in an interview for the film's promotion.

Filming continued, but soon the original director Julien Seri was replaced with Ariel Zeitoun. The group assumed it was an everyday event in the film industry and turned up for filming and trained every other given minute of the day. Shooting wrapped after sixteen weeks and apart from a few scratches, bruises and a sprained ankle, everyone was fine.

The film was an overnight box-office success in France. The film's promotional machine was on full throttle. Interviews were requested and the Yamakasi were driven from one appointment to the next. Philippe Levasseur and Jérome Mignard from the *Sept á huit* (Seven to Eight) popular TV show wanted to interview them. The Sunday night show consisted of six stories of ten minutes each and averaged 4.5 million viewers. As Malik remembered, they explained to the journalists, 'It's a sport, it's an art, there's a pedagogy, there's a vocabulary, everything in a positive way.' They explained their concept so clearly making it all the more shocking for the group and everyone associated with the film when they saw what was in the final TV piece when it aired.

If David had felt wronged, then he couldn't have picked a more public way to express it. More than half of the TV report was dedicated to him communicating a clear message that the seven Yamakasi are currently the stars but the guy who created the discipline can't make a living and is in the shadows, living with his mum. It went on to state that he was starting a solo career with a new team as the Yamakasi had left him.

How the public loves an unsung hero! Whatever David told the journalists, they were convinced by it as the narration announced that 'among Parkour practitioners, David Belle is recognised as a master but in the south suburb of Paris, he is not the famous one.' David was portrayed as the star and the Yamakasi were misrepresented through a negatively biased edit. 'It's a quest, linked to my father, it's my story,' David explained during the piece. 'Inside my own story, I turn back and I've got followers! It's awesome.'

Even though the first Stade 2 television report had shown that the group of friends created it together, the public had a short memory, it seemed. If it was David's intention to delete that version of the past, then the new report helped consolidate his version of the story. The Yamakasi decided to say nothing. They knew the truth of the past decade. Why retaliate and instigate a feud with journalists who couldn't be trusted anyway?

15

Just one more thing . . .

If David told me 'Do this and I'm here', I was . . . blind faith.
I know nothing is going to happen to me, David will hold me.
DAVID BELLE, he's holding me, I'm fine.

Stéphane Vigroux

'David, what would be the craziest thing I could do?' asked Stéphane. If he had known what would happen next, would he have still asked? Probably. As they sat in David's bedroom at his brother's Jean-François's house, Stéphane eagerly awaited the reply.

'OK, I think you're ready now. You've shown me a lot of stuff and you're serious about Parkour. There is a warrior training that my father told me about. I'll train you in this special way. My aim will be to make you give up. I tried with someone before. I thought they were a warrior but they cried after a few days. They didn't last. You can quit at any time. It's OK.'

Of course he wasn't going to quit. David knew Stéphane only too well.

In 2001, after three years of training together, Stéphane would be at David's beck and call twenty-four-seven for fifteen days. If he didn't answer his phone, it was over. Whatever David asked of him, morning, noon or night, he would have to do or admit defeat. He did it or he didn't.

If he failed, then he wasn't a warrior or a man, just a weak piece of shit. Stéphane tried to prepare himself mentally. This was going to be his moment. No way was he going to give up! He was now on a crazy kung fu mission heading into the unknown to experience legendary mystical training. Every day for the last three years, he had been at David's side and now he would really be able to show him how good he was. No matter how much David wanted him to give up, Stéphane wanted to finish the challenge even more. It would be a battle of wills as much as anything physical. As Stéphane remembered, 'Only a young ignorant imbecile would have such enthusiasm for that kind of challenge.'

It started predictably hard. Every day was a different type of 'crazy shit'. Conditioning – a thousand leg pistols, running, hanging. It was only the start and it was more intense than anything he had done before and it was happening every day. The days were long, the nights short and the winter temperatures were freezing. The antisocial times of day at which they trained and having to be available twenty-four-seven added a new and unfamiliar element. Such a small thing as recharging his phone and knowing where it was had never been so important. Stéphane's nerves were on edge.

The phone rang. It was 4.30 a.m. 'Be in front of the Dame du Lac at five.' Stéphane could just make it. David stood waiting, posture upright, chest proud, hands behind his back. Anyone passing by could see exactly who was in control. The build-up and sequence of everything Stéphane had experienced was 'an actual piece of art', he recalled. One that was only appreciated with the beauty of hindsight. In the alley that led towards the lake stood a series of concrete bollards, thigh-high. David wanted a hundred precision jumps in a row, no falling or failing. Stéphane began, maintaining his composure and accurately jumping as his mentor looked on. The area was quiet, with no light breaking through at this time of the morning, and a few stars still visible in the dark blue sky. A man jogged past, stopped and shook hands with David. It was Laurent Piemontesi from the Yamakasi. If they expected to see anyone at that time of day, it was Laurent: 5 a.m. was his time of day, the lake his second home. Stéphane felt so proud to be there with David training before dawn and now the Yamakasi would know how dedicated he was. David smiled; he had his student and look how hard and well he worked.

Stéphane rested at every opportunity. There was no socialising, none of the usual hanging out, smoking weed and listening to David's heroic tales of his father; just sleep. Two hours after the precisions were completed he was called back to the Dame du Lac, this time to repeat some routes. Up from the left to the right, the middle to the right, wall runs from the ground to the hammer, hammer to the chimney, and then climb the chimney and jump to the canopy. Repeat, repeat, repeat. Hanging from the top platform and traversing around the edge, first to the left then next time to the right. Vertigo games, repeat, repeat. His fingers and forearms were bleeding. Everything ached, but all the time his will to continue endured.

'Ah, I know, you'll like this,' David said with a smile. Stéphane knew that of course he wouldn't, but whatever it was he would do it. L-sits from the platform. David was right: he hated these. The top of the Dame du Lac was home to so many tears and fears. He had nearly died but had saved himself before. He had conquered so much, but there were always new fears waiting just beneath the surface and

David knew exactly where to find them. Stéphane lay flat on his stomach on the top platform, shuffling his body forward so he could reach with his hands underneath and hold on to the underside of the edge. He started to do what looked like a forward roll and rolled over his neck with his body ending up suspended, hanging in the void with his legs straight in front of him. People did the L-sit on the parallel rings or hanging from a bar, not from an overhang above a void fifteen metres high. Getting to it was a commitment, not for the first action but how to return. There he was again, vulnerable, relying solely on his mind and body to stay calm and find the strength and technique to then lift his legs back up over the edge and be able to roll back on to the safety of the platform.

Later that day he was back at the top of the climbing wall. This time he was not asked to move, but instead to hold static postures in precarious places that were equally terrifying and disturbing. Just below the platform to the right side he had to remain still in a crouched, seated position for up to an hour facing the void. Body stiff and cold, he wasn't hiding from an enemy, just facing his own physical and mental limits, pushing himself to continue and not dying in the process. What was the point of staying there and not moving? To experience the sensations of what happened when eventually he did. David told him to get back on the top of the platform. Slowly his semi-paralysed body moved back to the relative safety of the top of the Dame du Lac.

Every day there was a horror to face yet Stéphane's determination remained resolute. He was rarely at home and when he was, he looked more fried than normal. On one occasion, David wasn't going to be around the next day but he sent Stéphane a text message with very clear ideas of what he wanted him to do. 'Starting at 8 a.m. until 8 p.m., every hour do the following routine: one running lap of your neighbourhood; the quadrupedal up and down your stairs twice, with ten push-ups at the end of each; three drop jumps from your bedroom window; five handstands. Have a good day.'

At least Stéphane didn't have to go far. David was being kind. The first round took thirty minutes, but after the first few hours, with tiredness once again seeping through his every cell, the whole combo took up to forty minutes. After each one Stéphane went straight to the lounge and lay on the sofa. No sooner had he cooled down from the set than it was time to warm up and go again. The alarm on the phone was set. Beep, beep, beep, 'Ah shit' . . . that time again already.

His parents got up for work and his brothers and sister left for school and college. Nobody dared asked. The time had long passed when anyone tried to make sense of what Stéphane was doing. Johann had an idea but said nothing. Neighbours watched with curiosity; what *was* he doing now? Whatever it was, he did it like clockwork, running round the neighbourhood and disappearing again. Would the phone ring and David stop it or would he add more? He hated his phone and he hated what he was having to do. He hated that he felt so exhausted, but he had stopped thinking about how hard it was. He simply did it. He didn't have any spare energy to use on hating anything. The cumulative effect was taking its toll, but nobody was giving up today. Late that night, David rang. 'OK, stop now.'

A few hours later, when Stéphane was in his bed finally getting more than twenty minutes' rest, the dreaded call came again. 'Do a handstand now.' Out of his bed, still half-asleep he didn't even bother to rub his eyes. There was no point. His feet pushed a pile of clothes to the side and created a space where he could start from a crouched position. He gently moved into the handstand. He was dizzy and uncoordinated, his legs were fully vertical above him for only a few seconds before they fell to the side hitting the bedroom wall. '*Ah merde!* Stéphane what the hell are you doing?' his father shouted from the other side of the wall. It was a good question. He went back into the crouch and slowly raised his legs to a perfect handstand position, held it for thirty seconds, then lowered his body back down and crawled back into his bed.

He had wept, bled and vomited but had not stopped. What day it was, he didn't know. How many were left, he didn't know. Survival and pride were running the show. What was on the menu next? Serving David.

Stéphane was a lowly servant presenting goods to his master who sat waiting at the end of the route. He had to carry an imaginary dish, a meal of imaginary food. An arm-jump and then a precision jump were required before presenting the imagined dish and offering a forced pose as he balanced along a ledge to the master. David loved this one. The repetitions continued and his smile grew, pacing, waiting, enjoying being served.

Snow was on the ground in the forest at Courcouronnes when Stéphane arrived the following morning. He had already done climbing drills, drop jumps and a sprinting session as they walked to the parallel bars in the fitness trail. Their breath was crisp and visible in the air. 'Go over and under the bars, in and out, fifty times, fast and without stopping,' David told him with his usual charismatic blend of authority and confidence as he gazed at his exhausted follower, student and friend.

Stéphane had to move his body in a figure of eight over

and under the bars like a lithe fluid form of strength and agility. Where most gymnasts would start with their body in the middle, Stéphane had to vault the first waist-high bar, then go under the second. Over and under, again and again as he struggled to breathe. His gasping breaths were a soundtrack to the effort. The accumulation of the previous days and weeks were visibly and audibly taking its toll. The rhythm of the reps slowed, but David's instructions were clear. If he stopped moving, then he would have failed the task and therefore given up. David watched and instructed, setting the pace of the reps. Twenty-five done, halfway there, time to up the pace. David was really pushing things. 'Do it, do it, do it, do it, stop,' commanded David. Stéphane felt a pressure building up in his chest and throat, the cold morning air not seeming to find its way in. Disorientated, he wobbled and fell to the ground, having passed out.

David looked on, waiting for the submission, but slowly Stéphane crawled back to his knees and then on to his feet, regaining his composure. He again started to move in a figure of eight around the bars. As he neared the final ten, his breaths again became shorter and more accelerated. Overheated on the cold morning, he removed his T-shirt for any last chance of energy. He gasped for life. He needed something to fuel his empty frame. 'Don't stop, don't stop,' said David. This rare moment of encouragement was the last thing Stéphane heard before he finished the set and passed out again in the snow-covered bush next to the bars. His chest was blocked; there was no more air, no more anything as his half-naked body lay in the snow. Fainting twice during a drill was a new experience for both the participant and observer.

'OK, you've done it. Good job. That's it for this morning.'

They were at Stéphane's car when David's next words shattered any semblance of calm and recovery in him. 'Oh just one more thing.' David knew how to play with his emotions. 'Just one more, one more thing, then it's over.' Stéphane had been picturing the hot shower, food and bed awaiting him, but with those few words the images vanished from his mind and the nightmare continued. His spirit was breaking, but there was no way he would allow David to see his pain and disappointment. Any show of weakness was ammunition for David's brilliant yet twisted strategy.

On a normal day it would have been such an easy drill but, with a broken body in a state of exhaustion, the series of jumps in between the small concrete rectangular bollards was torturous. 'You just have to do that and then we can go home or you start again,' said David as he pointed out the four-hundred-metre-long stretch. Stéphane knew if he missed one, the chances of things improving the second time around were slim. It would be even worse. With as much focus as he could draw upon, he very slowly and accurately jumped the one-and-half-metre distance between the small concrete pieces. It had never before and would never again take him so long, but time was the only thing on his side as he completed the route.

He had made it through another day. He had made it back into the sanctuary of his car, his hands shaking as they grabbed the wheel to drive away. 'If this is too hard, you can quit, Steph. Have a nice rest at home, some hot chocolate and croissant. And you don't have to come back tonight for the second session,' David told him. 'Will you buy me a croissant?' Stéphane asked in reply. David laughed and said no. Nothing else was said until they reached McDonald's. David bought his protégé a coffee.

David was an enigma for Stéphane. Somehow he was

like Bruce Wayne in *Batman*. He loved and loathed him, depending on what he was asked him to do, but once the action was over he was always grateful for the experiences. David could do so many amazing things but, on another level, he didn't know how to make his own bed or cash a cheque at the post office. Whatever anger issues Stéphane had, he had found in David someone even angrier at the world than he was.

After seeing him pass out twice in one session, David eased off a bit for the remaining days. David could see that Stéphane would severely damage himself rather than admit defeat. The two weeks were a blur of pain and excess but, on Day Fifteen, Stéphane was proud. Everyone in Lisses knew that he had completed the challenge.

David and Stéphane's relationship was all-consuming. David even introduced Stephane to the girl who would become the new love of his life, David's cousin Katty. David guided him on what to think, who to talk to, where to be and what to do. Theirs was a life of all-day and then late-night training sessions, mostly alone, though David had a group of avid followers who would join in – those who could keep up; Kazuma, Romain, Cisco, and Rudy had stayed with David over the months and now years. They always followed and found themselves jumping blindly into trees in the dark. At the end of each session they had nothing left – they were unable to walk down the stairs or their hands were covered in blood from the endless traverses.

There wasn't always a lot of talk when training. There was work to be done, but during the downtime there was a constant soundtrack of listening to David's tales of his father. He spoke less about his other family, Jean-François the firefighter and his older half-brother Daniel, who had died of a drug overdose. No matter what the scenario or story, there was only ever one conclusion – Raymond Belle was the man, a legend. The things he'd seen, and the records he'd broken . . . He was David's hero.

The young minds wandered and dreams were explored. 'What if one day we could travel the world doing Parkour, what if we had a place for it? What if . . .' They talked about Parkour and of course, the routes, the *parcours*. One evening Romain had started a discussion about how a bullet would 'trace' a straight line. The discussion drifted to the fact that a *parcours* could also be called *un tracé* and therefore the person who creates it is a *traceur*. The word and name stuck, they were *traceurs* and the name of their group was *Traceur*.

David was built on habits, not just his training. Cannabis was one of them. Now Stéphane, the previously 'clean monk', also smoked the night away. The jump they'd tried to break all afternoon was hard in the rain, but what about now, at night, after smoking a joint? After so much talk of Parkour, there was only one thing for it. 'OK, let's go!' Outside they went. It didn't matter if they could do it when they felt well; could they do it when they didn't or if there was a problem with their legs full of tiredness from the day's training? Even if they were out late at night, and weren't training, David would have his 'shitty shoes' on and could go and break a jump that he'd wanted to do for ten years. His level was unlike anything any of them had ever seen. He showed them what was possible and he enjoyed impressing this on them.

Being a *traceur* wasn't just about jumping for David and Stéphane. It was as much about how something was done as what was done. Hours on hours were spent throwing knives at trees. Accuracy, precision and timing. Skill and quality counted. They also fought.

As well as the technical perfectionism of their training,

Stéphane had to be able to endure a certain amount of physical pain. Normally this was tolerable and he never complained, but something had happened to his leg and the pain felt different than the usual bodily aches he knew so well. The pain on the side of his leg screamed every time he rolled over at night, to the point where neither him nor Katty could sleep. Enough was enough. They went to the hospital the next day. The doctors said everything was fine, which seemed really surprising considering the continuing pain – but, hey, if it was, then it was. Stéphane knew he had pushed and teased David in their muay thai-styled sparring and he should have known that there could be consequences. David's sideways kick had been an instantly painful shock . . . boom! Stéphane continued to move and jump but the side of his leg hurt like hell. Two months later an X-ray revealed a break that had happened the night he had teased David. It had just broken again with insufficient time to heal. If you play with fire, at some point you'll probably get burnt.

Stéphane's life was fully consumed by his passion for Parkour. His training and mindset was being moulded into an approach to Parkour that only few had experienced. While he felt as though it was a path to freedom, many aspects of what he and David were cultivating were far from positive.

16

Sleeping Dragons & Revelations

The way I see my fear . . . It's a personal thing. I tell myself, either I decide to be happy, or I decide to be 'unhappy'. If I don't break the jump . . . Why can't I break it? I try to understand why, and what I should do to break it.

Serika Kingmen

Just a few miles away in Evry, at 5 a.m. the ringtone of fear struck excitement and anxiety into the hearts of Sami Saula, Serika Kingmen, Brahim Meslem, Emmanuel Kizayilawoko and Fabrice Luzukamu. 'You know that if you answer, your body will regret it later on! But there was this thing, the way he knew us so well and pushing us in what felt the right way to us, that we kept wanting some more,' recalled Sami. The 'Revelation' crew loved and hated it but wouldn't change it for the world. Yann and his girl-friend were living in the Bois Sauvage area of Evry; the fifteen-year-olds lived on the same estate and had met Yann six months before the release of the film *Yamakasi*. Yann was twenty-eight years old and had more energy than all five teenagers put together.

Their journey into the world of *L'Art du Déplacement* hadn't started with hard, physical training as Yann was more of a 'guide' and father figure. He didn't want to just be a coach. If they were together for six hours, Yann would talk for three, covering everything from life, their goals, who they wanted to become, their names and lineage and how they should react in front of an obstacle. Yann had told them how the practice had evolved, how long it had taken them and that he could train them. It was never to be just about their physical training. Learning how to train to overcome obstacles was a way to improve their lives. Their progress would be far quicker than that of the founders, but the most important thing was that they were to train in the right way; otherwise they would not last. The young guys soaked up every word for weeks and were hungry, ready for anything Yann wanted to share. Yann was paternal, brotherly and the instigator of the craziest games of their lives.

They met up two or three times after school and then all day on Sundays, starting in the early hours of the morning. The first year of training had been about creating a physical base and completing 'jumps from the heart'. This required tapping into a mix of unbridled energy, self-belief and a lot of motivation to overcome the obstacle. Combining these factors allowed them to make small yet very tricky and psychologically demanding single jumps. These were the kind that messed with your mind, hence the will to do it had to come from the heart. You had to trust yourself as well as everyone else. According to Yann it was a way of training the senses, emotions and experiences to real life. 'Your mother is being attacked right now! There! Can you respond, will you jump?' Motivational, imaginary scenarios were a regular testing ground. 'You need to jump six metres from that bridge, will you save yourself?' He made them angry or fearful, or just instigated a sheer sense of panic, playing on both positive and negative emotions. It was about how to overcome the difficulties of life as much it was about jumping. Whatever Yann had learnt and benefitted from through his hardships, he wanted to share and pass on. Like sleeping dragons with the potential for fire and flight, the teenagers were dormant creatures that Yann awoke with his words and actions. 'Do I want to become a strong person? Do I want to be free with my thoughts?' Yann repeatedly asked of them. He wanted to teach them how to break away from societal expectations and free up their energy to be able to save themselves.

None of them could ever have envisioned doing the things they did on their own. Together they were more friends sharing and supporting one another. There was a simple principle of endurance that Yann encouraged: 'We never stop.' According to Yann, if they achieved that kind of endurance, then it would save them physically for whatever life had in store. There were different types of fears to face and being scared of the training sessions was just one of them. It was exactly what Yann wanted. He wanted them to give everything, not hide their emotions and never to give up. He would show his own weaknesses so they wouldn't be afraid to reveal theirs. Serika described his first year of training: 'You knew you'd be tired. And, I don't know why, you're afraid but you want to go anyway. You know you're not going on holiday, you're going to suffer, but you know you'll get something out of it, and you're going to share a crazy moment with your friends, and you're going to make some real progress. So then we did the jumps . . . We tried to repeat them three times, the good jumps, just to confirm it wasn't pure luck.'

Quantity and giving your all came first; quality would follow. They were wild. They suffered, bled and cried together. Their legs cramped and their hands were raw and they answered the phone every time it rang. As David did with Stéphane, Yann did with the group of friends. They trained others in a way they wished they themselves could have been trained; and their methods reflected both their priorities and personalities. If they were ready to share and pass on the practice, then they had reached a certain level with their own personal research and in pursuit of their goals. Like many of their age who search for adventure, this work provided Sami and his friends with a sense of belonging that they could not find on the streets of Evry, or with their hard-working parents and in the boredom of school.

Certain aspects of Yann's training were somewhat confusing for friends and family as well as for those doing them. In an attempt to teach his pupils about mental control, days were devoted to aspects of their emotional behaviour. One day they had to be happy and laughing all the time, on another they had to be cold and offish with people for no apparent reason. It was painful and upsetting to inflict this behaviour on unknowing friends, but this was training and, of course, they couldn't talk about it or offer any explanation. There were times when they wanted to laugh but couldn't, and then there were the silent sessions, which were equally hard for a group of close friends in their mid to late teens bursting with comments and jokes.

There were days when talking was enforced when playing the 'sandbox game'. With increased physical strengths came bigger egos, but the mea culpa of letting it all out and laying their emotions bare kept the friends grounded and balanced. 'You're an asshole because . . .', 'You may be my friend but your words upset me . . .' 'This isn't good . . .' They hid nothing and stomached the raw honesty of the good, bad and ugly feelings they'd been harbouring. They ended each session stronger and more united.

On a physical level, Yann's training was about strength and was brutal on the body yet somewhat elegant. He referred to everything acrobatic or technical as an 'illusion'. They could try to recreate whatever they wanted.

Alongside all of the various aspects of the group's training which Yann guided the group through, the most important element that Yann wanted them to retain was the 'Yamak spirit'. All of the Yamakasi group promoted the same thing: to share, give your all and leave no man behind. 'Stay together, community and sharing' were among Yann's most frequently used words. If a group of them had started a challenge together, they would finish together. If you finished first, great! The next thing to do was help those who were still training and ensure that they finished too. While the experiences of the Yamakasi had been a contradiction of both elitist and open behaviour during their early days, the values they wanted to pass to the next generation had evolved. *L'Art du Déplacement* was a culture of effort, not just one of personal advancement and incredible actions.

The group told Yann that they were ready to train harder. Yann listened, observed and picked their first big jump, *le saut de la maison de quartier*, (the leap of the community centre) in Bois Sauvage. It was far and high; between four and five metres across and four metres up. Whatever they had been expecting, it wasn't *that*.

'That was the test? Ouch . . . what a gap!' thought Sami. 'I could die on that jump.' They rehearsed the jump on the side but still . . . They knew that once they had committed to it there would be no opportunity to change their mind mid-air. It was all or nothing. They were scared but told themselves they could do it. Yann thought they were ready, all except Brahim. It was too early in his training, so he was not allowed to attempt it.

Yann's voice changed tone and he chose his words wisely. The peaceful, calm voice clicked into warrior-spirit mode. One by one each of them had to tell Yann that they wanted to do the jump; even up until a minute before they did it, all the while listening to Yann say, 'You want to be a man? You want to train harder? You want to be somebody someday? For yourself? For your friends and family? Well . . . it starts here. It's now!' And with that, one by one, Sami, Serika and Fabrice made the jump and changed their lives.

Sami went home in a haze of fear, peace and pride with an underlying sense of disbelief in what they had just done. He had to share his experience and, without too much thought, relayed the whole story to his father. His ramblings were so incoherent it was hard for his father to comprehend fully that his son had just jumped from one building to another. He had seen Sami and his friends training with Yann in front of their building and that all looked fine. He felt proud of his son, but this big jump was a shock.

Yann had three stages that he wanted the Revelation crew to experience. The first, the big jump, had tested their commitment. They were ready for Phase Two.

Fighting and aggression were always in the air in Evry and having physical abilities gave the Revelation crew the confidence to be themselves in that environment. If Yann had lived and survived it, then they must too. They never knew who they might have to fight or run away from. On the other hand, they always felt safe with Yann; he was a one-man life insurance policy. He knew all the bad guys in town anyway! If Yann could have fought ten of the biggest and hardest badasses all at once, he would have done.

It would have been his dream come true. However, Yann had realised that to win fights was more about using certain techniques than just strength.

It was time for Phase Two. At the staircase by the gym in Lisses, Yann asked, 'OK, who wants to go first?' For what, he didn't say, but as they looked on, Sami spoke up. 'What do we have to do?' 'That's not important, you have to commit first, then there's no coming back from it.' 'Yes, ummm, OK . . .' said Sami as Brahim, Serika and Fabrice looked on nervously. 'There's another level waiting for you,' Yann said as he positioned Sami's back against the wall, leaving him stood up straight. Yann looked him in the eyes and without warning punched him in the stomach. Sami bent forward, almost falling to his knees at which moment Yann took both his arms and lifted them above his head allowing air to flow back into his lungs more swiftly. 'I'm not done yet,' said Yann ominously. Time stood still for Sami. 'What?' was the only thought that went through his mind. He didn't cower away despite knowing full well the pain he was again about to experience as Yann prepared to deliver the second blow. Sami had made the commitment. He had to have the *esprit guerrier*, the warrior spirit. He knew he had to take it like a man.

The expression on the others' faces was worse than that on Sami's. Informed anticipation could be crueller than a surprise blow. One by one they all went through the painful and winding experience. Fighters were spiritual and physical, Yann explained to them afterwards, and because they were being trained by him, in some way they would somehow represent him. Because of this, they had to be like him. For Yann, this meant they had to move and jump and fight like a beast. There would be more fighting in their training, but in the act of receiving punches, not inflicting them.

Yann's plan was to cultivate the warrior spirit within them so they would all be ready to jump anytime, anywhere. Regardless of who was ready to go first and take it, they all needed to be able to instigate action at any moment. There may not be anyone there to set an example or go before them. They all had to be leaders, prepared to go first even if deep inside they were all thinking: 'Oh shit, not me!'

Sami was relieved that he was going first again but still his stomach tensed and his throat swallowed in anticipation of the unknown. 'Stand straight!' Yann said to Fabrice standing on the side of him as – bam! – he delivered a low kick on the side of his leg. Bam again, the other side had to be done too, of course. Each of them went through the experience until it was time to go home and rest. Their training was about to become more hardcore, Yann told them. There would be more physical training, pushing their limits, cardio and big jumps. They were ready.

Their physical conditioning circuits were intense. They combined small and large jumps, exchanged punches to the stomach, fifty at a time, then did squats and push ups-until they couldn't do anymore. Then it was time to run into town, where Yann would find the biggest, potentially most painful jumps possible. They weren't technical rail-precision type jumps but ones that had an impact and a brutal consequence if you failed. Yann would designate the jumps per person each time, reading and assessing their abilities on the day. Every day had to hold some new challenge that would push them beyond their comfort zone. It was in those moments – poised on the edge of a jump between two buildings – that Yann would drop one of his many sayings:

'When people lose their minds, I don't. When people cry, I smile. When they are in pain, I feel good. Because it is me and I recognise myself through it.'

In the moment, it wasn't fun but afterwards the sensations were unique. Their bruised and exhausted bodies, full of lactic acid, had never felt so alive. They would live to train and train to last. Yann had told them not to live obsessively, just to jump. That was the theory they were taught, but to be not obsessed was easier said than done.

17

Exit Stage Left

Real killers, machines! To me they weren't human. They were supernatural. It didn't make sense. When we were with them and they gave us instructions for a session, push-ups and all that. From the beginning we were exhausted. We couldn't continue but they would carry on with smiles on their faces. 'We start together, we finish together!' But we were drained. We couldn't even start, we were already tired . . . Superhumans!

Alexis Scogib

The friends had hoped that *Yamakasi: Les samouraïs des temps modernes* might touch people when the film was released in April 2001, but they hadn't expected such a positive reaction or the attention that followed. It became a cultural phenomenon in France. 'Oh my god, are you one of the Yamakasi?' yet another teenage girl squealed at Williams, while desperate for recognition or even a glance from her new heartthrob. 'No, no, no, that's my twin brother, it's not me, sorry!' Williams said, making his usual hasty retreat from the limelight. Several teen girl magazines requested an interview, but none was given. The film had shown some of what they were capable of, but Williams yearned for a documentary, something explaining how they had got to where they were. Nothing had come easy to any of them. It would give out the wrong message to think that. Against the odds the multicultural group had stepped out from negative stereotypes, discrimination, alienation, racism and lives where few opportunities were available. They had proven dreams were possible.

While the pubic searched for the Yamakasi, the group did what they normally did; trained like crazy, but it wasn't always as simple as before. During the filming, nobody knew who they were, but now training outside became problematic as people stopped and asked for photographs and autographs. Of course, they politely obliged, but it wasn't part of training. Some new elements were disturbing. Bodyguards were assigned to them for some of the press events. The most capable and 'ready for action' men had to be protected, according to the film's marketing team. It was surreal. They had never trained to be famous or sought individual recognition. They were motivated to be strong to help others, to improve themselves but not for the sake of celebrity. They wanted to pass on and share the positive values of the discipline. It was too much for some of the group and the peak of fame became the least confident, lonely and depressive of days. Friends from their neighbourhoods told them: 'You've changed', where in reality no such thing had happened. Their friends' perception of them was the thing that had changed. Judgements and envy brought out the worst in others. 'Ah you can buy me something,' friends demanded. 'What are you talking about? We're friends. I don't need to buy something for you. You work just like me.'

The Yamakasi had no plan to maximise on the publicity and attention, as they only ever had one simple goal – to train to be strong – and there was always more training they could do towards that. Bruno Girard, with whom they had worked on the film *Le Message*, advised the group to protect their name. They knew nothing about business, trademarks or ownership of anything they did. While Luc Besson was unhappy about the idea of having to pay a licence for the use of the name of his film, it gave the group a small share of something. They set up a company overseen by Malik's brother.

The film's success was perhaps most damaging for David. The education he delivered to his followers was very clear. The Yamakasi were traitors: they lacked talent and had stolen what should have been his. The cult of David lived and breathed his every word. His competitive side once again formed the difference between the groups – for the Yamakasi, the challenge was for all to complete a task. For David the challenge was to win.

Although it was only a ten-minute walk between Evry and Lisses, the paths of David and the Yamakasi had rarely crossed since his request to be in the film was rejected. Yann, Malik and Charles happened to be passing through Lisses one afternoon when Stéphane was training with David in the children's playground next to the Dame du Lac.

Stéphane looked up. He knew full well who they were. David had often told him that the Yamakasi couldn't do various jumps that Stéphane was now capable of. It was part motivation and partly a product of David's ongoing negative communication regarding anything about the Yamakasi.

Stéphane, the favoured student, knew he could do those jumps. With fire in his belly, he told David, 'I'm going to go there and challenge them. The Yamakasi should be better than me, I'm just a beginner. I've been doing Parkour with you for three years, they should be good, so I'm going to go and challenge them.' David smiled and said nothing as he folded his arms and watched his protégé approach the Yamakasi.

Ever the optimist and thinking the best of people, Malik smiled as he extended his hand to Stéphane. It was great to see new guys out training hard, he thought. Stéphane refused his handshake. 'Hey, guys, what's up with the Yamakasi? I'm just a normal guy training with David and you should be super-good. You should kick my ass. So show me. Show me what you can do! I want you to show me any move that I can't do.' Yann's eyes glared, piercing Stéphane's soul. Yann was speechless. He did nothing, but Stéphane recognised the look of a guy who wanted to punch him in the face and was glad he didn't follow through.

With a heavy heart, Malik sighed and calmly replied, 'No, you know what, man, it's OK. If you train with David, you must be good. There's no problem. We do the same thing.' To emphasise the point he repeated it to make sure the sentiment came through. 'Yeah, if you train with David, then I'm sure you are good. No problem.'

'Ah, OK, so are you refusing my challenge?' and with that Stéphane returned to David as the three Yamakasi looked on in disbelief. They felt sad that there were so many tensions and factions when the discipline was still in its infancy, and there were only a handful of people in the world who trained to do what they did.

Unless you had a friend who was a friend of a friend of the founders, finding and learning from any of them wasn't easy. Yet the Yamakasi film had lit the fuse; people were inspired and wanted to move.

The group, in turn, wanted people to know, experience and appreciate the values of *L'Art du Déplacement*. How to manage such a thing when there was still only a handful of people with any lived experience of it had not been thought through. The rest of the world was ready for the Yamakasi, but the Yamakasi weren't ready for them. There was no structured organisation, no membership card to sign, and certainly no plan. The Yamakasi were still developing their ideas and doing their personal research into the practice, even if it had been over a decade since they began exploring their methods. Success was great, but it was too much too soon. Just as they had no coach to guide them in their training, they also had no manager to guide them in exploiting the swell of publicity and attention. They knew nothing of marketing strategies, communications and PR. What they knew was that, through their actions, they had found a way to give meaning to their lives and they knew how to train.

While cinema and television had been an effective mainstream way to introduce *L'Art du Déplacement* to the public, a new medium was becoming ever more present. While David and Sébastien had not made it on to the big screen with their presence, they were soon aware of the potential of the internet. It was another way to be seen, but quite unlike cinema and television: once the content was there, it was available twenty-four-seven to be replayed, studied, obsessed over and discussed, and you never knew who could be watching. Whilst nobody fully understood its potential, it would have a huge impact on them over the next few years.

David had created his own showreel edit, the video *SpeedAirMan*, a play on the name of his favourite superhero, Spider-Man. A friend posted it online and soon people around the world were amazed at what they saw. In a bid to get the attention of the production office who were making the next Spider-Man film, another friend pretended to be a pizza delivery guy and left a VHS copy of the video at the office, but no one called back. Whatever hopes and dreams David had of being on the big screen were yet to materialise.

The success of the *Yamakasi* films meant times were changing even for the small group of next-generation loyal adventurers in Sarcelles. Williams was nineteen when the film was released but had started training the kids from his neighbourhood when he was fourteen. They'd seen him working out since he was young. His older brothers, cousin and their friends had helped and shared so much with him that he wanted to pass it on to others. He'd left school, was a Yamakasi and had a small group to train. His youngest students were his little sister Audrey and her school friends. The others were ten and eleven years old, with the group made up of four boys and two girls. They were all already sporty and had a passion for movement. They also practised Viet Vo Dau and athletics but looked to Williams for training and guidance.

Williams kept the sessions playful and helped the kids to find themselves. Their perseverance, courage, strength and willpower would improve the more they trained, but they played games and covered small routes on the wooden ship playground at the heart of the Ecouen forest mainly for fun. At the end of every session there would be a little strength training but nothing extreme: push-ups, pull-ups and sit-ups but never any pressure. Whatever the dreams and aspirations of the kids from Sarcelles, Williams was very clear; he would be happy to train them until they were eighteen and after that life was up to them. Sport was still one of the best career paths for the youth of Sarcelles, but as Williams told them, it was better still if you finished school and got your Baccalaureate – even if it hadn't quite worked out like that for him.

If the kids had their own way, they would have trained all day, every day but, apart from during the holidays, Williams limited it to weekends. They spent the whole day all over Sarcelles, in the town centre or in a park, but always finished in the woods of Ecouen, a mythical spot for all of them. They'd finish around 5 p.m. and gather at Williams's mother's house to eat and recover. Williams could relate to some of the kids, particularly the extremely shy ones who, like him, found a way to focus and express their potential in the world through exploring movement, even if they didn't say much.

Each training session started exactly the same way. 'Why do we train?' Williams would ask the group. What's the purpose?' Alexis Scogib, best friend to Williams's youngest sister, had a simple answer. 'I train because we're all together, and I enjoy being here. And in this sport I find myself. On your own it's all right but at times it's boring . . . So yes, sharing, we train in order to share. There aren't that many sports where you can gather so many people and share that one sport. For example, basketball, sure, but if you're limited in numbers . . . With football there's eleven people, but with this it can be two, it can be just you, or a hundred people, or a thousand, and so on. So it's really a great sport based on sharing.'

With only three years' difference between Williams and the oldest in the group, he was a big brother to them and they all thought he was special. 'He's a machine, he's not human! He's not normal! Sometimes he did moves that even to this day, I can't do,' recalled Alexis after ten years of training. Williams had it all: flexibility, endurance, creativity and a stamina and physicality that seemed unstoppable. They also thought he was wise, an attribute rarely applied to one so young. Sarcelles was a small neighbourhood and, whatever the locals thought young people should be doing, it wasn't what Williams's group did. They were obviously some sort of crazy cult. Some were so concerned they knocked on Alexis's parents' door to say that they'd seen their child doing strange things and to ask if everything was OK in the family.

People were always shocked to see some of the things they could do. There were certain occasions when it was reasonable to question their actions – for example, when some of the group chose to jump across the train tracks at the Châtelet train station instead of taking the longer route around. *L'Art du Déplacement* people have a different eye for opportunities and it was a small leap for them to make. They did it because they could and to be on time for their next meeting. Their training was useful.

The guidance for the young guns of Sarcelles didn't only come from Williams. Sometimes they went to Evry to train with Yann and Laurent. Compared to Williams's approach, it felt like military service, but there were always good times because they inevitably ended up at Laurent's grandmother's apartment for food and rest.

Williams's style was distinct and his priorities for the group were clear. 'You are training for yourself, not for me.' They did not represent or mirror him; they had to individuate and become the best versions of who they could be. 'If you know what you're capable of you'll be able to do it; otherwise, train in order to find out,' Williams told them. His words had a great impact on the younger minds as he never put pressure on anyone to do anything. Williams was also smart; he knew they were of an age and mentality where raising his voice and shouting orders would be ineffective. 'If you want to do it, you do it for yourself, otherwise don't do it.' Williams could not have been clearer. He wanted them to be perfect in everything, not simply their strength; it was equally important to be flexible, have endurance and be creative.

Chau also kept a watchful eye on them, his little sister being part of the group. There was no distinction between what she and the boys should try. Any girls who trained with them were treated respectfully, which meant that they had to do the same. 'You're mean, we're girls, you should . . .' some of the girls would say, but to Williams it was simple: 'Just the fact that you're here, I respect you. You know or you train towards it.' The girls moved, did vaults, rolls, big drops and arm-jumps just the same as everyone else. There was Path A that Williams would do, and if the others couldn't do it, they had a path B that Williams suggested to them. They did it their way so as to be able to follow him. Nobody ever said, 'Williams, I can't do it, I quit,' even if Williams did something the others couldn't do. They always did something else until another move came up. 'That one, yes, I can do it!'

Chau was very happy with the level of the group as they progressed. They were very similar to the young guys in Evry or those in nearby Torcy where he now lived. In Evry, there were jumps to test you everywhere whereas in Sarcelles it was still mainly the Ecouen wall and the ship playground.

There was no gym in Sarcelles for the group to experiment in and try out new ideas. Everything they did was outside and the grass was their only crash mat. When they saw some of the things the Evry guys were doing, they'd try it out back in Sarcelles. Without the luxury of an indoor environment and obstacles that could be adapted to their needs, they could only adapt to the existing surroundings. Sometimes it resulted in an injury, but still they'd keep trying.

Each one of Williams's training sessions would also include the 'meditation moment' – height training on top of the three-metre wall at Ecouen. Standing on the top of the wall, they closed their eyes and went up on their tiptoes. The aim was to stay there for as long as they could, losing track of their spatial awareness and conquering their fears. Within a few years, Alexis was doing handstands on top of forty-metre-high buildings. Even though his body was being pushed by the wind, his mind remained calm and still.

At times, the thorny issue of competition would be discussed as more people started to train. Sometimes in La Défense, there were groups training who were eager to impress and wanted to compete, but Williams had educated his group in a particular way. 'There is no point competing. Competition is an exchange for a future injury,' he told them. 'People didn't understand when we said we didn't want to compete,' Alexis recalled. '"OK, sure, you're better than us. No worries. Congratulations." They didn't understand why we didn't want to do that. Williams completely closed off that path for us. No competitive exchanges. He didn't even want us to put videos online because he didn't want people commenting or inciting us to compete. He was protecting us.'

However, this did not stop people noticing them. 'Hey, Yamakasi, go on, jump from rooftop to rooftop . . .' It was annoying and caused them some pretty poor training sessions, especially when they went to Paris where people asked for photos and autographs. Some thought they were crazy while others wanted to join in.

'It's open to everyone, but you'll have to train on your own. You can train, we'll give you advice, but you can't join this group,' Williams told people. He never wanted to reject anyone but he was wary of giving access to newcomers. Within their group they knew each other well and what everyone was capable of. They had tried bringing in new people before, but it was a bad experience that caused chaos and lost the group time. Some followed and mocked them nevertheless. 'Ah, why are you doing this? It looks simple. I can do it easily . . .' This was generally the last thing said before missing their landing and badly performing whatever it was they were trying to do. The copycats were generally harmful only to themselves.

Amongst the endless wannabes and bandwagon-jumpers, there were many who claimed to have been training their own version of Parkour for years. Whilst there might have been some parallels, none had been through the long, shared processes of discovery and near-masochistic levels of discipline that the friends had created for themselves. No one had suffered, experimented and undergone the complete perceptual shift that their training had forged. Some could produce comparable movements, albeit at a much lower intensity, and some might have been equally strong and resilient, but no one could claim to have experienced anything even close to that which the Yamakasi experienced. There was, however, perhaps one exception: Erwan Le Corre, a young man from the southwest of Paris, who had spent seven years as a disciple of Combat Vital, a methodology and philosophy developed by Don Jean Habrey, a then 48-year-old Frenchman with a strange past involving childhood psychiatric institutions, the military, musical performances, martial arts, extreme stunts, naturopaths and a rejection of everything that popular culture had to offer.

Habrey's adventurous cult-like world of Combat Vital

took place mainly at night in central Paris and was a mentally darker affair than the philosophies of *L'Art du Déplacement*. Habrey's followers caused mischief and mayhem while living by his guidelines. Habrey wanted the world to change and had some very distinct ideas on how. He wasn't looking for acceptance from anyone.

Erwan had resigned himself to the idea that what he had done with Habrey was a part of his youth, a rite of passage that he had thrived and survived on. After seven loyal and devoted years, he left aged twenty-five. For three years he lived in China, but he was now back in Paris. He had never stopped his physical training and continued to explore new movement worlds, throwing himself into Olympic lifting, rock climbing, trail running, sailing and triathlon. He never thought he would find other people to train with in the way he used to, but after seeing the recent Stade 2 report on television and the Yamakasi film, he was really happy to know he wasn't alone. 'This is amazing!' he thought. 'What are the chances . . . the movements, the locations, and all in and around Paris! How cool that these guys had done something with this. Where did they train?' He had to meet them.

Luckily for Erwan, the Luc Besson marketing machine was in full swing, which meant that the Yamakasi were making various public appearances to promote the film. They would be at FNAC, one of Paris's well known book shops, on a Saturday afternoon for a Q&A. As soon as the Yamakasi arrived, they were swarmed by fans trying to get a glimpse of what real ninjas look like. The group smiled and answered with somewhat abstract phrases, particularly if Yann was passed the mic. Erwan patiently waited his turn and made his way towards the front to speak to them. 'I've been doing the same sort of thing as you,' Erwan said enthusiastically. 'Hard training, moving on rooftops,' he began to tell Chau, who was always a little reserved and somewhat distant on first encounters. Erwan just wanted to connect with these guys. 'Ah, OK,' said Chau. He had heard similar things before, but the guy looked fit and strong. Chau kept an open mind and shared his contact details.

Erwan called and emailed, but Chau never replied. Although he never got to train with the Yamakasi, seeing their film had relit the fuse. He used to train like that, even more completely, he thought. It was time to move like that again.

18

Combat Vital

You find the scared urban dweller, you find tribes where every individual feels safer, you find wild bunches who can attack the weak. You find lone wolves, but you also find the free man, the new warriors, those who are not afraid of adventure, who are self-sufficient and who can survive in this new forest . . . Because the city is still nature, you find water, earth, trees. The city is alive. It's an incredible source of energy.

Don Jean Habrey, *Combat Vital*

It was another cold, wet and windy winter's night in December 1990. Erwan Le Corre was barefoot, dressed head to toe in black and meeting a group at Châtelet in the centre of Paris. His stomach was empty and now beyond hunger after fasting all day. Three cars pulled up: twelve guys and three women all in their early twenties. No brands, labels or shoes: 'minimalist tactical meets mime'. Whilst others their age got their kicks from fast cars, parties and getting high, this group were simply looking for adventure. Some laughed and made jokes whilst others were silent, the atmosphere a heady mix of excitement, fear and anticipation. For the next seven hours, no one knew what would or could happen.

There was no special equipment, bags, water or snacks to keep you going. Just you. Don Jean Habrey had organised the meeting and led them in silence towards 'point zero', the geographically mapped centre of Paris, in front of the Notre Dame cathedral.

For them, what was considered to be one of the most famous churches in the world represented little more than a high-level playground to be conquered. Security wasn't a serious threat, but if the cops came, even better. The weak and unfit establishment was no suitable opponent for their feats or pace. As part of the ongoing project to clean the structure, scaffolding had been erected. One by one, the group began to climb; the cold metal stung, almost burning as it rested in the arches of their naked feet. Their hands grabbed tightly, but sweat made the bars more slippery the higher they climbed. As their breath became ever more visible against the cold blue-black of the night sky, they found their rhythm on the structure. The forty-eight-year old Habrey was as nimble as a cat, moving with ease as he intuitively found the most secure positions for his limbs without hesitation or fear. After a twenty-minute climb, the equivalent of walking the three hundred-and-eighty-seven interior steps, they ventured to the side of the scaffolding with only sky above them. They quickly gained access to the high north tower and looked out across a city of lights, the Eiffel Tower glowing in the distance, stooped gargoyles their only witnesses. The rooftops of Paris were Habrey's magical kingdom and spiritual home.

In through the nose and out through the mouth, his breath was audible as Habrey inched towards the edge of the cathedral wall thirty-five metres up. He took off his T-shirt and his stomach rippled as it changed from extended and bloated on the in-breath to concave as if starved on the out breath. 'If you can't control your breathing, then you can't control your focus,' he had told them on many occasions. The breath was core to Habrey's methods; breathing was focus and focus was discipline. The rhythm and sounds increased as his flesh rolled in and out like the tide. There's always a price to pay to gain something of value and when you choose to go that high, you *have* to look down. He didn't just look, he leant forward as if to touch his toes but rose up again quickly on the in breath as though rising from the dead. The movement quickened to a high-speed yoga-esque moon salutation. He danced with death and closed his eyes, feeling the moment as the pace increased. A state of heightened yet unconscious aware-ness. Not everyone in the group had begun their training from a place of health and strength, but for all who dared to try, the slightest changes in balance, breath, body sensa-tions or the wind were felt. Barely perceptible sounds and precise sensations created a drug-free, optimal, altered state of mind. For Habrey this was lucidity. If there had ever been a style of breathing and body relaxation or Chi Gong for daredevils, this was it.

In his wild ways, Habrey had eliminated all of the usual systems the body relies on for maintaining balance: the constant visual feedback from the eyes, keeping the head still, thereby allowing the inner ear to let us know where our bodies are in space – the key things that make up the body's vestibular system. By purposefully creating blind disorientation through bending forward, flowing up and down, all the while situating this in the fear of a poten-tially fatal fall, the resulting mental and physical balance training at height was incredible. The mind could fly, be at peace, explore and always *breathe*.

Exhilarated from the climb, the group made their way towards the Passerelle Débilly, a large, arched footbridge that crossed the Seine in front of the Eiffel Tower. 'Respect matter. Matter means elements. Elements mean the universe. The universe means force. Respect the force that is in everything,' Habrey had lectured as they arrived.

The bridge was a regular haunt offering climbing, balancing, hanging upside down and other such antics on its large metallic frame, but tonight they would go under the bridge not over.

There were many ways to immerse oneself in the water, but it was always fast, never gradual. 'Don't half-ass it. Don't stay in your head thinking of it. Just stop thinking, *feel*, relax, exhale and plunge swiftly,' Habrey instructed as they waited by the edge. Erwan loved a challenge. He was keen and always willing. He waited and continued listening. 'Exhale to relax just before you enter the water. People's reflex is to breath in, because they're afraid. Breathing in makes them think they will stay alive, in control but they, in fact, tense a lot because of it. It's like they think that exhaling equals dying, whereas exhaling is the most important aspect of breathing.' And so Erwan exhaled and, feet first, entered the dark waters. There was no conscious thinking, just feeling, the intense shock of the skin instantly dressed in a liquid so cold that changes had to be happening.

Once under water, why make such an experience so brief, he thought. Erwan glided through the darkness, hands outstretched to avoid any debris, the mind silent and calm, knowing it felt good. He swam for as long as his breath would take him. Onshore the group worried – was it natural to be gone for minutes? He rose to the surface as calmly as if in a warm bath with a grin as broad as could be. One inhalation and he swam back to shore.

To warm up after the plunges, Habrey orchestrated among his followers rounds of striking skills: punches, elbows and Thai boxing-style leg kicks. The sun rose and the majority of the group would slip back into the comfortable façade of their 'other' lives; university, work, shopping, friends and families.

From the moment that Erwan could stand upright and walk, his father had instilled in him a love of, and connection to, moving in nature. School sports occupied him for several hours a week, but even then rules and set formats didn't ignite his passion in the way that being outside and adapting to his environment did. Running up hills, climbing trees, swimming and jumping from boulder to boulder felt challenging and real. These were the normal things to do in the forests and rivers of Etréchy, a pretty, quiet and somewhat idyllic rural town in the district of Essonne, twenty-six miles southwest of Paris.

'You can do it. Just try,' his father always told him. Erwan was shy and lacking self-confidence, but his father knew he could be braver than Erwan himself ever believed. When he was aged ten, the family moved closer to Paris to Epinay-sur-Orge and with his father's continuing encouragement, Erwan grew more athletically daring year by year. However, as Erwan entered his teenage years, his father moved less while drinking and smoking more. Erwan trained judo and karate, earning his black belts by the age of eighteen and competing at national level. The seeds of discipline and commitment had been sown.

Things looked good on the surface: he was eighteen and enrolled in a psychology degree. The reality, however, was that he was bored and lost. Like many his age, he simply questioned the meaning of life. His father was no longer the figure of inspiration and his quest for inner strength, for finding mental and physical resilience, was going nowhere. He may not have known what he wanted but he knew what he didn't want – a desk job in an industry such as marketing. Somewhere there must be a path.

Not much awoke or excited his soul these days, but when he saw the 1986 TV clip of a man jump out of a helicopter half-naked into the freezing sea in Greenland, it lit a flame. The segment had been filmed two years earlier as part of a commercial for the French underwear company Hom. The client felt that it probably went a bit too far and perhaps just a little too extreme for the French market at that time because the commercial was never signed off.

The snow might as well have been sand for the ease with which Don Jean Habrey had trained and moved barefoot and bare-chested in the freezing temperatures against the arctic backdrop. Rope skipping, running, push-ups, yogic-styled breathing rituals – he had prepared his body for the record-breaking ultimate cold plunge. For the stunt, the helicopter circled the serene landscape of dark blue ocean, turquoise sky and sparkling, frosted white icebergs before holding its position five metres above the ice-cold water. The vista was beautiful yet uninviting. Inside the helicopter, Habrey stripped down to a pair of shorts. He then stepped out, raised his arms above his head and jumped feet first.

What the ad didn't show was that the cameras were in the wrong position first time around. They had to go for another take, but first the doctors wanted to check that Habrey was OK. None of Habrey's preparations for the jump had involved spending any time in the water. His blood pressure levels indicated that he should have been in a coma, but he wasn't. Against the doctors' wishes, he refused an injection to stimulate his heart. He believed in his methods and would jump again.

The helicopter circled and held its position. He jumped. Upon surfacing he swam to the waiting lifecraft, no flailing arms or indication of shock or alarm. He could have been swimming in the Mediterranean on a sunny afternoon.

One fateful afternoon years later, while killing time in FNAC, Erwan recognised the picture of the Arctic jumper as he stumbled randomly upon the book *Combat Vital* by Don Jean Habrey. There was a residential address at the back of the book. Erwan wrote and waited.

Habrey replied and the two men arranged to meet. Under the cover of darkness, Erwan waited eagerly for his elusive figure in the underground tunnel beneath the l'Arc de Triumph. Nothing was normal that night. Soon the two men were in a car, Erwan listening intently to a two-hour monologue on the physical and mental degeneration of society. 'Westerners have almost no needs,' his new friend explained. 'They don't need anything essential, and therefore they lose the need to surpass themselves; no effort, no courage. He is constantly assisted and is therefore not a warrior. He is scared, alone and isolated. He has lost his consciousness of belonging to the universe.'

The voice and rhythm captivated Erwan, but more importantly the sentiments rang true. He had seen people around him become increasingly weak and sick; blissfully numb and content to consume comfort and settle for a life lacking fulfilment.

Part rock star, part renegade soldier action hero, this man had a face that was chiselled, lean and strong, framed by shoulder-length hair. Aside from being barefoot, his clothing was a classic ensemble of jeans, shirt and leather jacket. He was the same age as Erwan's father.

Born in a small village near Leipzig in Germany towards the end of the Second World War, Habrey had never known his father. His French mother, Clementine, despaired; her son was wild – walking on all fours, feral in his behaviour, always craving contact with the earth and digging holes. The French pre-school system brought out the worst in him: whenever he was placed inside the four walls of a building, he was prone to outbursts of uncontrollable rage and had to be accompanied by an adult at all times, both for his safety and that of others. Rivers, nature and churches were Habrey's only sanctuary. Years later in the book *Combat Vital*, he claimed that he had been embracing the energy and healing virtues from the sacred sites of telluric currents (ley lines) on which many of the French churches and cathedrals were built.

His mother couldn't manage his behaviour and after failed experiences with foster families he was eventually institutionalised. He continued to fight whatever systems were put in place to enclose him and he never swallowed his medication.

He survived his institutionalised school years with time spent outside, finding adventure. He was a natural leader for anyone willing to follow. With the onset of adulthood, the troubled youth took up various jobs, working as a labourer and a waiter, as well as playing percussion with various immigrant communities. At nineteen, the mandatory military national service called and he joined as a frogman in the airforce, training in Lahr in Germany. He was fit, strong, looked good, was musical and wanted to perform.

In Lyon he worked as a singer and drummer in small nightclubs and venues. To make the show more spectacular, he added some stunts, arriving on stage by jumping on to a moving motorcycle. Following his success in Lyon, the bright lights of Paris were calling.

Paris was not Lyon. He was unsuccessful but continued to explore and absorb the city. He took up combat sports and martial arts, discovering a stark difference between the teachings of eastern philosophies and the everyday realities of western living. The body and fitness cultures baffled him. Why were people jogging? The same benefits could be gained from fast walking for thirty minutes, three times a week. Body building made no sense – why spend energy building muscles which then require more energy to maintain and quickly turn to fat as soon as you stop training? Aerobics was dangerous —a sweaty room full of bacteria, a breeding ground for sickness. There was no nature or sense to it. It was these thought processes that developed someone ready to be taken in by a new type of life.

He was also a kick-boxer and once went 17 fights undefeated. He was still fighting at 38, when he suffered a serious injury and doctors told him he wouldn't walk again. He refused their diagnosis and medications, which led him to an encounter in an organic food store with a seventy -year-old naturopath called 'Master George'.

The mysterious Master George took Habrey under his wing and paid for his ticket to go to a small village near Ajaccio in Corsica. Under Master George's guidance, he spent the first twenty-one days in a fasted state (no food, just water) taking regular cold water plunges in rivers, trying to walk and swim. He then began eating and on day twenty-seven walked pain free. Resurrected and healed, Habrey had a renewed sense of purpose. He invested his time creating and maintaining a holistic lifestyle that could make people healthier and stronger: a raw vegetarian diet, breathing exercises, fasting, cold plunges and movement. Habrey had a vision of how his system of living could benefit society.

Returning to Paris, he utilised the city's environment to facilitate his training and ideas. Soon a few young adventurers found him out and came in search of new experiences.

Habrey introduced them to the type of training not available in any sport. Rooftop challenges included blindfolded-balancing as well as dramatic getaways. The group were chased by Dobermans and security guards, arrested yet never charged. Action films and popular culture had nothing on what they were up to. Life was thrilling and challenging with what Habrey had to offer. There were audacious acts, including a group of twenty breaking into the Louvre art gallery. If society was broken, then this was a sure-fire way to make it exciting again. However, members came and went as life's responsibilities and priorities changed.

Over time, the training and adventures intensified. As a result, during Erwan's first three years of training, the membership of the secret club shrank from around twenty to five or six. The strict diet – organic raw vegetables with some eggs, seafood, no grains or sugar, no processed food and a handful of fruit and nuts – wasn't to everyone's taste. If that wasn't enough of a fun filter, there was a frugal, stoic minimalist lifestyle that accompanied the eating, or lack thereof. Discipline was present in every detail of life – the way you had to eat, not eat, talk, breathe – with the group even silently standing still for long periods of time just to be able then to experience the elixir of movement. It was even recommended that you slept as close to the floor as possible without blankets or comfort of any sort. There were no TV or radio shows. Popular culture was to be avoided; stupid people saying stupid things on stupid shows. By exploring silence instead, you could repel such polluting influences. If you experienced discomfort on a regular basis, then anything could be comfortable.

The years of adventures that Erwan experienced with Habrey were wild. He had broken into the zoo, fed wolves raw meat directly from his mouth and experienced countless encounters with the authorities – both the police and fire brigade – and always came back for more. The group relished their superiority of their skills over the authorities who tried to follow them at height.

Erwan was fully dedicated to Habrey. He believed in the message and tirelessly embraced every element of the lifestyle thrown at him. Habrey himself was proof of the benefits of what could be achieved by following his way of life. He was far more able, daring, strong, impressive and charismatic than anyone Erwan had ever known or seen. However, if you didn't conform or agree, then you were not welcome.

There was only a small group who believed strongly enough to continue to live by Habrey's marginal code, shunning conventions and habits, not to be different for the sake of it, but for conscious lifestyle choices, personal freedom, wellbeing and health. 'Know thyself and you will know the universe and the gods,' the Ancient Greeks had said and so it was for Erwan. He put in the hours, the days, months and years and his self-knowledge was advancing. He had challenged every convention that his psyche had been built on, revealing to himself the raw matter that made him who he was and who he wanted to be.

Habrey was helping to build him physically and soon he could keep up with his mentor but, with that balance, came imbalances. Habrey was no longer the only one who could achieve the long rope-traverses that tied the boats together. When they sparred, Erwan could fight and hold his own.

His balancing at height and breath-holding in freezing water were equal to his mentor's. He faced and managed all of the fears that Habrey had put in his path.

However, it was the connection with the mainstream, 'normal' people that brought Erwan a sense of outward self-confidence. He worked part-time selling unique hand-made soaps and was eloquent and charming. His interactions selling roses to couples in restaurants, those enjoying the best of fine dining that Paris could offer, actually gave Erwan an even greater sense of strength. What's the use in being able to hang upside down blindfolded from a bridge if you don't feel comfortable talking to a stranger? He wanted and needed to exude a sense of self-confidence.

Over time, Habrey was no longer on such a pedestal for Erwan. He saw the cracks appear in his character. The reality of there being a system and an ability to reach, change and help people – Habrey's original mission statement – seemed less of a priority than the frequency of creating opportunities for Habrey to be seen and to perform. Why carry a kettle drum to the top of Notre Dame so Habrey could play to the New Year's Eve revellers? Yes, it was an adventure and unique, but where was the benefit and for whom?

Erwan wrestled with his doubts. He didn't want to stay but didn't know what to do if he left. 'At least I'm having some fun with this guy and we do some crazy trainings,' he thought.

Insecurities grew within Habrey as he relied on others not just through his need to impress and teach, but for financial support. Some of them had part-time work, but he was reliant solely on their donations, a precarious set-up even for the most marginal urban adventurer. 'You're going to betray me!' became an uncomfortable, all too common statement as Habrey's insecurities revealed themselves more frequently. Erwan's loyalty was beyond questioning and he had never felt more insulted. He warned Habrey that continually doubting his dedication would make him leave.

A new pattern had evolved as Habrey continued to try and maintain more followers. He would find a new guy to bring to the group and the others watched on as the predictable cycle of awe and wonder at this alternative adventure led to a series of personal revelations followed by doubt and despair as an individual whose every convention, habit and previous relationships were thrown into question. Like many before them, eventually they would crack and leave.

Life had been more original, exhilarating and unique than Erwan could ever have imagined. For seven years, he had loyally followed Habrey's hierarchy and training regime. He had run, jumped, climbed, swum and fought the majority of the norms society had to offer. He had explored the inaccessible, hidden and lesser known sights of central Paris, but now was the time to step away. However free and independent he thought he was, he would never truly know and understand his own nature and sense of personal freedom while next to Habrey. The teacher/student roles would never be reversed. Habrey's paranoia continued and, despite the warnings, Habrey persisted in questioning Erwan's loyalty. It was the final insult because Erwan had been pure and honest in his dedication; but this part of his life had come to an end. Enlightened, his inner voice told him that it was time to leave.

Erwan believed that should never be about a person. It should be about *the* person. It should never be about anyone looking up to anyone else. It should be about people inspiring themselves to improve, to be a better person, to have a better quality of life. A method should be designed, nothing else.

'Maybe one day I'm going to do something with that whole experience, but for now I just want to live my own life on my own terms and we'll see,' thought Erwan. In 1997, just as the Yamakasi were about to go public with the firefighters' performance and then receive national attention on TV with the Stade 2 report, Erwan packed his bags and left for China.

19

The Most Famous Ghosts in France

I was always very scared about everything. I was very determined to get through it but scared at the same time. It was like two great forces in my mind fighting against each other and it would take ages, but the guys were very patient, they knew and understood what I was going through and they were fine with it.

Thomas Couetdic, aka Thomas des Bois.

There was no 'intro to Parkour' class or 'come train with the Yamakasi' advertised or accessible to anyone. Living in Paris gave some a head start in terms of being able to access anything related to the Yamakasi or Parkour, but even then serendipity had to be on your side. For those living elsewhere in France, the internet was their only hope in finding a way to learn Parkour and meet its founders. It would take a lot of dedication and patience, but some were very determined.

'Hey wake up, Yamakasi!' Mrs Couetdic whispered to her son. He was wide awake and couldn't wait to get going. There was a big day ahead. From the sleepy town of Tours in the midwest of France, Thomas Couetdic was going to travel to Paris. Not quite Paris; rather, the suburbs that weren't so obviously inviting but home to the mysterious, infamous and inspiring Parkour. Finding the Yamakasi, David Belle or Sébastien Foucan was like searching for a needle in a haystack.

Thomas had only recently moved to Tours. He had met a few people at school, but there was no one to hang out with at the weekends. He was seventeen years old, alone, unhappy and longed to be anyone but himself. A few years ago he had seen the Stade 2 feature on TV and more recently they had been featured on the *Sept à huit* (*Seven to eight*) show. That segment had featured a piece on both the Yamakasi and David Belle.

Already a big Jackie Chan fan, Thomas liked the idea of moving in the environment. 'I mean, why wouldn't you do that?' he thought. Just watching what those guys could do was humbling for him. If he could just learn, gain a small chance to be exposed to a little bit of the Yamakasi and Parkour magic, then maybe something would rub off on him.

The Yamakasi had a webpage with one of their names and numbers on – Laurent Piemontesi. Thomas began to prepare himself mentally for the prospect of being able to talk to one of them. He needed to think about what he was going to say. He didn't want to mess it up. It mattered. After several days of contemplation, he had his script. He would tell them that he simply wanted to learn from them. That's all he was asking for, and he didn't mean to impose or bother them. He would be a dedicated and humble student. There was no point in rushing such an important call and messing up first impressions, he thought. He would practise saying it just for one more day. He had the deepest of respect for these people and what they did and he knew he would be starting from scratch. Eventually, he nervously dialled the number whilst still running the sentences over in his head. He held his breath with anticipation. 'Number no longer in service.'

Thomas had no idea of how to do Parkour, but he wanted to be a Yamakasi. With a heavy heart after the unsuccessful call, he went outside to the garden to try to move around. He didn't know how to train. His bedroom was on the first floor with a small balcony outside. Without knowing the name for it, he did a turn-vault over the rail and landed facing the opposite direction. He crouched down and lowered his body. Hanging from the rail, he then let go, dropping down into the garden. Practice continued. Some days he would just jump down from the balcony. These were big drops that made his ankles swell and shins hurt. He eased off after a while, again disappointed.

The Yamakasi webpage listed a few techniques that he tried his best to emulate and piece together. 'This little definition list was all the help we had at that point to learn Parkour,' remembered Thomas. 'It was our only foot in the door so trying to make sense of it was of paramount importance to me.' Sometimes he would go into town and try to jump over things and do big drops on to small surfaces. These were precision jumps – landing on a small target. He imagined a target from a dartboard laid out on the ground and he needed to land on the bull's-eye. He chose a spot and dropped. The concept of landing on a rail or other such surfaces seemed beyond the realm of human possibility at the time.

Other techniques included: the blind jump where you can't see the landing, the *saut de détente* (broad jump), *saut de bras* (arm-jump or cat-leap) and *saut de fond* (depth jump). Nobody had ever actually met any of the Yamakasi, David Belle or Sébastien Foucan, but that didn't stop everyone commenting, writing and becoming an authority on the subject on the various Internet forums that were springing up. Everything around Parkour was a bit of a mystery for those trying to find out about it. The Stade 2 report had referred to the 'cat men' and then 'the spider men'. Were these other groups who were training? Nothing was clear, but whoever was doing it was the stuff of urban legend.

Watching the videos *SpeedAirMan* and *Xtrm-Up* blew Thomas's mind. He didn't just like it. He wanted it. They were interacting with everyday life. The seriousness of the training appealed to Thomas. It was more than a sport or leisure activity; it was rough, thrilling and had elements of danger that necessitated a certain, disciplined approach. Thomas had to know more. It was the only way he could *be* more. In his mind, David looked especially amazing and Thomas repeated David's lines from the original Stade 2 feature. 'Everything that's an obstacle is part of our art. When we're walking and we encounter a challenge, that's what we work on. It's a way of saying, "I'm breaking free, I'm free and I can go where I want." No one can tell you, "You have to go this way because that's the way it is." I follow my own path.'

There were others like Thomas who'd seen the Stade 2 reports and were inspired to find out more. Tim Vogel-Gourgand (later known as Tim Pisteur) created the website Parkour.fr.st, a 'golden book' for the practice. Although designed with the intention that people would leave suggestions about the Yamakasi and Parkour, the handful of people using the website treated it as a forum. The number of people interested was so small that everyone knew everyone. Most used their real names but of course there were exceptions; 'Ninja Shaka' and the 'Wakazai brothers'. It was a friendly and welcoming group with a shared passion. Most were from somewhere near Paris, but there were a couple, like Thomas, from further afield.

Three months into his fascination with all things Parkour and Yamakasi, Thomas made plans to go to Lisses. It would be amazing! He tried again to contact some of the locals from Lisses on the website forum. Michael Ramdani had posted a message as had Johann Vigroux, Stéphane's younger brother. Thomas had seen Stéphane with David Belle in one of the TV reports.

'You don't know how to train. You don't know what training is. You don't push yourself. It's not serious training. Parkour is about overcoming every obstacle,' Johann told him on MSN Messenger. 'Wow, these guys aren't very friendly', Thomas thought. 'No one can overcome every obstacle, you know, not even if you are David Belle,' Thomas replied, getting a bit agitated by Johann's tone. He just wanted to learn, but this guy was arrogant and a bit aggressive. The secretive Lisses guys knew it all, it seemed. 'I just want to train, that's all. I want to learn. I don't know anything and I want to learn everything, that's all I want.' 'OK, then you can come. Drop by and train with us.'.

Finally! Stéphane hadn't said much but it was enough. At last there was a contact in Lisses with whom Thomas could train. His quest was getting closer. Like the young man who packs his bags, heads for the mountains and stays for two years learning the wisdom and ways of the wise elders, Thomas wanted to return a changed man. His stomach grumbled with nervous tension as the train pulled into the station at Evry. It was the first time he had travelled to Paris on his own and he didn't know what to expect. He patiently waited outside for Johann and Mike, checking his watch every five minutes. The train was on time. Maybe these guys were unreliable and being late was their style. 'Hey, I'm here, where are you?' Johann asked on the phone.

'At the taxi place outside,' Thomas replied

'No, you're not . . .' Evry has three train stations and Thomas was at the wrong one. After some confusion, Thomas eventually found himself in the back of Johann's small car with Mike.

'Hungry?' asked Johann.

'No, I'm good thanks,' replied Thomas, his sandwich still making itself known.

'Hey, look, that's the Manpower jump over there,' Mike pointed out the window as they took Thomas on a white-knuckle ride around the training spots. Johann only had one driving speed: fast. They made their way from the station and parked at the estate in Lisses.

As they walked and then crawled down what Thomas would later refer to as 'quadrupedie alley', Thomas tried to take it all in. They stopped at a large tree. Thomas was sure he had seen it in one of the videos.

'OK, we just climb it,' Johann said with a big smile and a shrug of the shoulders to help normalise things. Thomas tilted his neck skywards and watched Johann navigate the remains of sawn-off branches with confidence and experience. Thomas had never seen trees climbed liked this before. At the top, Johann swung from a branch with both hands, then let go and caught another branch one metre below. Thomas watched and tried to remember the route. The climb was high and he knew that, after the first two metres, any fall could have serious consequences.

'OK, now move your left foot to the lower branch stump, then get a better grip with your hands on the one above,' Johann told him as he patiently guided Thomas through the climb. Thomas felt exposed trying to move around the wooden stumps. With their heads tilted back, Johann and Mike kept their eyes on the new guy who seemed willing to try everything. Each hand and foot placement scared Thomas as he hesitantly followed every instruction. His trainers had little grip on the slippery surface and the spaces where he could put them were often only large enough for his big toe. The tree's diameter was too broad to wrap your arms around for any added sense of security. He tried to stay calm despite an all-encompassing fear that questioned both his and the tree's strength. 'It's cool, you've got this, nearly there,' Mike and Johann told him from below. Thomas continued to the top. While Johann had swung down and caught another branch Thomas was too scared to hang. Just getting there had been petrifying and now he had to get back down, which was even worse. It was harder to see what was underneath you than in front and above, so he needed more guidance on the way down. Thomas listened, followed and trusted their instructions back to terra firma.

As they continued on their way, Thomas glanced back at the tree he'd climbed only moments before. It was such an achievement and he'd stepped out of the car only fifteen minutes earlier.

'Oh, for example, you can jump from here to there,' Mike pointed out as they arrived at the gymnasium stairs. 'Really?! There's no way . . .' but before Thomas had finished his sentence, Mike was perched on the edge of the metal railings halfway up the staircase two metres above the ground and facing the wall opposite. He balanced and smiled down to Thomas. 'See?' he said with a grin and then took off, stretching his arms out in front of him and landed, grabbing hold of the wall opposite. Ah, so this was a *saut de bras* – an arm-jump, Thomas realised. Piece by piece things were coming together.

Karim Mouhous was already training at the stairs and was happy to see the guys when they arrived. Thomas walked up the first section of stairs and climbed on to the thin railing. He found his balance and looked across to the wall. He'd just seen Mike do it, so one part of him knew that it could be done. However, the idea of jumping towards the wall and being able to catch it seemed like a distant, fantastical act. He could jump, but there was no way he'd make it to the wall. It wouldn't end well. He climbed down from the rail while constantly staring at the wall, walking back down the stairs to get a different angle. From below it didn't look too bad, but from the side it wasn't so good. On the ground he marked out the distance and stood the same distance as the rail was, looking towards the wall. The others smiled knowingly as he looked over to them for signs of impatience or annoyance. There was none. Thomas had never experienced a mind-set that valued effort over achievement when being taught a new skill before. It fuelled his will to continue.

Thomas imagined taking off, first from both feet and then from just one to see which might feel better. He swung his arms forward and imagined catching the wall. He was scared; the wall was far. Just standing on the thin rail corner was challenging enough, let alone the idea of taking off from it. He also couldn't imagine that there was enough strength in his fingers to be able to catch his weight when he landed on the other side. None of his thoughts gave him confidence. Again he walked back up the stairs and stood staring at the wall. He climbed on to the rail and back down again, always staring and thinking about the act of committing to taking off. It was possible. He'd just seen someone do it. But then why did he not feel it was possible for him? Could he do it? Was it a question of belief more than ability? He started to feel upset but desperately didn't want to show it. He was angry and frustrated at his lack of emotional control. This is what he had come here for, but now he was just a mess. He tried to emulate the jump at ground level and proved to himself that he had the distance. Rationally he knew he was strong enough to make it to the wall. Technically he had to keep his balance on the rail and then catch the wall firmly. If his balance was good at the start, then the technique shouldn't stop him from trying, but still he didn't feel capable. He was afraid. It was everything he didn't want to be. He yearned to control who he was. Only then could he be more. The more the realisation hit him, the angrier he became. Anger meant more determination, but still he didn't jump.

Thomas had never faced such fear in his life nor had he been in a position to try to overcome it. The encounter felt like a puzzle, an emotional riddle that only he was capable of solving. He asked himself why he felt so scared and why was it consuming him in this way. 'Why can't I control it if I'm the cause of it?' he continued to ask himself.

He didn't want to let these guys down, so he had to try. After the false start with online communications, Johann and Mike couldn't have been more welcoming in person. He would repay their time and patience at least by trying. Back up the stairs, back on the rail. 'Damn you. Fear! Damn me! Why the fuck can't I just . . .' For the next two hours Thomas paced, stared and worked himself into a rage. The jump was terrifying. 'Oh look, if you arrive a bit short on that one, you are going to go like this,' Johann joked and pretended to knock his face upwards. 'You'll hit your chin, your teeth will jump out, you know,' he teased, trying to relax the proceedings. While his voice said one thing, his eyes told Thomas another; he too had been on the rail and knew the fear and uncertainty of committing to the jump. Thomas appreciated the jokes and reassuring looks. These guys were funny. The jump was serious, but they knew how to lighten the mood. The forces of fear and determination continued to battle it out in his mind. Was he ready for this kind of jump? Was it too soon for him? If not today, then when? He tried to think of everything and then nothing, to blank it all out, a peaceful mind, a busy mind, but it always came back to the same conclusion: he was scared. The jump wasn't without risk. With a big sigh of anxiety, he continued to think, not think, talk, joke, be silent, stare, walk, pace and be at the spot.

When his fingers made contact with the edge of the opposite wall, they grabbed on with all his life's worth. His feet slid down after making contact, but then he instinctively moved them higher up on the wall to take some of the strain off his arms. He'd done it! No sooner had Thomas marvelled at his own achievements than it was time to head to his budget, Formule 1 hotel nearby. 'It'll be some time around 3 or 4 a.m. when we head out again. Relax and get some rest; you'll need your energy.' Johann and Mike smiled and were gone.

Time passed slowly for the rest of the day as Thomas lay on his bed unable to relax. His body's biochemical adrenaline dump tired him, but his mind was racing, hungry for more. However long it had taken him to do it, he had jumped.

Back on the road again, this time to explore Evry. Seb Goudot was along for the ride. Before they experienced the night-time spots in Evry, there was just the little matter of crossing the bridge.

The Avenue du Lac marked the border between Lisses and Evry and passed over the A6 highway. The edge of the wall was slightly more than Thomas's hand span. The concrete surface had small stones embedded within it, giving reasonable grip. Seb jumped up on to the wall and walked along as if out for a Sunday stroll. It would have been easy to do had it not been for the eleven-lane highway of fast-moving traffic twenty metres below. Thomas watched in a state of disbelief as his eyes kept being drawn to the speeding vehicles that were ready to flatten him should he get in their way. It was so impressive to see the calm, controlled movements of the others in such an alarming context. They wanted Thomas to try.

He moved on to the wall at the beginning of the bridge with Johann standing nearby. From his crouched position, with his body consciously leaning towards the side of the pavement, Thomas was reluctant to stand up. Whereas some people might have thought: 'Are you crazy? I'm a beginner! Do you want me to die?' Thomas felt flattered by the fact that they trusted him enough to ask him to do this challenge. As terrifying as the task seemed, it gave him an incredible sense of personal responsibility. He felt empowered by the fact that only he could decide whether to walk or not.

He stood up at the very beginning of the bridge, his stomach sick with fear and vertigo. The game of logic had begun in his mind again. Was it possible? Yes, he had just seen it. Could he physically walk in a straight line on that width of wall? Yes. It was too much, though. He wanted to change who he was and he had made a commitment to do exactly that. After all, he had travelled to meet these guys and try new things. However, this was too much. No amount of jokes could lighten the mood or shift his all-consuming fear.

'How is it?' asked Johann.

'Fucking horrible,' Thomas muttered as he jumped back down to the safety of the ground. He had reached a limit and taken responsibility for his actions and wellbeing. He had chosen not to walk the bridge that night. Given the risks involved, he had to be sure of his own abilities – and he wasn't. It was a great lesson in responsibility.

The next spot seemed more reasonable. 'This is real Parkour,' explained Mike as he showed Thomas the route. 'This is what Parkour is really about. People think that Parkour is when you jump from a rooftop to another but, no, Parkour is this.' Before them was a concrete sleeping policeman – the kind that stops the car from going on the grass – and a tree. Tree, concrete block, tree, without ever touching the ground. An arm-jump to the tree, climb around to the side, then a precision jump back down on to the concrete thing and then repeat, over and over again. As the evening progressed, they lifted construction cones, traversed around the edge of a bus shelter and generally moved around as many obstacles as they could find. Thomas didn't feel well after his vertigo on the bridge had prevented him from crossing it, but he was still having the time of his life.

On the first night, when Johann was driving Thomas to the hotel, he had pointed out David Belle's house and honked the horn to see if he was around. Thomas had hoped to meet his hero on his visit, so just to know and see where he lived was exciting new information. As they drove off, Thomas looked back thinking, 'Maybe he's going to come out just as we're leaving'. He looked for as long as he could but David didn't emerge. The following evening, as Thomas drifted off in a haze of physical and mental exhaustion in the back of the car, they stopped at a junction and another car pulled up alongside them. Johann started chatting to its occupant. Only vaguely aware of what was going on, Thomas's attention was brought to full alert with the words, 'Hey Thomas, this is David.'

Thomas looked and saw David waving at him from the other car. It was surreal and unexpected. 'Hey, how's it going?' David asked. 'Good' was all Thomas could muster before the cars drove off. It was a brief encounter and Thomas's debilitating shyness had masked how starstruck he felt, but still he thought, 'Wow, I had seen David Belle! 'If I didn't get to talk to him I saw him.'

Thomas had seen how amazing David was on videos, but until his visit, he had been unaware of how good so many other people were. The Lisses collective were like a new breed of people and possibility. Johann, Seb and Mike had been training for two years and were only a couple of years older than him. It was a good reference for what he could become.

Thomas got lucky on his last night and again caught a glimpse of David and Stéphane hanging out, talking under a streetlight by the edge of the Dame du Lac park. As Thomas approached, he started to tremble with nerves. He was sure David could see what a shivering wreck he was, but David smiled, appreciating the humility Thomas demonstrated towards him. Although very shy, Thomas reached out and they shook hands, then briefly said a few words about what training they'd been doing. 'What a night!' thought Thomas.

He couldn't believe he'd actually spoken to David, who had been really nice and friendly. It was impressive. Johann and Seb walked over and together they all made their way to the children's playground. David jumped lightly from wooden post to wooden post in almost pitch darkness. 'What, do you need some airport runway lights?' David joked to the others who complained about not being able to see the landing. It was playful and inspiring and Thomas joined in as best he could as they took turns to dive roll through the hole in the middle of the children's train. He banged his head and they laughed, but it felt OK; he was with them and they knew he was trying.

Over the three days Mike, Johann and Seb had given him their time and energy while asking nothing in return. Their manner and the situations they put him in gave him a method to forge a new version of himself shaped from the inside out. It was the first steps. Their actions said, 'It's OK, it doesn't matter if you miss, if you're scared or if you don't do it, there's no shame. Take your time. There's no hurry.'

Armed with a few more techniques and a little knowledge, Thomas was even more determined to apply everything to his training back in Tours. He would push himself and go back to Lisses in six months' time to show them his progress. 'I wanted something that would change my life, to go through a process that would change me as a person, like some sort of an initiation into something that's going to change me forever,' he recalled.

That first trip was more than he could ever have hoped for. As he sat on the train back to Tours he looked down at his hands. They were destroyed. He was destroyed and had never been happier.

20

By Head,
Hand and Heart

*It was all practical stuff. Why? Because that's the way you train
soldiers: practical stuff. Soldiers don't freaking need to do a flag,
you don't need to do handstands. You need to run and sprint and
vault over obstacles. They need to balance on stuff, and they need
to climb to crawl to lift and carry, throw and catch. They need to
do all these things. They need to fight, to swim.*

Erwan Le Corre

While internet discussions had led Thomas Couetdic
to find his heroes and train in Lisses and Evry, it led
Erwan to the website Parkour.net (an evolution of Tim
Pisteur's golden book website), run by Jérome LeBret.
Jérome was one of the wild bunch from Lisses whom
Johann Vigroux had first met when he began training, and
Jérome was passionate about sharing everything around
Parkour. Parkour.net was the most credible and interesting
site for those in search of anything Parkour-related. Erwan
still wanted to connect with the guys who were doing
similar training to his despite having been unsuccessful so
far. What he found on the website was a connection to
someone far more interesting – a picture of a twentieth
-century French naval officer named George Hébert.

First and foremost, Hébert was an educator who had done what Habrey had talked about with Combat Vital but never achieved: Hébert had created a system, *Méthode Naturelle*, the Natural Method. His system didn't involve just training outdoors in functional, interesting and challenging ways; there was a method of progressions that made it accessible to all. 'He became my overnight hero and I wanted to learn everything I could about this guy, about his system,' remembered Erwan.

Although the participants on Parkour.net were keen to appoint Hébert as the one precursor to Parkour, he wasn't the first to combine physical, mental and moral fortitude. Many educators across northern and western Europe had been developing similar methods for the past two centuries. Even though the training was later used as a way to create and train armies, the motivations for a lot of the work in the late eighteenth century came from a will to create social and political autonomy. Compared to the genteel and aristocratic associations of fencing and dancing, these far more vigorous physical exercises aimed to promote more egalitarian social interactions. Many of the early gymnastic programmes emphasised that it was not only about gaining physical strength and a beautiful physique; rather it was for the influence that it would have on one's mentality. You could become braver, improve your aptitude for mental work and be of use to others.

Hébert was a Commissioned Officer Fusilier of the French Navy who reformed the gymnastics systems that had been in place in France at the time, a programme pioneered by Colonel Don Francisco Amorós. Previously, Amorós had developed specific training for firefighters as well as the military and civilian populations. Hébert's method provided a renewed focus on functionality and an altruistic approach to training. He also stressed the necessity of being outdoors and simplified the equipment. He maintained much of the work and methods created by Amorós and the physical educators before him such as the Prussians Johann Christoph Friedrich GutsMuths and Friederich Ludwig Jahn.

In 1902, while travelling by ship to Martinique, Hébert experienced a sequence of events that would influence how he reformed the navy's training. On 8 May the volcano in the city of Saint-Pierre erupted, killing 14,000 people within just a few minutes. Being in good physical shape with a strong will to survive separated some of those who had a chance of living from those who didn't.

In 1903 he was transferred to the Marines school in Lorient, Brittany, and by 1904 started to apply his new thinking to its 1,200 students. It was here that he began to develop the *Méthode Naturelle*, named very closely after Amorós's 1838 publication *Nouveau Manuel d'Education Physique, Gymnastique et Morale*.

Hébert established no complex rules and required no expensive equipment. There was no competition, no doping, no stadium and no specific field needed. He set out ten families of skills and movements all very similar to the educational components that GutsMuths used in 1793: walking, running, jumping, quadrupedal movement, climbing, balancing, lifting, throwing, defending and swimming.

In 1909, following positive results, Hébert extended his method to all the navy and had a team of 350 sailors performing demonstrations throughout France. The displays at the 1913 International Congress of Physical Education in Paris were well received and there was great enthusiasm for his method. He soon became the director of the Collège d'athlètes de Reims, sponsored by the French aristocrat and military captain the Marquis de Polignac.

His method revolutionised physical education in the army and gave it an altruistic goal for peacetime. He was inspired by the indigenous people that he had witnessed on his travels, who were far more active and athletic in their day-to-day living. Hébert trained men in how to perform rescues at sea, carry the wounded and on what to do during natural disasters. He adapted his method for a limited space such as the deck of a navy ship by having people working in rows, one behind the other. On land, the training could be done in a square. *Méthode Naturelle* could also be done in a natural environment where natural obstacles such as trees created opportunities for activities such as jumping, climbing and crawling. Stones could be lifted, carried and thrown.

Continuous movement and being outside were important. Hébert believed that physical education was something that everyone should do. It wasn't just an activity for elite level athletes who took part in competitive sport. According to Hébert, everyone has their own rhythm and ability and should be given their own goals; a freedom to choose what they want to work on. He believed that the training should be varied and, similar to the *parcours du combatant*, he built a *parcours Hébert*, an obstacle course made of wood and rope that ensured you never stopped moving.

The outbreak of the First World War sent Hébert with a company of fusilier marines into battle. He was badly injured, almost losing the use of one arm, but continued to train soldiers. By the end of the war, the college in Reims had been destroyed and left in ruins. The majority of his coaches had been killed in battle. Hébert started to take care of the physical education of women and children but the post-war French youth had little enthusiasm for his method. Audience-based spectacles and records held the next generation's interest.

Not everyone shared Hébert's approach to non-competitive, physical activities. Pierre de Coubertin was the French aristocrat, educator and historian who established the International Olympic Committee and would become known as the founder of the modern Olympics, with Paris hosting the first modern Olympics outside of Greece in 1900. Coubertin promoted organised sports and competition between amateur athletes. In contrast to Hébert, Coubertin not only advocated the importance of participation over winning, he also believed that organised sports would provide one with moral and social strength.

Hébert started fighting against organised competitive sports, which he felt lacked any altruistic ideals, and wrote the book *Sport vs Physical Education*. In 1936 he wrote *Physical, Manly and Moral Education through the Natural Method* and started Hébertiste centres across France. By 1940, with no army in France because it was occupied by Germany, the government used *Méthode Naturelle* to train young people. Hébert died in August 1957.

Everything about Hébert's approach resonated with Erwan: the free use of space, egalitarian principles, an anti-competitive stance and altruistic aims that focused on the functionality of the method. There was no show or performance. Creating any sort of spectacle was the opposite of education and functionality.

Erwan and his fellow free-spirited, late twentieth-century civilian warriors of the Parisian suburbs had unknowingly gone back to a time of valuing the belief in an individual's responsibility for their own moral, physical and intellectual condition. To create a strong body, they chose to develop their resilience rather than lean towards comfort and convenience. If there were a more difficult and challenging path, you should take it. They chose nature and training outdoors over a covered gymnasium. With a little imagination, any environment could offer up opportunities to explore your limits. Like the original purpose of gymnastics, theirs was a social movement; their own philosophical, educational and personal revolutionary tool. They strived to be both in harmony with their environment and autonomous over it.

Like Hébert, Erwan wanted to be strong to be useful. Could the ideas they explored help to rediscover the old values of physical education and return it to a time when it employed a free and playful approach to methods designed to develop a strong and resilient mind and body?

The current state of physical education and sport could gain a lot from *Méthode Naturelle*, *L'Art du Déplacement* and Parkour – if explained properly and if someone would simply stop and listen.

21

The Chicken,
the Lover and the Cat

*I was very much under David's influence. I was very arrogant, and
when you are too arrogant in Parkour you get slapped in the face.*

Stéphane Vigroux

The chicken, the lover and the cat was an unlikely
trilogy. If that wasn't interesting enough, the chicken
was angry and the cat was scary. The sports-loving public
would enjoy the new, action-packed Nike Presto campaign.
The American advertising agency Wieden+Kennedy had
found the talent to perform in it. They were some of the
new wave of French urban tumblers and outdoor gymnasts. The agency didn't really know how to describe them
but were sure that the campaign was going to look great.

There had been a few live Parkour performances and
commercials by David's group that had been very well
received, but for Johann Vigroux it had never been about
money or fame. He just wanted acknowledgement from his
peers. He had trained hard and was now good enough to be
allowed to move alongside them. By contrast, Parkour was
David Belle's life and future. He was trying to build something with his Parkour group and there were marketing
people coming from Germany to see them about a live

performance at a car show. Johann was so proud when David asked him to be part of the team for the video and live performance for Ford. 'Yeah, Johann, I'm going to take care of you for a few weeks,' David told him.

Nearly a year earlier, the three young guns – Johann, Seb Goudot and Mike Ramdani – had somehow become absorbed into the larger pack and were training with David and his group: Stéphane, Kazuma, Cisco and Romain. There was nothing formally offered to them or spoken of and, as with many elements of the early Parkour scene, the loose, informal nature of who was involved and how was rarely said out loud. Things just happened organically.

Both Vigroux brothers, Stéphane and Johann, longed to show the world what they could do. In 2000 they instigated the Traceurs team's first video, *La Relève*, meaning The Succession. It was Stéphane's homage to his master, David. The six-minute action video showed David and Sébastien along with the next generation; Seb, Mike, Rudy Duong, Romain Moutault, Jérôme Ben Aoues, Karim Mouhous and Johann. It depicted a raw frenzy of jumps they had broken specifically to impress on video – and to impress David. They took on every obstacle in their path as they tore up the streets of Evry. Kazuma and Thomas Couetdic would also have featured had they been able to attend the filming.

Stéphane and the others had started their Parkour journey after being inspired by what they had seen on video. It was normal for them to want to share what they could now do. They put a huge effort into the short films to create the highest production values possible. As well as demonstrating what they could do, they were also unknowingly communicating something subtler: we are not in the cinema, not in the movies; we are in real life, in the streets training. If they were going to try to make a living from Parkour, then they had to show people that they existed. The availability of cheap digital cameras and video-editing software had provided opportunities that hadn't been available several years before. Technology was moving fast and had democratised the possibilities of who could be seen and who could create an audience. The next generation were happy to use it.

Sébastien had been away from both David and the Parkour scene for a while, instead concentrating on athletics and doing part-time security work. He was twenty-seven years old and had worked as a doorman at the Royal Opera. He watched the performers come and go, wondering what it would be like to lead a professional artistic life. Could he and his childhood friends have done something with their practice? Like everyone else in France, he was aware of the success of the Yamakasi film.

Now Sébastien was back. He wasn't extreme like David, but then Johann had never met anyone as extreme as David. Sébastien was the healthy one; a fun, smiling kind of guy, training diligently, always early to bed and early to rise.

Johann knew adventure, flow and jumps, but Sébastien knew more. 'He wasn't the best in movement, but he was more. He was better in whole training, the philosophy, the values. He got it,' remembered Johann. 'His whole way of life was disciplined. He cared about being healthy in every way. It wasn't just about training. Why something is done and what it brings you.' Sébastien's way of structured training and exercises with a real purpose opened a new approach to Johann even though he still craved the movement adventures and extremes of David's world. Johann was eighteen years old and, for the first time in his life, decided to go against his parents' wishes. It was a tense time in the Vigroux household as Johann told them that he wanted to commit himself to make a living out of a sport that nobody knew about. He had got his Baccalaureate and left school and, through Parkour, he had been introduced to shooting and editing videos. He completed a year at a private film school, but his heart was on the streets of Lisses.

The career choices for Johann at eighteen were the same for nearly all of the Traceurs group with the exception of Seb Goudot, who maintained full-time, postgraduate education, eventually leading to a PhD. They wanted to make a life out of Parkour. David was twenty-eight years old, Stéphane was twenty-one, and they had the talent and time to try to make something of the opportunities that appeared, with one video project leading to another.

People were starting to find their videos online and gradually an audience for Parkour was beginning to grow with more commercial opportunities coming their way as a result. Marketing agencies saw the potential in how they could appropriate Parkour to sell a whole host of products and services that would appeal to a youth audience.

The next project for the Traceurs was the *Xtrm-Up* video, a nine-minute documentary for a French lifestyle and alternative sports magazine webstreaming tv channel tv-up.com. The inner-city drum and bass soundtrack provided the appropriate rhythm to the edit as it showed off the skills of the group in and around their usual haunts. They wore white track pants and a black sweatshirt with the white silhouette of David and the word Parkour emblazoned on the back. David's attire was slightly different.

Sébastien took a moment to step back and watch. He was energised to see the young blood carrying on the passion of what him and his friends had begun years before. They all seemed a little less wild than the original Yamakasi, but that was no bad thing. David had instilled high standards of quality in his new Traceurs group and at last he had his followers. However, no matter the years Sébastien and David had spent together as best friends and their training experiences; regardless of the insights, philosophies and structure that Sébastien contributed, David's shadow remained all-consuming. It would not allow Sébastien or anyone else to shine. If you trained with David, he viewed you as inferior.

The good vibes between the two former best friends had been short-lived and soon the tensions Sébastien had felt around the time of the *Notre Dame de Paris* opportunity surfaced again. Sébastien had been there; he knew what had gone on and what everyone had shared. How easy it was to rewrite history when only one voice is heard, he thought. However, David had charisma and a strong presence and there would always be many willing to follow him. He could talk and demonstrate the discipline better than any other. *La parole c'est l'homme* – A man is as good as his word – was David's favourite phrase, but the noble values he spoke of were often absent in his actions.

The *Sept à huit* ten-minute documentary on TF1 had been damaging not only for David's relationship with the Yamakasi but also for Sébastien. Although present for the filming, he barely featured in the final cut. He was unfairly portrayed as the sidekick of the 'master of Parkour', David Belle. Sébastien was insignificant, and according to the report, had nothing to say.

Yet Sébastien wanted to spread the word of Parkour and felt that more of those who were training needed to speak up and talk about themselves and the practice. For Parkour to be passed on and benefit others, it couldn't and shouldn't be just about David and his version of events.

In wanting to show it in a different light, Sébastien worked with Jérome LeBret, Johann and Mike Ramdani, whose IT skills helped them to create a simple flash-based website, Parkour.com. It was at least one place where people could read about the philosophy of Parkour and have some idea of the basic moves. It would be a small presence on the internet amongst the growing cacophony of voices, and there were no grand ideas about creating a community. There was a news page, but there was no news as they were always outside training. Who was looking at it and what they thought didn't really matter to them. If you already knew how to train Parkour, then you probably had little interest in being indoors and online.

Parkour.com stated, 'Parkour is more than a sport, it is an art that develops body and mind. This discipline con- sists in seeing in the environment, urban or natural, obstacles to vanquish, overcome and clear with ease and fluidity. This requires showing proof of an excellent physi- cal condition and imagination. Parkour is, above all, a sports discipline.'

The website spoke of some of the quests or internal con- flicts that had to be navigated when training Parkour. 'The mind becomes indecisive and the body blocked. One strug- gles against one's ego and interior demons; at no other time do I feel so divided within myself, but what a sensation when I join the two!'

The word 'Parkour' could easily have been replaced by *L'Art du Déplacement* despite Sébastien and David having left the group five years ago. By contrast, the Yamakasi believed that going online wasn't a good decision and stayed away. The word Parkour was becoming more well-known online regardless of the millions who had seen their stage and feature film work. If people wanted to find them, it wouldn't be facilitated by the internet; they were on the streets. 'They wanted to be sure about everything they put on the internet, they wanted to train and foolproof everything first before releasing anything,' remembered Bruno Girard, the producer of the short film *Le Message*.

Although David and Sébastien's friendship was under a lot of stress, there was still the Nike job to complete. The ad agency wanted one commercial for David, one for Sébastien and one that would feature the whole group. When the time came to agree who would do what, David was on holiday in Thailand. It was obvious which of the ads had the cool factor. Sébastien took the angry chicken. David would be the lover and together the group would chase a scary cat.

The scenarios were simple and original in style: an angry chicken would chase Sébastien through the concrete land-scapes of District 13 in Paris. The abilities of both man and bird would be displayed in all their glory. For his solo role, David would use his skills to repeatedly reclaim a dropped ring from his lover, thereby demonstrating his commit-ment, patience and adoration. In the final ad, the group of young men would go in search of a 'scary cat', traversing the urban landscape while asking and alarming pedestri-ans en route. Meanwhile the scary cat, a man dressed in a cat costume with arms constantly raised in a state of alarm, discusses 'a lifestyle choice' in a café where the group even-tually find him. With a 1970s public information-styled narration, the campaign hit gold for Nike and the agency. The angry chicken segment won several awards, including gold at the Cannes Lions International Festival of Creativity in 2003, the biggest annual awards festival in the global creative communication industry.

On the shoot, the rehearsal days had gone well and the media machine of a high-end commercial production had set up camp for another day in District 13, home to many of Paris's Asian community. The area was another ambitious post-war architectural project. The Olympiades project of high-rise towers, multi-level platforms with walkways, and a raised esplanade was supposed to be the 'Champs-Elysées of the South' according to its creator Michel Holley. Similar to Evry, the Olympiades area had been created in the 1960s to accommodate immigrants, baby boomers and cars. The large pedestrian concrete platforms and walkways provided numerous opportunities for Parkour, but the dimensions of the urban landscape meant that many of these movements were huge in scale.

The athletes had checked the spots and gone over the action shots with the crew. One of the biggest drop jumps had been scheduled for Day Two. It involved a lot of impact but wasn't technically hard for any of them. Stéphane had done it twice the day before, while Johann preferred to wait for the big day, wanting to make use of the added pressure of performing for camera. Stéphane, Sébastien, Johann, Kazuma and Jérome hung out in the trailer while David was alone. He kept himself to himself. Things were tense between David and most of the Traceurs group, not just Sébastien. However, as soon as they all started to move, the cracks smoothed over. Once their bodies were in motion, they understood each other better than anyone else in the world.

'First positions, going for a take,' the first assistant director announced as everyone readied themselves for the jump. They had all warmed up, but the rhythm of a commercial shoot was quite different from their normal hours of training. The stop/start and waiting could kill the energy of even the most hyperactive athlete as well as taking its toll on the body. Stéphane felt tired that day but, hey, he was Stéphane Vigroux and he'd be performing for Nike.

'Roll sound!' Speed, the sound recordist confirmed. 'Roll camera. Action!' shouted the director.

The five men ran and vaulted over the wall. They dropped and landed with a roll on the walkway four metres below. The ease with which they landed from height on to the hard surface made it seem like they had landed on a soft mat, not concrete. However, the surface was unforgiving. Stéphane hadn't landed well and felt some pain in his knee.

'Hey David, I don't feel good. I'm not going to do it again,' Stéphane explained as he rubbed his knee and tried to shake his leg out. He didn't know anything about injuries or how his body worked; it just did.

'No problem, you've done it. They got it, it's in the camera. Don't worry,' David replied.

Was he crying wolf? Stéphane wondered. Was it another test, another game? 'OK, don't worry, you can give up now, go and get some breakfast, have a croissant, relax.' There had been so many times David had tested him that Stéphane really didn't know what to think.

The others lined up again for a second take as Stéphane sat in discomfort nearby. 'OK, ready to go again, positions everyone . . .' Before he knew it, Stéphane thought, 'I'm doing it again.' He was on his feet and boom!

The weird noise he heard on landing couldn't mean anything good. His knee twisted on the inside as he came out of the roll. Again his landing was weak and painful. It was one jump too many for the young Jedi who had been caught up in the moment.

He could still walk, albeit painfully, so his own diagnosis was that it should be fine. His biggest fear was always that he could break his leg. He knew his leg wasn't broken, as a broken leg meant he wouldn't be able to walk. No one had ever mentioned ligaments . . .

Johann was worried. It was so rare for his brother to even say he was in pain, but nobody seemed to care, least of all his brother. He had told the others he was injured and in pain but, in a culture where your worth was valued on being super-strong, there was no way he was going to cry or make anything out of it. He'd see the doctor afterwards. His knee began to swell and he wrapped it in a bandage and carried on moving, doing the smaller jumps and hiding his limp as best he could from everyone for the next two days.

On returning home, Stephane was told that he had torn the anterior cruciate ligament in his left knee and a tiny part of the meniscus. He would need surgery. Stéphane had no choice: they had to replace the ligament.

The rehabilitation centre in Evry was used mainly for professional athletes, but the large white building would be Stéphane's home for the next three months. He was given a timescale of the expected recovery and various stages after the operation. He had physio to do and needed to be patient so he could heal.

He was angrier and more negative than he'd ever been before. He hated hospitals and the rehab centre wasn't any better. Johann visited him every day and for him it was tragic to see his older brother, role model and friend so broken and alone. Stéphane's family and girlfriend Katty visited, but the rest of the Parkour people and his world for the last few years were markedly absent.

The attitude from the elitist Parkour scene in Lisses towards Stéphane was harsh. Stéphane had messed up. The accident was his mistake and he therefore somehow deserved it. He had said that his knee was hurting, didn't need to jump again yet decided to go ahead regardless. If he was strong, then he'll recover and get over it. If he wasn't strong enough, then he would quit Parkour. In a culture based on strength not compassion, you were relevant only if you were moving. The reality of seeing one of them change from being a mover to someone less than able most probably terrified the rest of the group. Regardless of the rhetoric and bravado, silently they all knew that none of them was immune to the potential of such an injury, but still they never visited.

Stéphane spent three months in the hospital and rehab centre. It was upsetting to think that he wasn't on his friends' minds. How deep was the bond they shared, after all? He miserably whiled away the days in his small white room, occasionally limping around the centre's outdoor area. Emotionally disturbed, alone and scared; in one jump he had gone from an arrogant and aspiring Parkour name and athlete, riding the wave of success, to a discarded nobody who was unsure of his future.

Would he be able to come back? How long would it take? He had so many questions and so few answers, only fears. He had shared the best part of the last five years of his life in extreme and exhilarating situations with friends who were now nowhere to be seen. In Parkour he had found something for the first time in his life to which he had given his heart and soul. It was the only thing that had made sense to him in his life. Society had nothing to offer apart from Parkour, so now what? He had begun to find who he was, but now his addictive passion no longer seemed a possibility.

His recovery was behind schedule. After one month, he still couldn't straighten his leg. His knee was swollen and painful and he could only walk with a limp. Johann checked each day to see if he needed anything and tried cracking bad jokes to lighten his mood, but nothing worked. Stéphane's hot summer months were physically and emotionally painful. Pain and anger consumed his every moment, even after leaving the rehab centre and returning home. The payment from the Nike job would tide him over, but he took some part-time factory work putting things in boxes, stamping and shipping them out. On a conveyor belt to nowhere with a bent leg, he felt desperate. There was only one thing to do that could help: it was time to go back to training.

The tensions prior to the Nike shoot with David hadn't healed during his time spent injured, alone and away from everyone. It felt for Sébastien, and others, that friendship with David was largely one-sided. You give, and depending on his mood, you might get something back. Obstacles were to be overcome, but the obstacles were always of David's choosing. One by one the Traceurs group disbanded as the love affair came to an end. Sébastien had already left. He had tried to share a path with David twice, but now Sébastien knew he had to be his own person and have his own voice.

Stéphane wrestled with his feelings, but he knew he too had to talk to David. Even after everything – all the pain he left him to go through alone in the hospital, the demands on who he should and shouldn't speak to, who he could and couldn't train with —David was his friend, a big brother and master. The pain of the injury had given him time to think and face the reality of who he was – and he didn't know who that was anymore. He was lost, young and needed space to grow. That was only possible away from David's influence.

It wasn't going to be easy, but Stéphane had to tell David how he was feeling. No individual had ever had such an impact on him before. The decision hadn't come easily. 'He was my teacher, my mentor, a good friend and also because he was older than me I looked up to him for more than just Parkour. Views about life, everyday behaviour, relationships with others and the world outside Parkour,' remembered Stéphane. 'If I was not training with him, we were at his place chilling, talking about Parkour, life, dreams or at mine doing the very same. I spent most of my time in his company and due to the nature of our "teacher/student" relationship I was absorbing a lot from him. David is a charismatic man, driven, with strong beliefs and views on how to live his life.'

Stéphane had felt pressured by David in nearly every aspect of his life. He had seen how he had treated friends and family recently and, during his spell in the hospital, felt it himself. He told David: 'All the good people you had in your life, you kind of hurt them in some way, and they left you. They are all good people, I know them, so there's maybe something wrong with you, you should think about it, and I feel the same now, so I need to leave.'

Later that evening, David arrived at Stéphane's parents' house with the material remains of their relationship: a box of DVDs and a book. David turned and left.

22

Flowing on Rails

I don't think you need to jump from a building to another to be strong or to find answers in your life. That's our story, and all this extreme part, that's where you can say that there was a lot of suffering. Because the pain was big, we would make ourselves suffer even more. It's a bit masochistic . . .

Williams Belle

Williams had mastered all of the techniques they had played with at the time – the palm spin, double kong vault, all of them. Not only was he extremely strong but his approach was open to a wider set of influences and was more gentle than the hardcore energy that Yann and the others had lived for so long. 'With Williams, it wasn't just the jump which was beautiful; it was before and after the jump. It was strong in its individuality,' recalled Yann. From the outside Williams didn't look exceptional, but mentally, physically and technically he did, Yann said, 'extraordinary things'.

Soon after the release of the film *Yamakasi*, Williams had been inspired by a picture of the martial artist Mark Dacascos in the magazine *Karate Bushido*. The trick looked beautiful. It spoke to him in a way that reconciled challenge, mastery of technique and a non-violent approach, and so Williams started learning capoeira. The flexibility

238

required, its aesthetic, the games, fun and the personal expression ensured it complemented his practice.

After the first film, Williams had helped to keep the Yamakasi grounded, with little interest in chasing fame and fortune. Away from any attention, he continued to explore the basics of what was possible with his agility and techniques and was committed to teaching his young students. For others, the artistic element could enhance their professional performances, but for Williams it was merely another standard to test himself against.

Even if he mastered the aesthetic quality of a movement, there was still a nagging question. 'What's the point of it all?' he asked himself. Why was their training so hard? Does any of this have a meaning? Williams had struggled with these thoughts since he became famous three years earlier and constantly reflected on his motivations and actions. From the first jump in the ship playground with his brothers, cousin and Sébastien, the questions had never ceased. What had been a tool for facing his fears continued to have a brutal effect on him. The violence he had feared as a child had not returned, but here he was still enduring so much pain and confronting death in his training – perhaps a little too often. Was it an illusion? Had he really achieved a better understanding of himself or was he just hiding behind a mask of physical achievements and reflection?

'Why have I done all this, why have I confronted death so much? Why am I playing like this with my life?' he thought. 'After all, it was only through being alive that change could happen.' Williams knew he could endure suffering, of that there was no doubt. He was concerned that by continuing to do so he would only continue to nurture more suffering rather than happiness and joy.

He wanted to share the promise and dreams of

possibilities they had all fought so hard to achieve. He wholeheartedly believed in *L'Art du Déplacement*, but his concern had recently turned to that of longevity and therefore protection. How he could protect people whilst still offering them very hard training? He wanted to be able to offer the same progress that he had when he was confronting death but in a setting that corresponded to each person's context and needs. Everyone's battles were different but there must be a way that would allow people to be safe while still making quick progress and going far . . . It had to be useful to others.

Williams knew that there was some training where you needed to take impacts because sometimes you miss, or some jumps were violent. You had to be able to resist the pain, but not all of the training should be like that. Sometimes you could be light and other times you had to be as hard as stone. If the impact was potentially violent, you had to be like a stone, but at the same time you needed to know how to release energy on landing; to absorb or be flexible: your body should know both ways. You had to be able to respond as the context dictated, to adapt and find your way.

As the youngest member of the Yamakasi group, he was never in a position to question the ways of his elders and peers but he could not ignore his persistent doubts any longer. If you worked only on joy, then you'll just have results related to joy. It was the same with pain, he concluded. Pain will only breed more pain. You must be honest with yourself, he thought. At times, life would be hard and far from perfect. You'll be in good health and then at other times not, but as hard as life could be, why add to the pain? Where was the joy, love and openness? If a person could tap into that, then surely it could help reduce fear and build more trust in and instead of pouring pain on top of pain, this would enable a person to be more resistant to pain.

The first person Williams applied his thinking to was himself.

The 'lab' – the *Usines Center* car park in Evry – had been their all-weather and night-time training hideout for years. The rails that marked the edge of the wall where the cars parked was the new setting for what would be a change to a more fluid yet resistant style of strength training.

He experimented and played with every technique he had ever seen. Using his body weight, he found ways to increase the loads on his arms, wrists and hands as he traversed across the top of a rail, then moved his legs in circles as though stirring the air with a spoon. Twisting his body in and out of the spaces between the bars on the rail, he snaked lithely, creating new movements – new lines of action. The moves soon became more dynamic as he jumped at the rails from various angles, twisting his body under the bar then muscling up to get on top of it. One set of rails could provide endless options.

The results of his training were the same – increased strength – yet the approach was more compliant, creative and less brutal. Williams had redefined his approach. If he was going to continue sharing their discipline, his teaching goals were to allow his students to learn to discover themselves, learn to know who they are and to improve their lives. By overcoming obstacles, they would be ready and better prepared for life.

23

Generation Yamakasi

We were together, we grew together, so we needed a project together. And when we did the film, I felt like I had completed a collective work to show people that it's possible to be different. We're from different cultures. We don't agree all the time, but we can work together.

Williams Belle

After the success of the first film, Luc Besson wanted to make a sequel and possibly more. As well as Besson's Leeloo Productions, the production company UGC was interested in a follow-up Yamakasi film project. Charles Perrière, who had been given a writing credit on the first film, had subsequently and unbeknown to the rest of the group, been offered a sizeable payment to be the co-writer on the UGC production.

By contrast, Besson wanted to invite the whole team to be involved in the writing process for his sequel. However, only Charles and Malik attended the meeting with him and Charles didn't want to tell the others the details of Besson's offer: it was in his personal interest to be the only writer on the next project. The Yamakasi had a decision to make: to go with Besson or UGC (based on what each of them knew).

The first film had provided Williams with his dream of

all seven Yamakasi doing something together. The group had been offered a lot of projects, but few included all the members. However, he now felt it was time to move on and didn't want to be involved with either of the proposed sequels. He asked the others if he could leave the group. 'No, we need you. You have to stay.' Without all seven Yamakasi there was no film. The remuneration they'd received from the first film wasn't huge and many of them had spent the money. Besson had not offered a retainer yet still expected exclusivity and patience. UGC was ready to go while Besson's proposal still wasn't finalised. Malik thought it was the best opportunity for the group and pleaded with the others to wait for Besson, but financial necessity made it hard for some.

After the first film, the group had done a lot of unpaid performances. They were very much in demand and wanted to promote the positive pillars of the practice. With help from Bruno Girard, they set up the Yamakasi Association in 2001. They were also training a lot of people. 'It was a really nice era!' remembered Williams. 'We were all from modest social backgrounds, so money went away [ran out] really quickly. . . So, we always had to work a lot.' Financial matters began to put a lot of strain on the group's internal relationships. There were various other projects that were being discussed such as ongoing talks with Cirque du Soleil, but at the time the only deal with money on the table was the one from UGC.

To turn their backs on the filmmaker who had given them such a huge opportunity wasn't an easy decision, but they had to survive. They could wait only for so long and their everyday needs took precedence. Apart from Malik and Williams, the group decided to go with UGC and signed their contracts. They optimistically waited for the response from the remaining two. Malik and Williams knew they couldn't let their friends down and signed two weeks later.

Besson was furious; not only had he invested money in the new project, he had given them a great opportunity yet they couldn't or wouldn't wait for him. Their new project had better be a great success, he told them, as from then on they were going to be on a blacklist as far as he was concerned. Leeloo Productions had been renamed EuropaCorp, and it never did another project with any of the Yamakasi. Instead Besson started developing his next project, *Banlieue 13*. It was time to honour his promise and give David Belle a chance to shine.

When Williams signed, he told the others that it would be the last project he wanted to do with them all together. Apart from the material benefits, he couldn't see the value of making a second film. It would take up a year of his life and wouldn't move him on personally. He felt it was the same for the others too. He was searching for a way of life in which he could be strong and that allowed him to be mentally and spiritually sound.

Individually each of the Yamakasi had their own projects and objectives that they wanted to achieve, but the collective goal of the group still took priority. Even before they started shooting on the second film, they weren't functioning well as a group, even though they agreed on the objectives for the practice. When news of Charles's personal arrangements came to light, there was predictable anger and resentment. In addition, there were conflicts over who would manage their future projects. It led to an unstable situation and, mid shoot, the group decided to split up. Charles, Malik and Guylain would go their separate ways once filming was completed . . .

The documentary producer Philippe Alfonso had been researching projects with the Yamakasi and was also making a series of films about Franco Dragone, an influential theatre director who was pivotal in combining various elements from theatre and circus performances that would evolve into a very distinct style of Cirque du Soleil in Las Vegas. Alfonso had a good understanding of the Yamakasi and helped to forge the link between the two. After several years of on and off meetings and discussions, Cirque du Soleil were finally ready to make an offer.

They wanted to include elements of *L'Art du Déplacement* in their new show, *Ka*. As the Yamakasi were still busy shooting the second film, they asked Bruno to help organise things back in Evry. Based on Yann and Laurent's recommendations, ten of their trainees were invited to attend three days of casting. The Revelation Crew were happy to step up. Eighteen-year olds Sami, Brahim, Fabrice and Emmanuel were selected and accepted the offer. Two of Laurent Piemontesi's trainees, Teng-Meng Ly and Tej Limlas Ly, also joined the cast. Fabrice was injured during a promotional event for Cirque du Soleil in Montreal a month before the show opened and Serika was offered a part but stayed in Evry due to family commitments.

By the end of the second film, the Yamakasi were completely fragmented. Their individual concerns had risen above the group's as a whole.

Prior to all of the feature film work, Malik had studied brand marketing and back in 2001 set up his own company. He had always dreamed of creating a Parkour brand for clothing and other lifestyle elements around the discipline. Under the name Gravity Style, Malik and Charles started offering indoor as well as outdoor training at Kremlin-Bicêtre in Paris.

They wanted to find a way that would allow people to explore the discipline in a progressive and safe manner. 'We created the discipline, we did the movie and we wanted to come back to teaching,' Malik recalled. 'Everybody said teaching indoors was rubbish, nobody believed in that. Everybody laughed at us, they thought it was a bad idea. For us, it was important to think responsibly about people who wanted to learn Parkour. To teach them, we needed to find a place, a safe place that was like the outdoors, but indoors with mats and everything as a way to teach the discipline. This is how Gravity Style was born and we never stopped.'

Charles and Malik also wanted to show how the discipline was evolving outside of France. In 2006, they set off to various European countries to start filming for their own documentary project, *Gravity Style: Come Fly With Us.*

Guylain N'Guba-Boyeke was friends with everyone. He was the street kid from Kinshasa who was happy to build a life in France and didn't particularly care if he was in a movie or not. He was still the smiling, easy-going guy who felt that each day was an adventure. He set up a small team, World Movement Team, and took various part-time jobs to get by.

Williams had made the decision to live his life based on his own choices and a vision of what he wanted his life to be. He had still struggled with his stutter even after the first film, but as soon as the group split, his body started to unlock itself. He felt total release and let go of so many elements in his past; the childhood violence and the painful family secrets that he couldn't reveal but had kept close. There were still so many different disciplines to try, experience and learn from and he still wanted to communicate what being a Yamakasi and practising *L'Art du Déplacement* meant. He told Chau, Yann and Laurent about the objectives he had set for the practice.

'The four of us were in the same state of mind,' Williams remembered. 'We wanted the association to live on . . . to transmit the practice. That's what I was interested in, what I thought was important. At the time, all I wanted was to train.'

While the first film had been a surprise success, the second one didn't do so well. Fans of the film *Yamakasi – Les samouraïs des temps modernes* had expected an adventure of a similar style to the first film, with the group working together against the forces of evil against a backdrop of spectacular action. However, when *Les fils du vent* (English language title: *The Great Challenge*) was released in June 2004, many felt that it didn't deliver. It wasn't the film that they or the group themselves had wanted.

The name Yamakasi was well known in France, but the two feature films had never portrayed the raison d'être for the group and the meaning of *L'Art du Déplacement*. They had inspired a young generation who could relate to the disenfranchised lives of young men from the outskirts of Paris. *Yamakasi, Les samouraïs . . .* had shown the suburbs of Lisses and Evry in a positive light, as a multicultural group who worked together to fight for a just cause. The concrete playgrounds of the banlieues provided more opportunities than the general public realised, but where was the influence of Sarcelles and the importance of being in nature? If the film mirrored certain elements of the group's story, it missed the endless days and years of training in the Ecouen forest. As Yann would later say, the art may have grown up in Lisses and Evry but the spirit came from Sarcelles. The beauty, exploration and adaptation in the forest had been key.

Yann, Chau and Laurent joined with producer Bruno
Girard and other artists to form a creative collective called
Majestic Force. Williams was happy to step in and out of
projects with them as he saw fit. Together the four Yamakasi
had an idea; to make a documentary to communicate the
meaning behind the practice. They wanted to show what
they meant by 'strong mind, strong body, strong man'.
While France 2 had rejected the idea of a four-man
Yamakasi documentary, the idea of doing one around the
discipline itself rather than focusing on the group appealed.
It would be a Majestic Force co-production with Phillippe
Alfonsi for API Productions and directed by the celebrated
documentary-maker Mark Daniels. For the next four years,
they worked on the documentary. It was broadcast on
France 2 and distributed by the national TV network TF1.

In the seventy-minute documentary Yann, Laurent,
Chau and Williams explained their past, present and hopes
for the future. 'We were barbarians!' Chau explained. 'Such
as playing volley ball using rocks; we took rocks and we
threw it to each other, we played volley with it. Everywhere
was our playground. We adapted ourselves really to every
environment. It's imagination. Because we were many to
do it, I think each person gave something. "You jump like
that", "I'm going to try this way . . . with a reverse." So gradually, imagination becomes wider. With very little things
we could create things.'

In contrast to the action-packed fast edits on the silver
screen, their training sections within the documentary
showed the audience a far more considered side to their
approach and movements: the contemplation and reflection; the imagined lines they drew with their fingers before
they created them for real; the training that occurred at
ground level and of course Williams flowing on rails. The

fear and the conditioning work they did at height by traversing the tops of tall buildings were seen in the context of the landscape rather than from a sensational-ised perspective designed to instigate vertigo in the viewer. Their approach was neither reckless nor carefree and instead focused on the precise drilling of a movement over and over again. The responsibilities and reality of knowing when to break a jump or not were displayed and discussed for the first time. Their bodies flew through the air as they had done in performances, promos and the fictional exploits of the feature film work, but their message and values were explained explicitly in the documentary too. They weren't escaping or chasing, just seeking out, asking and answering questions of themselves in their own par-ticular way. It showed the simplicity with which Williams had always viewed the discipline.

Génération Yamakasi directly addressed the stereotypes of the suburbs and how the group had figuratively, as well as literally, elevated themselves above the antisocial unrest and tensions of their environment. The film embraced the wild and brutal style of Yann's movement and his abstract and poetic style of communication. They were warriors whose motivation was to fight to improve themselves. Laurent expressed *L'Art du Déplacement* as an extension of man's need to move, the art to chase, search and escape. They had adapted to different environments and found ways to go from A to B. Chau acknowledged the complexi-ties of defining something that seemed so aloof to many. It was a mind-body practice in which you overcame obstacles both external and internal.

The documentary also showed Williams demonstrating the fluidity, power and grace of his style of movement with only two walls as his obstacles. It visited his spiritual home, where it had all begun for him, the walled forest of Ecouen. And it followed Williams and the other Yamakasi while they worked with their growing body of students. Without training others, the art would stop when they did.

The four Yamakasi had a message to communicate and, unlike in the past, their story did not have to fit a script. There was no artificial narrative arc designed to subject the viewer to emotional peaks and troughs. Instead, this time the Yamakasi chose the words and produced a film that was about the human values behind spectacular physical acts. *L'Art du Déplacement* was more than a series of jumps; it was a way of thinking, seeing and being that could be lived twenty-four-seven.

24

Finding A Voice

He's just here. He's the philosophy, the dreamy one. He's the smart guy but he's not training like us or he's maybe not as tough as we are.

Johann Vigroux

The shirt collar pressed against his neck. It had never felt good. He checked his watch again and glanced over at the Chinese warrior ornament on the desk, a distant reminder of times gone by. Suit jacket and trousers off, shirt and tie undone, the toned and tattooed torso in track pants opened the window, stepped through and made his way outside. Like a 1920s stuntman, he scaled two walls, a bridged climbing technique made to look easy. One final step and he had reached the rooftop. He shook his arms and muscles rippled. Time to change gears. First a handstand on a set of corner rails high above the streets where only birds and bystanders in the adjoining towers had tickets to his private show. His form was as straight and still as the architecture itself. A back somersault and he was on his way. He vaulted over a small wall and rolled on landing, never taking a predicted route. Drop jump, body snaking effortlessly through a gap in the railings. He was elevated, athletic and creative while those below barely moved. He flew across a gap, spinning his body in mid-air for the pure expressive joy of motion. A fire escape provided poles to climb and edges to launch from. He ran, jumped, flew and rolled to safety from one rooftop to the next. A fence did nothing to stop him, running up and along the wall. A final slide down a slanted smooth metal roof before climbing in through a window. Home at last. A palm spin around the edge of the sofa and his route was complete. In one minute and thirty-two seconds, the ident commissioned to capture the "new spirit" of the BBC One television channel wowed and was about to cause waves across a new and largely unknown Parkour landscape.

Newspapers wrote of the 'real Spider-Man' while kids watched in awe. Special effects? Apparently not. 'BBC film's rooftop stunts "real",' the BBC wrote in its entertainment magazine. CGI wasn't that advanced in 2002. Crash mats yes, safety wires no. This was TV, not underground guerrilla shoots on handycams. The handstand on a rail was performed thirty-six metres above the street. 'At one point in his journey the twenty-eight-year-old leaps a seven metre gap between two buildings eighteen metres," the BBC proudly stated as people trawled the internet in search of information.

With beautiful cinematography set to a remix of Dean Martin's classic 'Sway', the ident Rush Hour was original, exciting and excelled. A full film unit with a high-end budget had spent twelve days working with the star David Belle and his stunt double Kazuma, with Cyril Raffaelli as choreographer.

'We want to do a programme but we don't know what it is.' It wasn't the kind of message a television director usually receives, but Mike Christie was interested. Although only five years into his TV career, he had established a reputation for both architectural and cutting-edge documentaries through work such as *Around the World in 80 Raves* for Channel 4 and an architecture series called *From Here to Modernity* for the BBC. He knew how to make buildings look beautiful and Channel 4 liked that.

Simon Andreae, the head of Science at Channel 4, had had a spark of inspiration, the first green shoots of an idea for a science documentary with the working title *Leap*. 'What if we were to do that sort of sport, whatever it is, that thing, with landmarks and do a science programme,' he suggested. 'Muscles and how the body works.' He allocated a small amount of money to a production company, Optomen, to spend a few weeks researching the viability of the project based on Rush Hour. He wanted to know what was it and who did it. It was called Parkour and David Belle did it.

Growing up, Mike Christie had been a classic sensitive loner from a broken, impoverished home. Materially he had nothing but he revelled in the wealth of his own incredibly vivid escapist imagination. Mike was an artist, not an athlete or authority on sport. His interest lay in what was behind the jump.

For four weeks Mike Christie and his friend and producer Mike Smith set up base in Optomen. 'I can't find a single newspaper article, let alone a television article. I can't find any piece of journalism that talks about the philosophy of Parkour,' Mike told Simon. It was a storyteller's dream: a cultural vacuum. The UK didn't know anything about Parkour. Now Mike just had to find a way to communicate what this weird nebulous thing was.

The internet revealed little about David Belle, but various links led to a commercial where a man had been chased by a chicken. David didn't respond to any of the communications the production company sent. But there were others who did Parkour in a small town called Lisses. The man chased by the chicken replied.

After parting company with David Belle, Sébastien Foucan created a new team; the Taori. Stéphane, Kazuma and Johann had joined him. Johann had seen the extreme side of David's character and now he saw the worth in the values that Sébastien spoke of and lived by.

Mike wanted to take Parkour from underground and place it centre stage on mainstream TV. If the 'slightly Wild West stunt thing', as Mike referred to it, was going to work they needed to show more than just the movements, spectacle and entertainment. The question that Mike wanted asked and answered was: 'How should we use the city we live in?'.

To do so, involved an unlikely collaboration of influences. There were the Parkour practitioners, including one of the original pioneers (Sébastien), an injured yet eloquent athlete (Stéphane), a dedicated follower (Jerome) and a young gun with masses of enthusiasm and passion (Johann). Added to the mix was the renowned architect Will Alsop, prima ballerina Darcey Bussell, professional footballer Robert Pirès and the group Pet Shop Boys (one of whom had trained as an architect). If his years in marketing and the music industry had taught Mike Christie one thing, it was that sometimes you just had to try stuff. TV on the whole was formulaic, a science in itself, a game of numbers with carefully understood demographics and timings. Science and muscles? If anyone asked, the programme they were making was 'urban science'.

'You must unlearn what you have learned,' said Yoda in the Star Wars film *The Empire Strikes Back*; 'Let it all go, Neo. Fear. Doubt. Disbelief. Free your mind,' said the character Morpheus in the film *The Matrix*. Never before had Mike quoted Yoda and Morpheus in a proposal, but against all odds the people in positions of power had said yes. Now they had to put it together. The proposal was submitted in March 2003 and they received the green light just a few days afterwards. Production started in April with shooting in London scheduled to take place in May and June over a four- to five-week period.

'Johann, you have something to do.' His brother Stéphane called him into his bedroom. 'We have a documentary.' It should have been Sébastien, Jérome, Stéphane and Kazuma, but Kazuma had fallen out with the others, so it was Johann's chance to shine. After four years of training, Johann Vigroux would get the chance to help introduce a British audience to Parkour and describe to them, as well as show them, its beauty. They were in London two months later.

There was no product, car or sportswear. This time it was about them: they were the product. Someone wanted to listen and know who they were, what they saw and what they wanted to do. It was a dream opportunity and Johann was determined to give it his all. They needed someone for a recce? No problem, ask Johann. This jump? He was ready. Nothing was ever a problem for Johann even when rehearsal days were cancelled or a change in schedule meant there was only one hour to prepare. He was happy to be there and never complained.

The 'Wild West' of Lisses had taught him always to be ready, willing and strong. Changes in the schedule, less rest time, pressure, the extra push of 'Can you? Will you?' was what he thrived on. His was a diet of passion, crazy and *Yeah, whatever*!. Sébastien and Jérome were smarter and structured; for them television production was a world far from their ideal of how to train, prepare, rest and perform. Not everyone on set was as happy as Johann.

The action sequences took thirteen days to shoot and the whole programme wrapped after filming for an additional ten. Mike had to create eighteen minutes of action performance with the same amount of shooting days that the BBC ident Rush Hour had had to create a one-minute, thirty-two-second ident. The athletes decided what they did and where. Locations had been scouted with permissions sought at some of London's most esteemed architectural landmarks. Not all were granted; they either liked or loathed the idea. 'In the Parisian suburbs it had been practised long enough to become a nuisance, whereas in London it was still fresh. It hadn't been around long enough to annoy,' Mike Christie remembered as the French contingent were surprised at how welcome and respected they were in general. St. Paul's Cathedral were about to agree to the project when Johann checked something out during the recce. Instinctively he jumped up on to the wall of the cathedral's Stone Gallery – an exposed edge fifty-three metres up – to get a better look. St. Paul's pulled out.

The film would show a day from dawn to dusk experienced as a Parkour journey across a dozen of central London's best known landmarks, Mike presenting it as a 'melting pot of romantic dreams, strength, escape and freedom'. Inspired by Lars Von Trier's film *Dancer in the Dark* and in a bid to maximise the action, Mike used ten small DV cameras in addition to the two main cameras, tying them to drain pipes and placing them on the edges of walls and wherever anyone else could get to. Everything was set to record and the production team watched as it was up to the athletes to decide when they were ready to go. Nobody called action or cut. This was no ordinary shoot.

It was going to be an epic edit. They had filmed four hundred hours of rushes with three hundred and twenty hours of nothing. The cameras had been left running 'to find the moment when the foot went past or the hand grabbed'. Together Mike Christie and his editor Olivia Baldwin spent eleven weeks locked away in a post-production house in central London. Occasionally someone would pass by, but nobody really knew what they were up to.

Sébastien Foucan didn't speak English but he had proudly shared his story. With his manager Guilleme, they had decided that for Parkour to have a life outside of France it had to have an English name: freerunning. As part of the process to legitimise and poeticise Parkour, Mike carefully scripted the programme so that the word Parkour appeared only once. It was easier to say 'the French sport of Parkour known as freerunning' and then call it freerunning for the rest of the film. It was simply a way of making it memorable and palatable for an English-speaking audience.

'Do you think more than twelve people will watch it?' Mike asked Olivia as the final touches were being put to the edit. The forty-nine-minute programme was finished in July and scheduled to air six weeks later. Two weeks later came a call. 'There's a problem. Scheduling don't like it. We can't show it in primetime. The first ten minutes is in French and isn't in London.'

'It's going out at midnight unless you make the changes,' Simon Andreae told Mike at his office at Channel 4 HQ. Mike called ahead and got an editor to load up the programme in the edit suite. After a three-hour meeting, it was decided that they wanted Mike to try a new edit. He reluctantly did his best but still felt the original edit was the better programme. Simon Andreae attentively watched the new version, then asked to see the original again. Mike was right; the story was about something new and you had to explain its origins even if that meant it started in French and outside of London. Simon fought their corner and a compromise was reached with the schedulers.

The programme was set to air at 10 p.m. Mike Christie was excited and nervous, just as he always was when new work was about to be broadcast. The hybrid performance documentary about the 'weird' French guys and their new art was definitely something different. Channel 4 ran a trailer all week – a compilation of jumps with the tagline 'Do you believe men can fly?'

As was customary, Mike had invited a few friends around to his place to watch the programme. The black cab pulled up to the wine shop in Soho and the driver was happy to wait. 'Any plans for tonight?' the cabbie asked jovially. 'No, just a few friends coming round,' Mike replied, with typical understatement. 'I'm going to go home soon,' the driver added. 'I want to watch that thing, have you seen that trailer? That *Jump London* programme? I've got to go and watch, it looks amazing.' Mike paid the driver and smiled. It was amazing how one moment could change everything. He left the taxi a happier man. Maybe more than twelve people would be watching after all.

25

Breaking the Jump

We all dream of finding our own form of Le Parkour.

Mike Christie

'You didn't try,' said Thomas Couetdic at the end of another night of Parkour training. Never before had so few words had such a deep and lasting effect on me. I hadn't been able to do 'just one more push-up' when he asked me to. I tensed and tried, but still only part of my upper body was raised off the ground as my back began to arch, my elbows weakened and I collapsed on the floor. 'I can't do it,' I said, prompting Thomas's response, which he delivered with a gentle but knowing smile as he squatted down to look me in the eye. Thomas wasn't angry or frustrated at my efforts, he was simply telling me what he thought. His expression and tone were as youthful, calm and serene as ever. Unbeknown to him, his words would haunt me for weeks.

What did it mean to try? Did I have one more push-up in me? Had I been too quick to give up and submit to tiredness? Had I ever *really* tried to achieve something physically and go beyond my perceived limits? If my life had counted on it, would I have been able to do it?

I knew I had a certain capacity for artistic and intellectual endurance, but I didn't know what I was really capable of in terms of the more physical aspects of my life. It was easy to document others' experiences of Parkour, but what did I know of it? Thomas had set in motion a chain reaction of questions and doubts in my mind. His statement made me aware that, if I wanted to explore Parkour, it wasn't enough that I had started moving again. I also needed to be able to invest more effort in what I did.

Thomas's comments cast a shadow over my daily life. I scrutinised everything that involved physical effort, from how I cycled up a hill to whether I carried as many shopping bags as I could in one go.

Training with Thomas was always interesting because you knew he would mess with your mind somehow. It could be a tricky jump or a passing statement that would provoke an existential crisis. Calm and quiet on the outside, he had an ability to see my human frailty through every façade and excuse, which was as challenging as it was rewarding. To have a friend so brutally honest yet kind was rare. His comments were genuinely constructive and not cruel. His early days with the wild bunch of Lisses – Johann Vigroux, Seb Goudot and Mike Ramdani to name a few – had shaped the demanding standards and approach to training that he was happy to share with others.

Thomas, Annty Marais and Yao Gogloy and I were at one of my favourite training spots: the children's playground nestled away within a block of flats at Westbourne Grove in west London. Yao had helped me to sing on railings and Annty was the least competitive and encouraging natural athlete I'd ever met. The first day we had met she had vaulted a high railing with a smile that demonstrated such genuine joy. 'Ah, is this what you meant?' she asked, after gliding effortlessly over the rail and landing with a perfect and silent technique.

Together with Thomas, these three friends were happy for someone older and far less able to hang out and train with them. Thomas set the challenges. The first thing we had to do was drop jumps from a small wall on to a line on the floor. Each one had to be accurate and we had to do ten in a row at varying distances. Quality mattered. I had the tendency to jump up, which only contributed to an unnecessarily heavier impact on landing. My friends would correct my inefficiencies with kindness. Even when jumping down I was inefficient. Why fight gravity, they asked. Just let the body go down and control the landing. It was better almost to step down, they told me.

In the middle of the play area was a brightly coloured, metal climbing structure. The next challenge involved utilising a cylindrical section of the climbing frame that looked like a giant slinky frozen in time. We had to hang from the top and then drop down through the inside of the shape. The only problem was that the structure was curved at the top. It wasn't a matter of stepping into it, holding on at the top and dropping down in a straight line. The curve meant your body had to adapt and follow the same shape as the structure. To start the move, you had to stand on a platform, lean across and grab hold of the rungs on the structure in front of you. The more you leaned forward and held on to the furthest rungs, the easier the move. It meant you had the added security of holding on to the bars while moving through the curved section with more control. Thomas's challenge was to hold on from the rungs nearest the take-off platform and then drop down, so you were effectively curving your body when it was moving freely in space rather than whilst holding on. It was the harder route, of course. It challenged your self-belief; you had to know that your body would not slam into the frame. I had to trust in the idea that my body knew what to do. That I knew what to do.

Over the past few years I'd overcome many obstacles and faced physical challenges of the kind I hadn't encountered since I was a child. I had jumped, balanced, crawled and climbed. Progressively I was getting stronger and, as much as everything still scared the hell out of me, I was getting accustomed to such uneasy feelings and aware of the kinds of steps I could take in my own conversation with fear. I knew now when I wasn't physically ready as opposed to being not in the mood, tired or lazy. I knew when I was relaxed enough to have the best mind-set with which to try and when to leave my albeit small sporting ego at home. Experience had taught me not to judge what I could or couldn't do based on first impressions. On many occasions, I'd been asked to do something and very clearly stated, 'No, I can't do that', only soon to prove myself wrong. I needed to be more open to the processes and possibilities and subdue the kneejerk 'I can't' reaction. 'I can't do it *yet* . . .' had turned out to be a far more appropriate Parkour phrase.

As much as I had originally seen Parkour as an obviously physical practice, it was becoming more apparent to me that my muscles had far less to do with it than my mind. Happy and relaxed days were good training days for me. Other times, simple movement drills were the switch that could change my mood. I realised that my academic stress also had a direct impact on my physical abilities. To experience a connection that holistic health experts would be familiar with was quite a revelation. As soon as I completed a deadline, I would be able to achieve new goals within my training without much apparent effort. My nerves weren't fried and I slept better.

I wasn't a warrior like Thomas but I knew the benefits

that came from moving across, adapting to, connecting with and exploring the environment. It was also a lot of fun.

Thomas, Annty and Yao completed the climbing frame cylindrical drop. To test it out the first time, they reached forward, grabbed the outer rung and their bodies flowed effortlessly down. Next time they went for the top rail – the more difficult take-off option that required the body to curve in mid-air – and everything was fine. Their bodies knew exactly what to do.

I stood on the square, flat platform of the climbing structure next to the top of the cylindrical tube. With my feet perched on the edge, I leaned forward and grabbed hold of the rungs furthest away from me. A gentle swing and arching of the back and I could let go. My body dropped down through the tube. There were no bangs and bumps as I smoothly went down. It felt great. It was such a nice movement for the body to bend its way through. Enthusiastically I went back to the top. It was time to work towards the Thomas challenge.

I placed my hands on the closer set of rungs. Although they were only twenty centimetres nearer, it was a game-changer. The enthusiasm I had felt for the movement immediately changed to absolute fear and reluctance.

Thomas watched as I leaned forward, grabbed the closer rungs and didn't move. He could see my mental block. I decided that another attempt back at the comfortable rung distance was what I needed. However, no matter how many times I did that, fear took over again as soon as I positioned my hands to go from the nearer rungs. I wasn't making any progress by continuing to go from the easy one and not attempting the hard. A compromise had to be found. I placed one hand on the easy rung and one on the hard.

I was such an unconscious cheater, it had turned out. Just before making the leap of faith and taking off from the platform, the hand on the hard rung swiftly moved to the one further away and down I dropped. Damn it! My body was on autopilot and liked to stay in the comfort zone. Shit! This was tricky. After even more repetitions, I managed to keep my hand on the hard rung for a few seconds more. It was a good job that I enjoyed the sensation of dropping down through the frame given the number of repetitions. I tried changing hands and my right-sided dominance seemed more cooperative than the left when it came to hanging on. At least one side of my body was doing what I wanted. Meanwhile Thomas, Yao and Annty were involved in their own challenges, occasionally checking in and giving me some encouragement: 'Yeah, you've got this. You've done it already; just trust yourself, let go. Nothing bad will happen.'

On the last note I had to disagree. Even though I'd been training for a few years, my overactive imagination hadn't let up in the slightest and the potential terrors that awaited me vividly played out in my mind. Such thoughts might have sounded ridiculous, but I had them nonetheless. I had no business thinking when trying to move.

I stared at the structure and the rungs from every conceivable angle. I walked around and came back to the platform. I couldn't flick the 'fuck it' switch and make my body move. My sense of self-preservation didn't allow it. It was time for Annty and Yao to leave. 'Good luck!' they shouted as they bade farewell. Thomas looked over and, much as I did not want to hear it, I knew what he was thinking before he said it. 'You know we can't leave until you do it.' I wish I hadn't been right about knowing what he was going to say, but I was. I knew I could physically do it, but to actually do it and let go of those goddam rungs was proving incredibly hard.

I paced, did the easier variations and dropped down time and time again, but still the final commitment wasn't forthcoming. 'What's wrong with me?' I asked myself. 'Why can't I do it? It's not hard. I want to be like the others; they made it look so easy. Why? Why?' I was bored with my inner moaning. 'Try something else and come back to it in a bit,' suggested Thomas. I had nothing to lose; I knew we wouldn't leave until I tried it and my current approach wasn't yielding any results. I balanced, did some small jumps on to steps and enjoyed moving for movement's sake.

It was starting to get colder, but Thomas wasn't joking when he said I had to do it before we left. Of course I could leave; I wasn't a prisoner held against my will, but the shame and disappointment of doing so would have been immense. I stared at the challenge again. For the next hour, I interspersed staring at the challenge with comfortable easy movements I knew I could complete.

I walked away again and did one more route of small jumps for joy. Then I was back on the platform at the top of the structure. I was so tired of it. I was feeling despondent about myself and utterly fed up with my inability to act on what I wanted to do.

How long was I prepared to wait for something to change? I wanted to be the kind of person who would try the movement. Externally very little could change beyond the environment. It could go from daylight to night and the temperature would drop further, but that was about it. I wasn't going to become stronger or have some new unexpected superpowers. The only real change that was possible had to come from within me. I was bored of myself. I grabbed the near rails and dropped down.

'I did it!' I said to Thomas, immediately looking over for recognition and praise. 'Cool,' said Thomas, 'so you can do it again.' Joy ran through my veins. 'Yep, you bet I can,' I thought as I skipped around the structure and made my way to the platform. Hands on bars and down I went. I repeated the move several times just to make sure I had it.

Something changed in who I was the day I broke that jump. I had broken a pattern of behaviour that said: 'I can't or won't.' I had made a break with fear as a foe; it was now a discussion I was happy to have and spend time looking into. To break a jump was to change from 'I can't' to 'I did'. To break a jump meant finding a way to overcome obstacles in every sense of the word. It was a change for the better. On my own I would have justified a multitude of excuses as to why that day was not the day to break the jump and would have left without attempting the harder option. I would have been OK with the idea that it was a better decision to stop trying and go home but, with my friend's gentle yet firm support, I achieved more by staying and going through the process of learning what it meant to try.

Thomas had been right all along. As he told me one day, 'I think most people give up before really trying and what I mean by really trying is that you don't just try a bit and say, "Oh, I'm scared I'm not going to do it now, I'm not ready." You go through all sorts of emotions; you know, anger, complete peace and quiet, and all the way to the point where you are just fed up. And sometimes, many times, that's what it takes to make you do a jump, you're just fed up. "I'm tired of this thing, I've been here for ages, I just want to go home, so I'll just do it, even if I break my leg I don't care, I'm just gonna do it. I'm just gonna go for it and we'll see." Not many people go all the way to that; they just reach that beginning point where they are like "Uuuuhhhh, it's kind of difficult, I'm not ready" and they stop there. They don't push themselves more to go all the way to these other emotions and that's a shame because I think you learn a lot through that.'

26

Starting Over

I learnt to be physically strong but I was missing the ... missing myself, my self-improvement, my relationship with life, and I was missing the mental aspect of Parkour. You know, we all talk about freedom and being strong as a person, take obstacles in life the same way and all that stuff, but it was just words for me.

Stéphane Vigroux

Katty Belle had tried everything to cheer him up, but the truth was that Stéphane was bad company. The rehab after his knee surgery hadn't gone well and he still wasn't able to straighten his leg. He had started training again but only his upper body.

'Come to Sarcelles; I want to show you the forest of Ecouen. I have so many good childhood memories there,' she told him. It would be a positive experience, she thought. After all, it was such a beautiful place.

Hand in hand, they made their way through the woods. Katty knew better than to suggest climbing and walking on the wall, as every action could trigger a potential bad mood. Physical challenges were painful reminders of his former self. As they walked deeper into the forest, they could hear people laughing as they neared the hanging bars on the fitness trail. 'Oh, seems like Williams is training and teaching the kids over there,' said Katty.

'*Salut!*' Katty was always happy to see her little brother. Williams was training his group of kids from the neighbourhood. He smiled and extended his hand to Stéphane. 'Oh no, not again,' thought Stéphane. He'd met Williams once before a few years ago when dropping Katty off at a family wedding in District 13 in Paris. It was the strongest handshake anyone had ever given him and nearly broke his hand. Williams communicated a very clear message that day: 'I'm here, I'm strong, I know who you are.' Williams was present, aware and protective of his sister. He knew Stéphane was his cousin David's student. A single handshake had left an impression.

Spending time with one of the Yamakasi was the last thing Stéphane was in the mood for. He had been a good student and followed all of David's directions. 'Anyone who has trained with David knows how it was back then and how for us it was impossible to like the Yamakasi,' he recalled.

In contrast to Stéphane, Williams's group were a happy bunch. The youngest had been given exercises to do whilst Williams did sets of ten muscle-ups. 'You want to train with us, Stéphane?' asked Williams, immune to Stéphane's bad mood and negative manner.

While Williams was happy to offer a chance simply to share some training, Stéphane took it as a challenge. He joined in and started doing the sets with Williams. Stéphane was a little bit stronger than Williams's students, but everything had been scaled and they all had their own number of repetitions. Unconsciously, Stéphane revealed the competitive streak that David had bred into him over the past five years. His ego silently whispered, 'Hey I'm Stéphane, I come from David.' Stéphane wanted to show Williams that he was strong, but the reality was that he was out of shape and mentally very low.

He just about made it through the first couple of sets of ten muscle-ups whilst Williams flew through them. Stéphane was impressed. Williams sweated, smiled and laughed, then took off his sweatshirt. 'What!' thought Stéphane – he was wearing a ten-kilogram weight vest!

Stéphane rested between sets and watched Williams. 'It's great! He's smiling, he's happy and helping the kids at the same time,' he thought. Williams was giving a lot of joy and fun to everybody while still knocking out his own ten muscle-ups with a ten-kilogram vest. 'Wow! He is impressive,' thought Stéphane as he readied himself for the next set and diligently began the all-familiar muscle-up. The first five were OK; he had managed to keep a baseline of upper body strength even though it had been eight months since the surgery and he couldn't bend his leg more than one hundred and twenty degrees. Rep six was a struggle and seven didn't come. 'I was disappointed, feeling crap, focusing on the performance and physical aspect of the situation. Williams in the meantime was helping the kids to do pull-ups with lots of encouragements, smiles and praise,' remembered Stéphane. Without invitation or warning, Stéphane felt a pair of hands placed below his feet that then lifted him up and assisted him in completing the final reps. 'C'mon man, you can do it. One more, don't give up,' said Williams.

For the next three sets, every time Stéphane struggled Williams supported and lifted him up literally and figuratively, each time giving him positive feedback: 'You can do it, you're strong.' Williams said everything with a big smile on his face and a lot of energy.

Stéphane had never before received such warmth and encouragement when training. 'He was not fighting me. He was helping me. It was a shock for me and I was overwhelmed by his genuine good, caring and loving intentions towards me. I was hating him and he was loving me,' Stéphane recalled. The kids were doing OK and, with a bit more encouragement and a few coaching cues here and there, Williams was back to another set of ten muscle-ups. Williams smiled and continued to take care of both his students and his own training with an open and peaceful approach.

Williams thought that Stéphane looked sad. He had heard about Stéphane's ability and knew it would have been nice if they'd been able to move more together. It was a shame about his injury. Williams had made offers to David's group to train together, but they were always rejected.

Williams could see Stéphane's competitive streak: he recognised so much of David in Stéphane's behaviour and movement. However, here he was: broken, down and alone. Williams had his own clear views on competitive behaviour. It could help people grow in some ways and maybe for a short while it could speed up someone's progress, but at some point the day always comes with the realisation that the struggle is with yourself. After all, if there is competition, then at some point there will be disappointment. Everyone gets beaten at some point but if the ego has constantly been fed with wins and high performance, then it will be unprepared when it has to deal suddenly with a lack of success or an injury-induced depletion of skills. If only Stéphane embraced the practice as a life art, thought Williams. If he could be patient, then he would be more at peace with himself and then surely he would recover more quickly and fully.

'How's the injury and rehab going?' Williams asked. Stéphane relayed his sorry tale of frustration and his depression was clear. Malik had suffered a similar thing, Williams told him, but everything would be OK. It had taken Malik two years to get back to his previous level but he did. "You'll be OK too," Williams assured him.

While Malik had been performing acrobatics during the run of *Notre Dame du Paris*, he had not taken years to build his body's resistance to the movements in the same way he had with his *L'Art du Déplacement* repertoire. Instead he had been on a rapid learning curve. In 1999, after a day of front flips, back flips and vaults before performing on stage, his knee gave out during the show. While filming *Taxi 2*, Malik had been more Robocop than ninja as he performed with a knee pad and cast on. The doctors told him he would have to change his career; sports and performance were over for him. In typical Malik style, he took it as just another challenge. 'You think it's finished for me? I'm going to show you it's not over!' was his approach.

'You saw the Yamakasi film in the theatre, right?' Williams said with a smile that communicated everything Stéphane wanted and needed to hear.

'OK, so it's not just me,' Stéphane thought. He had been isolated and so consumed in David's bubble for such a long time before the accident that he did not know of anyone who had gone through what he had. Williams was calm and reassuring. He told him it was normal to feel depressed during such a time but that he had to relax in life and give himself time to think about himself and try to be happy. 'Don't worry too much,' Williams told him. 'Of course the doctors don't understand how our bodies work and what kind of recovery we are capable of. They don't understand how we can move and do what we do in the first place, so why would they understand our potential for recovery? You'll come back. It'll take time but you will.'

Williams was ying to David's yang. Stéphane had never been exposed to the idea that, through Parkour, you could be happy and kind as well as strong. 'There were, of course, lots of moments of joy and fun, but best performances and peak moments were achieved mostly through the energy of anger,' remembered Stéphane. He had had the time of his life on his adventures with David but now he needed to look deeper at his motivations and state of mind. Driven, soul-searching, sometimes painful, but rewarding – all admirable attributes but being happy was never mentioned as a goal. Lasting strength was one perhaps, but strength and happiness were never paired. Stéphane had trained to be strong, ready, to face things *dans le vrai*, but he'd never saved anyone other than himself, from a life of potential delinquency. Physically he had explored the upper limits of his jumps but mentally he was only at the beginning of his journey.

David had given him so much: the quality and perfectionist standards in every move. He had an ego, but with David, you always had to be humble at the same time. They had lived the sort of lives that few could relate to, but ultimately it left Stéphane still angry at the world and alone. Despite his young years, Williams had an understanding about what he did and an ability to reflect that was new to Stéphane. The practice was as much about sharing and love as facing fears, suffering and overcoming obstacles. Such ideas may have sounded weak or irrelevant in the hyper-masculine and elitist Parkour scene that David had cultivated, but here someone incredibly strong and able expressed them. It had been a long time since Stéphane had a smile on his face and here was a guy excelling in pursuit of strength and happiness and in his willingness to share.

Williams intrigued Stéphane, who spent more time training with him after that day. It was rare to meet someone who trained with the same intensity as he had done with David. 'On the surface it was the same training school, but somehow the energy and feel when observing Williams was different,' recalled Stéphane. From the first jump Williams broke in the woods on the ship playground in the company of his brothers Phung and Chau, his cousin David, and his friend Sébastien, Williams had known that the discipline should be about helping and sharing with others. He had maintained the reflective state of mind he had always approached his life with, constantly asking himself: Why do I want to do this jump?

For all of his years of angst and societal dissatisfaction carefully hidden behind a mix of shyness, humility and exceptional physical talent, Stéphane still wasn't free of anything. When faced with an obstacle in life, he didn't have the skills and mind-set to work towards it positively. If his injury were a jump, his current approach would have been like running at a wall and slamming his shins into it time and time again, never stopping to ask himself, 'Why does my leg hurt?' Though he could move with power and grace, he didn't know how to face obstacles in life that were not of his choosing.

For the first time Stéphane had been exposed to a deeper meaning about what it meant to move. Williams had guided his thinking to consider: 'What am I looking to gain internally from a jump? What is missing for me to feel the need to do a jump?'

In one chance encounter in the woods, Stéphane had found both the antidote his mind and body needed and his second teacher on his Parkour journey. The afternoon of muscle-ups with Williams in Sarcelles set Stéphane on the road to a full recovery. His constant quest for bigger jumps, higher drops, more life-threatening encounters had trapped him into a cycle of feeding his ego and pursuing achievement but now he saw another path. He wanted to be like Williams, the peaceful warrior. This was *L'Art du Déplacement*, and Stephane finally understood it.

There was no mountain to climb or summit to conquer. It was not a race to be won. There were no medals or badges of honour beyond the physical and mental scars the practice inflicted. It was a journey of questions and answers to live and be continued.

The friends and families from Sarcelles, Evry and Lisses all gave something of themselves to the practice and fed into ideas of who they were and what they could do. On their journey towards enlightenment, they changed people's perception of what was physically possible and, in turn, created an international phenomenon.

Postscript

The discipline was born in France but, like other pioneering French activities before it such as scuba diving and high-wire walking, it became popular internationally and was absorbed into mainstream culture abroad more quickly than the country in which it started. What the Yamakasi call *L'Art du Déplacement*, what David Belle calls Parkour and Sébastien Foucan refers to as freerunning, continues a tradition of something within the French psyche that compels them to explore their limits in terms of physical creativity and resourcefulness. While the French absorb cultural influences from all over the world and mould them into something new, other nations then step in and maximise on what they created.

The phone didn't stop ringing at the Channel 4 offices the morning after the broadcast of the *Jump London* documentary. 'No, it is not possible to buy the programme on DVD' was the generic reply to hundreds of callers. The previous night, after the programme finished, many young men and women went outside and started jumping off things. They didn't necessarily understand how they should do it or even why they had started; they knew only that what they saw had simply compelled them to try.

Jump London was a great success. Its viewing figures broke Channel 4 records for an audience made up of 16-34 year olds and 'ABC1 shares', to use marketing speak. The chief scheduler sent Simon Andreae flowers with a card that said, 'Congratulations and sorry!' One of the UK's biggest television exports in 2004, it was sold to 70 countries, introducing the practice to millions around the globe. The word Parkour became widely known despite the use of the term 'freerunning' during the programme.

Young and old were equally inspired. Channel 4 commissioned a follow-up, *Jump Britain,* which was released 18 months later. Mike Christie had a feeling that the second Jump would trigger an even bigger response than the first. He was also sensitive to the idea that they should be showing the reality, skill and grace of Parkour – not just the spectacle. The programme included low level sequences mixed in with the TV-required spectacle and a gym scene – the first glimpse of how it was possible to transfer the practice to any environment. *Jump London* had introduced people to Parkour and *Jump Britain* showed them how to do it.

Not long after *Jump Britain* aired on 6 January 2005, Mike received a mysterious email. 'I am currently in the early stages of casting the latest Bond film and was wondering how I could get my hands on a copy of *Jump Britain,*' wrote Debbie McWilliams, the casting director for *Casino Royale.* 'And if possible, the making of. I can give more information at a later date.'

The James Bond team had been inspired. They tore up the script for the original opening scene and rewrote it to feature the coolest thing anyone in the stunt world had seen for years.

Mike connected them with Sébastien Foucan and forever changed the next chapter of his life. In 2006, he starred as the villain Mollaka in *Casino Royale* and from then on would always be 'the Parkour guy in the Bond film'. Sébastien went on to appear in numerous commercials and music videos for Madonna, before joining several other freerunners on her 2006 Confessions Tour. At the time of writing he currently lives in London, where he focuses on his Foucan Freerunning Academy as well as continuing to develop his acting and public speaking career.

10 November 2004 saw the release in France of the film *Banlieue 13*, produced by Luc Besson and featuring David Belle alongside French actor and acrobat Cyril Raffaelli. The opening chase scene set a new reference for stunts and action in both films and video games for the next decade. David Belle would go on to star in several other feature films by Besson's production company and continues his career as an actor and Parkour choreographer. Film credits include *Babylon A.D. District 13: Ultimatum*, *Brick Mansions* and choreography for *Prince of Persia*. Video games heavily influenced by Parkour include the Assassins Creed series, Mirror's Edge and Brink.

David was involved with various attempts to create Parkour organisations that he felt would both honour his father's legacy and distinguish his own style and methods of training from others. Organisations such as Parkour Worldwide Association and David Belle Productions came and went. There is currently no David Belle-run organisation as he focuses his career on acting, performing and choreographing. He lives in Lisses.

Members of the Yamakasi group spent years trying to persuade the French authorities of the value of their discipline and its potential to cross boundaries of ethnicity, age and ability. While cities were crying out for activities to engage young people, when the authorities were presented with one that did, they felt it was too different and not quite safe and clean enough to conform to their existing systems and ideas on sport and play. In 2008, the then mayor of Evry, Manuel Valls, played a key role in trying to help pave a way for *L'Art du Déplacement* to be recognised. 'I believe the spirit of Yamakasi incarnates urban life . . . They are a fantastic symbol of the town of which I am the mayor,' he told the *New York Times*. In Evry a space was made available to the Yamakasi Association to create an academy where they could train young people and help them work towards a coaching or performance career using the discipline. 'Without abolishing their philosophy, the idea is to integrate them into the city by giving them the possibility to develop themselves,' Valls said at the opening of the *Academie de l'Art du Déplacement* in Evry. Yann and Chau still run classes at the academy and are regularly invited to teach at Parkour training events around the world.

Manuel Valls became an influential figure in the French Socialist Party and the Prime Minister of France. Despite his attempts to persuade officials that *L'Art du Déplacement* could be a great opportunity to do something fresh and original that would appeal to young people in particular, French bureaucracy has yet to be persuaded that it could categorise and institutionalise the discipline. 'In France everything is complicated when it comes to the government and the institutions,' explained Bruno Girard. 'Maybe in 10 or 15 years they'll be able to understand the sport and make it a reality for the young people who want to practise.'

In 2006, Malik Diouf and Charles Perrière started

making their documentary, *Gravity Style: Come Fly with Us*, which showed how the discipline had spread and evolved in other countries. Malik flew to the UK to meet with Prodigal Theatre, whose new project The Urban Playground combined physical theatre, urban and contemporary dance with Parkour. Prodigal's co-directors, Miranda Henderson and Alister O'Loughlin, came from backgrounds in contemporary dance and physical theatre respectively. Like many others in the UK they had taken to the streets to explore the potential of their environment in a new way after watching *Jump London*. The Urban Playground Team had been running informal meet-ups and training sessions in Brighton and after winning a small grant from the city, had created their first Performance-Parkour show, which Malik wanted to check out. What he saw being shared with the audience reminded him of everything he had loved about working on *Notre Dame de Paris* in 1998: the open approach, creative expression and the utilisation of so many skills.

Malik and Charles joined Alister and Miranda for a 2006 project with the Dublin Fringe Festival, sharing their story and insights into *L'Art du Déplacement*. Over the next five years both of them performed with the Urban Playground in tours across the UK, in Botswana and in Alicante with organisations including the National Theatre and British Council. Charles left the group in 2011, but Malik continues as a central part of the team. The UPG Team has now toured performances and taught across five continents. They designed and opened the UK's first permanent Parkour site in 2009 and in 2013 founded the Performance-Parkour Network to support the development of this emergent art form. Their recent projects have included extensive UK tours and performance-residencies in Baltimore, Bosnia, Malaysia,

Thailand and India as they continue to promote Performance Parkour (2PK) as a tool for tackling social exclusion.

As well as his work with Urban Playground, Malik set up the Xtreme Gravity Parkour competition event in 2013, held in Paris at La Villette. It was an alternative to the injury-filled and divisive events sponsored by various energy drink companies. Further editions have taken place across France and on Reunion Island. Malik also began working as a Parkour coach in 2009 with the *Campus Univers Cascades* stunt school and continues to offer his services. 'And I still live in Evry, it's impossible to leave, I have all my bearings here!' he told reporters in 2013. He is the designer and director of the Gravity Style clothing brand selling Parkour apparel worldwide.

Charles Perrière continues to teach Parkour in Kremlin-Bicêtre and more recently began to collaborate with David Belle on various projects including the 2014 book *Le Parkour*.

Yann Hnautra, Chau Belle and Laurent Piemontesi continued to work with Majestic Force on various projects for many years. The film *Le Message* was screened in numerous film festivals thanks to funding from the Danielle Mitterrand Foundation. Bruno Girard put the film online on YouTube in 2006. In 2010, Laurent stopped collaborating with Majestic Force and moved to Formainarte, Italy, where he set up the country's first centre dedicated to *L'Art du Déplacement*.

In 2008 Yann, Chau and Majestic Force created the first 'A.D.D. (L'Art du Déplacement) events' in Evry. The first one had the support of the mayor of the city but also involved running workshops for all ages and hosting performances on a large stage built in front of the cathedral, as part of a weekend of activities where practitioners came to train from all around the world. The event also ran in 2010 and involved the premiere of the show *Darwin's Fantasy*, presented by Chau, Bruno and Yann; choreographed by Guylain.

Yann continues to live in Evry and, if you exit the train station, you are likely to find him either playing his guitar or training students at the cathedral walls nearby. He likes to keep life simple, still 'training, smiling and learning from life'. He continues to travel and share the Yamakasi spirit and values of the practice by running international as well as local workshops with his fellow Yamakasi brothers Laurent, Chau and Williams.

Chau is currently the general manager of the l'Art du Déplacement Academy in Paris. He continues sharing the discipline by training new coaches and *L'Art du Déplacement* artists. He has been involved in running summer camps for hundreds of young people which Majestic Force initiated in Courchevel, while also partnering with other international groups and projects such as Skochypstiks, a Balkan group who promote the use of the discipline to cross cultural and political borders on their Motion Tours in the Balkans, Asia and America. He is also pursuing his artistic life as an actor, choreographer and stunt co-ordinator.

Williams continues to train and develop his own approach to the practice. After Génération Yamakasi, he spent a year and a half in Hong Kong where he trained boxing and muay thai. He took up photography and cinematography and is working towards being a director as well as performing in films. Film credits include stunt work in the 2011 Rowan Atkinson film *Johnny English Reborn*. He lives in Paris, where he runs individual coaching as well as being involved in the l'Art du Déplacement Academy.

Laurent is currently based in Formainarte, Italy, where he teaches and trains a young team in the way that the

Yamakasi originally experienced. He collaborates with other movement artists and regularly travels internationally to deliver workshops and seminars to share the discipline and the original values of *L'Art du Déplacement*.

The next generation of trainees that Yann and Laurent had put forward for the Cirque du Soleil casting are still all with the show *Ka*, which opened in October 2004. It is currently running at its new permanent home at the MGM Grand in Las Vegas, where the friends from Evry perform five nights a week to a full house. Serika Kingmen from the Revelation crew continues to train, travel and teach with Yann, Laurent, Chau and Williams.

Following a second knee operation, an encounter with a Vietnamese doctor and time spent doing physical rehabilitation under the guidance of his friend Forrest, Stéphane Vigroux made a full recovery. It took him two years to start properly moving again. After his physical recovery he decided to leave France and follow his childhood dream of living in Thailand. He was based there until Chau and Forrest persuaded him to move to the UK to help guide the rapidly growing UK Parkour scene. Stéphane briefly joined the Urban Freeflow team but left to form Parkour Generations with Forrest and Dan Edwardes. Together with the help of Eugene Minogue from Westminster Sports Unit in London, they created a 'Parkour for Schools' programme that was seen as the first institutionalised example of how Parkour could be used within an educational establishment. Together with the help and guidance from Yann, Chau and Laurent, they created Europe's first Parkour Instructor certification, A.D.A.P.T. (*Art du Déplacement* and Parkour Training). After seven years Stéphane left Parkour Generations and as of 2015 is based in Dubai, where he offers individual and group training and classes through ParkourDXB.

After the success of *Jump London* and the role he played in it, Johann Vigroux had expected to be a part of the follow up *Jump Britain*, but Sébastien did not ask him to be involved. Johann left the Parkour world for two years. On his brother Stéphane's return to Europe, he began training again with Seb Goudot and then joined Stéphane in the UK and became a part of Parkour Generations for several years, along with other members of the Traceurs team including Kazuma and Seb Goudot. While based in London, Johann coached the up-and-coming British Parkour coaches while also travelling internationally to share his Parkour experiences in Brazil, USA, Spain, Germany, Finland, Denmark, Singapore, Bali and Thailand. He lives in Paris and continues to train Parkour.

Thomas Couetdic continued to train and travel while helping to build bridges online, particularly between the UK and French Parkour scene. Thomas was the first 'Parkour ambassador' of those who had trained in Lisses to go to the UK and several other countries to explain and demonstrate in person the style and approach to Parkour training and the importance of conditioning the body. He worked on various projects with David Belle, including the feature film *Babylon A.D.* and the pilot documentary project *Jump World: Madagascar*. He later became a member of Parkour Generations, helping to teach at international Parkour seminars and workshops all over the world, including in Indonesia, Brazil, Mexico and the United States. He applied his Parkour mind-set to his individual travels and adventures, which included cycling across Tibet, China and other countries in southeast Asia in the winter, and motorbike trips through India. He spent a year in the Territorial Special Forces and since 2014 has been working as a fire fighter in

Fontainebleau, France. He continues to train and occasionally teach Parkour.

Erwan Le Corre continued to research *Méthode Naturelle* and connect with various members of the Parkour community through the online forums of Parkour.net and UrbanFreeflow.com. He posted under the name 'Hébertiste' and became friends with Thomas Couetdic. They trained together and exchanged their experiences of Combat Vital and Parkour. Thomas introduced Erwan to David Belle. Erwan had been convinced that Parkour had somehow been influenced or inspired by Don Jean Habrey, but David confirmed that it had not. After training with David, Erwan offered to help him set up and organise Parkour as a method. Soon afterwards, David stopped replying to his emails. After seeing the struggles that Parkour had gone through in persuading the wider public that there was an educational value beyond the spectacle and behind the jump, Erwan focused his efforts on creating a physical education system. He sought permission from George Hébert's son Regis to use the name *Méthode Naturelle*, hoping to start actively promoting and bringing it up to date. Regis refused. Still inspired by *Méthode Naturelle* and drawing on its philosophy, Erwan created MovNat, an updated version of *Méthode Naturelle* including diet and lifestyle. In 2008, Erwan released the video *The Workout the World Forgot* but since then has rarely showcased his abilities, instead prioritising his educational intent by creating a MovNat trainer programme with help from Vic Verdier, an accomplished athlete with extensive experience in aquatics and combatives. They run workshops, retreats and certification courses all over the world. Erwan lives in Santa Fe, New Mexico.

Habrey is in his 60s and can still be found performing spectacles for the public and training in Paris. He currently goes by the name *Hors Humain* (Beyond Human). In 2014, David Belle began training with Habrey in Paris.

I continued to train Parkour in London and when I finished my PhD I treated myself to a trip to Thailand, where I learned MovNat with Erwan and Vic. I still train and move and am scared of everything, but that's OK; it just means I can't do some things yet.

Bibliography

This book is the result of ethnographic research, conversations, interviews and personal experiences over the past ten years. Special thanks to Yann Hnautra, Chau Belle, Malik Diouf, Laurent Piemontesi, Williams Belle, Stéphane Vigroux, Sami Saula, Serika Kingmen, Alexis Scogib, Johann Vigroux, Thomas Couetdic, Erwan Le Corre and Mike Christie. I am also extremely grateful for the help given by Tetsuiko Endo in the early stages of the project and the generous support from my translators Vic Verdier, Thomas Couetdic, Annty Marais and Gayle Welburn.

Belle, David. *Parkour,* Intervista, (2009)

Belle, David and Charles Perrière. *Le Parkour,* Amphora, (2014)

Habrey, Don Jean. *Combat Vital,* Éditions Robert Laffont, S.A., Paris, (1986)

Kolson, Kenneth. *Big Plans: The Allure and Folly of Urban Design,* The John Hopkins University Press, Baltimore and London, (2003)

Leone, Massimo. *The Semiotics of Parkour*, Department of Philosophy, University of Torino (2011)

Rozario, Rebecca-Anne c. Do. *The French Musicals: The Dramatic Impulse of* Spectacle, Journal of Dramatic Theory and Criticism, vol. 19 (2004)

Newspapers and Magazines

Allo Dix-Huit, no. 613 May 2003

Leonardo Vol. 10, 1977

The New Yorker

Acknowledgements

Be brave. To all those who have shared and trusted me with their story, I thank you from the bottom of my heart. Your story has changed mine.

For the past decade, the Parkour community have welcomed me in and showed endless patience and a belief in my abilities when I had not discovered them yet. Nothing has been the same since. There are those who have given me their time, knowledge, insights, feedback and brutal, comedy insults; and I have loved every moment.

Vic Verdier, Andy Day, Thomas Couetdic, Sheila Levine and Chris McDougall, I am forever grateful for the time, advice and encouragement you have constantly offered. Without you there would be no book; just a story rattling around my brain that I would tell for anyone with the time and will to listen.

Thank you to my editor Lucy Warburton for taking a chance and bringing the book to life.

To my family Vic, Pax, Brian, Margaret, Col, Gill, Emily, James and Sam, I love you.

Index